James R. Howard and the Farm Bureau

James R. Howard
A N D   T H E
Farm Bureau

ROBERT P. HOWARD

The Iowa State University Press
A M E S

ALLEN COUNTY PUBLIC LIBRARY
FORT WAYNE, INDIANA

ROBERT P. HOWARD, who lives now in Springfield, Illinois, is a former State Capitol correspondent for the *Chicago Tribune,* now retired, and the author also of *Illinois: A History of the Prairie State,* 1972.

Composed and printed by The Iowa State University Press, Ames, Iowa 50010

First edition, 1983

Library of Congress Cataloging in Publication Data

Howard, Robert P.
    James R. Howard and the Farm Bureau.

    Bibliography: p.
    Includes index.
        1. American Farm Bureau Federation—History. 2. Howard, James Raley, 1873–   . 3. Agriculturists—United States—Biography. I. Title.
HD1485.A45H6   1982   338.1′092′4 [B]   82-14837
ISBN 0-8138-0886-3

To James Raley Howard and Anna Pickrell Howard,
WHO BELIEVED THAT FARMERS SHOULD COOPERATE
WITH ONE ANOTHER FOR THEIR OWN GOOD
AND WITH CITY PEOPLE FOR AMERICA'S GOOD.

Henry C. Howard
Robert P. Howard
John H. Howard
Janet H. Paterson

CONTENTS

FOREWORDS

T H E personalities and ideals of the organizers tend to mold the character of the organization which they found. The biography of J. R. Howard is not only an interesting life story of a great man but it is a penetrating and analytical history of the first years of a major organization, the Farm Bureau. Through the years, many students of farm organizations have wondered why the American Farm Bureau Federation generally had followed conservative economic and political policies. This portrayal of the convictions, prejudices, and characteristics of J. R. Howard and the other leaders with whom he interacted helps answer these questions.

This biography is, in many respects, a history of a few important turning-point years in American agriculture. It describes the tremendous pressures that developed during the time that farming was changing from a way of life into a business. J. R. Howard was a tower of strength and wisdom in this period of unrest and instability. He accurately diagnosed the basic issues and lifted them up for thoughtful consideration by farm families and their representatives. This was a difficult task as there were many conflicting interests and ideologies seeking the support of farmers.

The J. R. Howard biography is the best-researched history of the early years of Farm Bureau that I have seen. This book will have value for farm operators and owners, rural business people, farm organization leaders, historians, and almost anyone who would like to know about the power structures within the nation's largest industry. This will also be a valuable reference source for students of economic history who seek to understand the trends of thinking that determined the course of agricultural political action. This biography of an intelligent and courageous man and history of significant agricultural events is also quite relevant to farm families.

United States agriculture is today suffering from the stresses caused by prolonged periods of rapid change. Many of the issues and problems so well described in the Howard biography remain unsolved and continue to plague modern farmers and ranchers. The greatest unsolved problem in American agriculture is the pricing and marketing of farm products—

just as it was sixty years ago during J. R. Howard's days. Adjusting farm production to the needs of the market is as frustrating today as it was in 1920. The role of government in agriculture has not been satisfactorily defined in the six decades during which it has been debated. Farm and ranch income has rather consistently ranged below the income of other occupational groups in the economy. The rapid pace of change creates economic hardship and emotional stress for farm and ranch families today as it did years ago.

Bob Howard has made a fine contribution to a better understanding of these unsolved problems but, most of all, he has given us the opportunity to explore an extremely interesting meeting of the personalities of the leaders whose purpose was to resolve these problems.

CHARLES B. SHUMAN

Sullivan, Illinois

A S World War I ended, many outstanding farmers in the United States foresaw an urgent need for an effective national agricultural organization. They were aware that consumers knew little about farmers, that powerful interests affecting agriculture were misinformed or hostile, and that government might as easily become ruinous as helpful.

Coming from farms in the Midwest and Northeast, twenty such men gathered in Ithaca, New York, in 1919 for a preliminary meeting. They talked of how to create a truly national organization and about what it might accomplish. Then with additional delegates from the West and South, at a meeting in Chicago in the same year they launched the American Farm Bureau Federation.

Obviously someone had to be chosen to head this new national body. The organizing pioneers were able men who had been observing each other. By a large majority they chose an unpretentious Iowa farmer, James R. Howard, to become the American Farm Bureau Federation's first president.

Not often in human affairs does a giant appear at the time and place he is needed. Jim Howard turned out to be the giant for whom U.S. agriculture called.

The leader they picked was a most unusual man. He had not sought the command. He bore the responsibilities of chief, but served as guide rather than boss. He was persuasive, because he could always comprehend an opposing viewpoint or interest, and could face it fair mindedly. The job was arduous, in no way easy, trifling, or merely honorary. He had to create an organizational framework that might endure through many years ahead, as it has done. He had to oversee the enlistment of individual and independent farmers by the tens of thousands, and did. He had to travel almost constantly. This was no desk job; participants in farm meetings from coast to coast wanted to see him in person. Meanwhile, it was urgent that the new organization show signs of being able to initiate measures through which practical farmers could see their dues pay off.

Jim Howard had enough stamina and character to face all such demands, and before long he raised the American Farm Bureau Federation to the position of respect and power for which its founders had hoped. Always able to comprehend an opponent's view, his sense of fairness allowed, even demanded, an avoidance of fruitless confrontations within and without the federation.

Then, after three strenuous years in the limelight of leadership, came the final evidence of an unusual man. Unlike most giants in public life and in history, he decided that his most important work had been done and that other men were fully able to fill his shoes. He retired from his office, from his nationwide labors, and quietly returned to the farm from which he had been called.

I should like here to record two sharp recollections from the years during which I knew Jim Howard.

The first time I saw or met him was in December 1922, when he was about to relinquish his presidency. The occasion was the annual convention in Chicago. A great attraction was the feature speaker, Georges Clemenceau, the statesman known throughout the world as the "Tiger of France," who had led his country through the critical days of World War I. To introduce him, as was Howard's duty, offered an opportunity for a few minutes of resounding rhetoric. The expected applause filled the auditorium as Howard led the renowned Frenchman to the rostrum. Howard moved to the podium, his own presence enough to impress any audience, and for a moment surveyed the assembly until an absolute hush settled around the big room.

"Ladies and Gentlemen," his resonant voice sounded. Then his introduction:

"Clemenceau!"

One word. More would have been needless. Few except Jim Howard would have known this.

With equal clarity I recall a visit, some years later, to a plain, dues-paying Farm Bureau member, at Jim's Homelands Farm, near Clemons,

Iowa. In working attire Jim made me welcome. Leaning against a wagon rack, he talked; he said nothing about the years of leadership—much about the farm, his family, and his helpers; and a little about general problems then besetting agriculture.

Then and later I was interviewing hundreds of farmers for magazine articles, mainly about their farms, methods, and ideas. Interviewing Jim Howard was no different, except in my consciousness of his great accomplishments. Jim Howard, who had led the building of the American Farm Bureau Federation, who had since seen it grow to become the prime spokesman for American farmers, had contentedly and happily laid aside his towering past to work again and live again as a productive Iowa farmer.

Although we met on a few occasions in later years, I shall remember most clearly the giant who on those two occasions fitted his time and place and was confident, when his work was done, that others should carry on.

His capable son, Robert P. Howard, after his own career in midwestern journalism, has put together just the right kind of book about his father. Here is no such eulogy as a son might be expected to write. He does not ignore the commonplace. Affectionate though he may be, his accounts are factual, forthright, and give full credit to other able men who helped Jim Howard during his Farm Bureau years.

This is a notably good book about a great American who deserves grateful memories.

WHEELER MCMILLEN

Lovettsville, Virginia

PREFACE

THIS book is a substitute for the autobiography my father did not write. A man of multiple talents and major achievements, James R. Howard had a sense of history and recognized that he had lived an uncommon life in an important time. An Iowa farmer who had not aspired to national attention, he had personally known four presidents and many other men of prominence in government. With them and with metropolitan bankers and corporation presidents he had held conferences that succeeded in improving the lot of the American farmer. Although untrained as an excecutive, he had played a significant role in making it possible for agriculture to have an effective and respected voice in the nation. He understood the importance of the printed word and during the last three decades of his life he wanted to be an author. He wanted to write about himself and the other founders of the American Farm Bureau Federation.

One of his legacies was a four-drawer filing cabinet overstuffed with partial records of his white-collar and agricultural careers. They included a series of essays that were to be the framework of the book he intended to write. The longest began with his birth in a prairie shanty and covered the first half of a productive lifetime. Shorter pieces, which were to be chapters or subchapters, told of the organizational problems of the Iowa and American Farm Bureau federations and of the adventures, adversities, and accomplishments of Jim Howard, John Coverdale, and Gray Silver, the men most responsible for the Farm Bureau's conservative foundation.

An effective public speaker, he also wrote capably on agricultural economics, as indicated by the year-end essays the *Annalist* printed in the 1930s about what was happening on Homelands Farm and its midwestern counterparts. A few other articles and one short story were printed in magazines and pamphlets, but autobiographical writing was not one of his specialties and, except for pamphlets, his name never appeared on a book cover.

When the contents of the filing cabinet were made available for publication by Howard's daughter, Janet Howard Paterson, the first thought was that they should be arranged in book form with editorial introductions, transitions, and explanations and that J. R. Howard should be named the author. That could not be. For one thing, the formal compositions omitted part of the pertinent information. As a paper hoarder, Howard had saved first, intermediate, and final drafts of essays, each of which might contain valuable information not found in the others. Also preserved were numerous single sheets of paper on some of which were written significant facts not found elsewhere. In his final years he wrote memoranda for posterity and some of the most revealing information is found in letters that were not mailed. These were raw material to be rewritten as biography.

Regrettably, Howard, Coverdale, and Silver were not diarists and the American Farm Bureau Federation's archives for the early years are limited largely to official transcripts of conventions and board meetings. The first president and his right-hand men left their official correspondence behind when they left office. Part of the personal files Howard accumulated in Chicago were lost in shipment back to Iowa. Only a few of the letters he received in retirement were preserved. Copies were not made of many of those mailed from Homelands Farm. The shortage of correspondence has been a major handicap in writing this biography, but the contents of the filing cabinet included the texts of many of Howard's speeches and a selection of other pertinent documents. Fortunately, Coverdale's private papers, although smaller in volume, include information Howard did not save.

The founding president's memory was sound in his eightieth year. Interviews with old-timers and research into Farm Bureau records and at university libraries have not conflicted with Howard's recollections. Doubtful cases for which documentation is incomplete on some questions have been omitted or identified as such. On some questions, such as Howard's backstage role in the passage of the Packer and Stockyards Act and in the negotiations with railroad presidents for reduced freight rates, he personally obtained verification. His word can be accepted that the notorious Gaston Means tried to blackmail him and that Boies Penrose, the most powerful eastern Republican, tapped Silver's telephone. When Howard prepared accounts of the latter incidents, he wrote: "I will vouch for their reasonable accuracy, since they were dramatic enough to be fixed permanently in memory."

This biography necessarily incorporates the early history of the Farm Bureau movement. For practical purposes that phase of the book ends with 1923, when the first president retired. Thereafter, he never faltered in his pride that the Farm Bureau was pursuing its original goals.

ACKNOWLEDGMENTS

Because he wanted someone to write a book such as this, James R. Howard preserved a record of his life. The immediate inspiration for the biography was a talk by his oldest son, Henry C. Howard, during the dedication of a plaque by the Marshall County Farm Bureau on October 23, 1977. Henry Howard's insight into his father's mental and emotional processes and his knowledge of an Iowa farm have been invaluable.

In addition to family members, many others have contributed information, points of view, and criticism. Special thanks go to those who read the manuscript at two points and urged its completion. The list begins with Charles B. Shuman, former president of the American Farm Bureau Federation, and Wheeler McMillen, the retired farm journal editor who is perhaps the last of the friends Jim Howard had on the eastern seaboard. Others are Roger Fleming, secretary of both the Iowa and American federations during the first president's last years; Dale W. Nelson, executive director of the Iowa federation; Wayne B. Rasmussen, historian for the United States Department of Agriculture; Richard T. Orr, farm editor of the *Chicago Tribune;* and Wendell Benson, managing editor of the *Marshalltown Times-Republican.*

Valuable assistance was provided by Morris S. Allton, Jack Angell, Joe M. Bohlen, William F. Farnsworth, Harold Gray, Peter T. Harstad, Kathleen Jacklin, Wilbur E. Jessup, Orville M. Kile, Allen B. Lauterbach, Fay J. Meade, Mary Louise Mitchell, Myrtle Robinson, Earl M. Rogers, John T. Schlebecker, Francis Silver, Gray Silver, Barbara A. Snedden, Andrew Stevenson, E. George Thiem, John D. Wagoner, Mary Anne S. Young, and many others.

In Iowa assistance and information were provided by staff members of the Herbert Hoover Presidential Library and by the libraries of the University of Iowa and Iowa State University; the Iowa State Historical Department, Division of Historical Museum and Archives; and the city of Marshalltown. In Illinois the same service was provided by the libraries of the State of Illinois, University of Illinois, Illinois State University, Chicago Historical Society, and the city of Springfield. The quest for information also led to the Library of Congress, the New York Public Library, the United States Department of Agriculture, the Smithsonian Institution, Cornell University, and Princeton University.

ROBERT P. HOWARD

James R. Howard and the Farm Bureau

1

◊◊◊◊◊◊◊◊◊◊◊◊◊◊◊◊◊◊◊◊◊◊◊◊◊◊◊◊◊◊◊◊

National Leader

JAMES RALEY HOWARD did not ask for the honor, responsibility, and work that went with being the first president of the American Farm Bureau Federation (AFBF). When delegates from thirty-four states gathered in Chicago's LaSalle Hotel on November 12, 1919, he knew there was some talk of electing him. He had been president of the Iowa Farm Bureau Federation since its founding ten and one-half months earlier, and during the three-day convention he probably was secretly pleased that his name was being mentioned by men who were sizing up the leadership material of the new national organization. In private he endorsed Oscar E. Bradfute of Ohio, whom he considered to be competent and deserving, but he did nothing to remove his own name from consideration.

On the third afternoon of the convention, John W. Coverdale, secretary of the Iowa federation, rushed into room 615 with news that Howard, who had packed his suitcase and was ready to leave the hotel, had just been elected. Genuinely surprised, Howard asked whether he should accept the office.

Coverdale's reply was brief and positive. The Iowan had been elected with a clear majority on the first ballot. As much as any of the leaders, Howard had kept the convention from being torn by dissension over issues of representation and financing. Some delegates already had left Chicago. If Jim didn't take the presidency, the trauma of a second election might wreck the national federation that he had worked so hard to establish.

His help with the corn picking on the southwest Rockhill forty would be delayed another day, for Howard did not take the next train to Marshalltown. Instead of checking out of the hotel, he went back to the Red Room and accepted responsibilities that changed his life. Years would pass before he would fully comprehend the immensity of the load that suddenly rested on his shoulders.

3

As the owner and operator of a 480-acre farm in central Iowa, J. R. Howard (he always signed his name with his initials, in imitation of his grandfather) had impeccable credentials for leadership of the Farm Bureau movement. It was important that he lived on his acres and that at home he wore overalls and worked harder than the men he hired. Absentee landlords were eligible for membership in county farm bureaus, but it was an article of rural faith that only actual farmers should be officers. A man who did not work his own land might not understand the universal problems of those who planted and harvested crops, fed and marketed livestock, and scraped up money to pay taxes, mortgage interest, and bills at village stores.

The new president came from the grass roots. Typical of rural Iowans, he followed a corn-corn-oats-clover rotation and marketed his corn "on the hoof," after feeding it to hogs that he raised and to feeder cattle and sheep that he bought at river markets. Most farmers didn't own 480 acres, and in the northern part of Liberty Township, in northwestern Marshall County, he was the largest landowner who operated his own farm. Half of his land he had inherited from his father and the contiguous other half he had purchased with savings and borrowed money. He had never attended an agricultural college, but he followed the recommendations of college-trained men who demonstrated scientific methods of husbandry. He was proud to be the third-generation owner of the quarter section on which his house stood. His grandfather, for whom he was named, had bought it from the government when Iowa was being settled.

Untypical was the background of the man who, at the age of forty-six, was given responsibility for launching a coast-to-coast farm organization. Eleven years earlier he had been the cashier of a village bank. Before that he had been a schoolteacher and, for one year, a college professor. He held a master's degree in English literature and, at the University of Chicago, he had enrolled for two quarters in English and education courses that could have led to a doctor of philosophy degree. In 1909, when U.S. agriculture was in a prosperous period, he turned his back on white-collar employment and planned to spend the rest of his life on his farm.

Early in his farming career he had shown interest in affairs beyond his fence lines. He had been president of a rural school board and, more than any other man, was responsible for the establishment of the crossroads consolidated school that his children attended. He had traveled, one trip in each direction, to the Atlantic, Pacific, and Gulf coasts. But he had never seen an American president or senator before he assumed volunteer leadership of a membership campaign that led to the formation of his county farm bureau. The Iowa Farm Bureau presidency had been a brief apprenticeship in dealing with state problems, but he had had no training in agricultural economics and his experience as a public speaker was limited. Howard never considered himself qualified for national leadership and he never quite understood how or why he had become the first president of the Marshall County Farm Bureau, the Iowa Farm Bureau Federation, and the American Farm Bureau Federation.

He had one explanation for his election. Charles W. Holman of the National Dairy Council, who attended the convention with his wife, quoted her as having predicted that Howard would be the first national Farm Bureau president because he looked more like a farmer than the active candidates. The winner regarded this as a compliment.

This description is provided by Orville M. Kile in *The Farm Bureau through Three Decades* (1948):

Tall and somewhat angular in build, generally with hair not too smoothly arranged and with clothes not too well pressed, with deep-set penetrating eyes boring into his questioner or auditor, speaking slowly and deliberately and emphasizing his key phrases with facial expressions, Mr. Howard was a veritable and convincing emissary of agriculture. His mere presence and expression before a non-agricultural audience went far to dispel the early rumors circulated against the Farm Bureau—that it was a creature of Wall Street, that it was controlled by big business and that it represented only big farmers.

One reason for his rise to leadership is found in his own words. Sometime in the early 1930s he discussed the Farm Bureau's organizational problems when he wrote a tribute to the man who succeeded him as state president in Iowa:

There was no trained leadership, so it was necessary to find men who knew the farm needs of Iowa, men indeed who could see beyond our border rivers, for the problems of the farmers know no state lines. The times demanded men who were coordinators, men who had that sense of balance which would enable them to consider the farm in its proper relationship with industry and commerce.

Howard could have been writing about himself, for he had a broad vision of what agriculture needed, how a united Farm Bureau could be achieved and what pitfalls must be avoided. He sensed that a populist or demagogic leadership would jeopardize the main goal of establishing a new type of farm organization, one that would be truly national in membership and programs, respected in government and business circles, and permanent in its representation of rural America.

Before 1916 he had never been a member of a farm organization. For a quarter of a century none had existed in central Iowa and, so far as he knew, no organizations in other states had programs involving such matters as marketing, finance, and transportation. He had been impressed with the potential of the county agent system that was spreading through the Corn Belt with the encouragement of the federal Department of Agriculture and the land-grant colleges. County agents were off-campus demonstrators of scientific agriculture and the government required that each be sponsored by a local organization.

Jim Howard believed in cooperation, at all levels by all classes and interests, for the ultimate good of mankind. Like many others, he believed that if farmers would cooperate locally they could solve neighborhood problems. If that were true, the principle of strength through united action could be applied to larger areas for the solution of county, state, and national problems. In the past, farmers had been unable to rectify their complaints about terminal markets, railroads, and banks. Another effort was needed and the Farm Bureau movement provided a potential avenue for success.

When some contended that regional federations would be a safer organizational road to follow, Howard had insisted that all states must be represented by a national federation. He would compromise on lesser points, but not in his belief that the new organization, whatever it was named, must be nationwide in its scope. He believed this so strongly that, at the hour of crisis, he accepted the presidency he had not sought.

Howard's unusual combination of character, intellect, and intuition, coupled with the talents of such able and far-sighted associates as John W. Coverdale and Gray Silver, provided the leadership the American Farm Bureau founders had hoped for. As national president, he believed that cooperation should not be restricted to the organization's membership and goals. To help agriculture, he was willing to work with the rival Grange and Farmers Union and with city people. Oddly, his greatest failure was in a major effort to obtain grain farmers' support of a large-scale cooperative marketing venture.

He was an adequate public speaker, but he had his greatest (if unappreciated) success as a behind-the-scenes negotiator with the influential men of finance, business, and government. Interested in the nation's welfare and conscious that new problems would arise tomorrow that would require more negotiations, he was a reasonable man who made a point of not demanding special privileges for his membership. But he insisted on fair treatment for agriculture. Because farmers had credit problems, he became personally acquainted with powerful New York financiers. When he demanded it, railroad presidents unwillingly reduced freight rates paid by farmers. He was suspicious of politicians, but during his administration the Farm Bureau experienced unusual success in having much of its legislative program enacted. One of the most important of the new laws was the direct outgrowth of a private conference with the presidents of two major packing companies. He recognized that meat packers have their own problems and he did not hesitate to join them in mutual efforts to benefit each other and the public at large.

As he had been twenty years earlier, the president of the American Farm Bureau Federation was a teacher. As a rural spokesman, he accepted many invitations to address conventions, participate in meetings, and talk privately with corporation presidents and millionaires about agriculture's proper relationship to industry and commerce.

One result of these activities was that Jim Howard was guest of honor at a dinner given in the Fifth Avenue mansion of Otto Herman Kahn, head of the second largest international banking house in New York City. The two men had become acquainted at conferences dealing with financial problems. Unusually versatile, Kahn had reached New York as an almost penniless immigrant and, among other distinctions, had become a financier, an economist, and a patron of the arts. He was one of a group consulted by Agriculture Secretary Henry C. Wallace when George N. Peek and Hugh S. Johnson announced a plan for equality for agriculture that became the McNary-Haugen bill.

After one of the conferences, Howard received word that Kahn wanted to invite him to a dinner at which he would be introduced to a few men whose attention should be directed to farm problems. That information came in a letter from G. Howard Davidson, an official of a farm journal in New York. Several weeks later Howard sent word that he was returning to New York.

The Iowa farmer was astonished when he saw that the guest list included such industrial giants as Judge Elbert H. Gary of United States Steel. Three members of the Rockefeller family attended. So did such financiers as Bernard M. Baruch and the presidents of several Manhattan banks. Henry W. Taft represented the legal profession. Publishers included Adolph S. Ochs of the *New York Times* and Frank A. Munsey, owner of magazines and dailies. Among editorial writers were Lewis Wiley and Walter Lippmann. Railroad presidents were A. H. Smith of the New York Central and Daniel Willard of the Baltimore and Ohio. Howard recalled that the presidents of the New York Life and Mutual Life of New York insurance companies were present. Kahn had assembled a roomful of the top figures in the business world and Howard made the most of the opportunity.

About eight o'clock, when the meal was finished, Kahn rose and told his guests that in his opinion the farm problem was their problem. It had been understood there would be no speeches, but the host asked the guest of honor to acquaint the city men with some of the operations on Homelands Farm. "So I took them down to the barn," Howard wrote several years later.

As we stood in the barn door I showed them my different fields and those of my neighbors, whom I referred to by name. In such a setting, I discussed with them not only my problems but those of my neighbors.

Then began an informal round table discussion that revealed a deep interest in agriculture. Occasionally some of those present showed a rather thorough knowledge about farm affairs, but more often they displayed an utter lack of information. But the keenness of interest in agriculture showed by those men was best indicated by the fact that not one of them left the room until well after midnight.

I was practically unknown and they all had doubtless seen enough of vaudeville so that a farmer would not be a curiosity. They were there because they were beginning to realize that the farmer and his problems were after all important to them. I was for the time acting as a teacher to one of the most influential groups of men ever assembled at a dinner in America. It would be presumptuous to say that the evening marked a turning of what had been a neglectful and in some cases an antagonistic attitude toward agriculture on the part of big business into a sympathetic one. But the change did come.

Six months later Davidson wrote to him that newspapers that had taken the side of the consumer previously had become more sympathetic with and in some cases exponents of the rural cause.

The dinner had been private and the Farm Bureau membership was not told about it. In its infancy the federation had limited facilities for public relations, and complaints would have been stirred up had it been known that its president had eaten dinner in the home of a millionaire. Howard was not boastful and he operated on the theory that he had more important things to do than to seek personal publicity.

A decade later, in a postscript, Howard commented that the business leaders of the eastern cities are not at heart hostile to agriculture. He said that they naturally look after their own affairs first and that they often forget their dependence on agriculture, but that they don't do it willfully or maliciously. A second point was that a farm organization can't succeed if it doesn't make contact with all classes of business. More than any other group, farmers are intimately involved with city men at all levels, he said. Several times the first Farm Bureau president commented that he had continually felt handicapped because he had no training for what he called conference work, the face-to-face meetings with corporation and association executives.

Howard had a vivid memory of an incident that occurred an hour after he had become head of the American Farm Bureau Federation. The president of one of the largest agricultural colleges told him this and nothing more: "I knew a dog once that every night the moon shone sat on his haunches in the front yard and howled all night. He didn't associate with other dogs or let any one sleep."

Howard, who never bayed at the moon, wrote that sometimes he thought he knew what the college president meant.

2

Quaker Heritage

F O R centuries the treeless and gently rolling land had been an unmapped part of the vast range of the American bison. Tall grasses and matted sod testified to Iowa's fertility, but the soil twelve miles north of Iowa's geographical center had been classified as second-rate by the government surveyor who inspected it in 1847. Possibly he meant that at places the surface was wet and that drainage must precede sod breaking. Muskrat lodges dotted the soggy bottom of Mud Creek a mile from its source and the tributary sloughs, which extended well up the slopes, were the habitats of geese, ducks, and sandhill cranes. The first settlers would find that only the higher parts could be cultivated until ditches, later replaced by tile lines, were dug to speed the runoff of excess water.

The first James Raley Howard, a cooper from the eastern edge of Ohio, nevertheless considered himself fortunate when, on the last day of October 1854, for $1.25 an acre paid at the Fort Des Moines land office, he became the first person to hold legal title to a wet quarter section, one-half mile square, whose southwestern corner was cut by the creek. He wanted to live somewhere near the Quaker settlement of Bangor and he did not care that the 160 acres had been passed over by speculators who had bought the rest of the Liberty Township prairie in northwestern Marshall County.

He was more fortunate than he realized. In the next century scientists discovered that the Howard farm was inside the irregular western boundary of the highly prized Tama-Muscatine loam. Not far away some of the land was less valuable.

Expanded several times in the next twelve decades, the 160 acres was the nucleus of a farm owned by four generations of the Howard family. The original owner's first grandson named it Homelands Farm.

On April 7, 1855, the pioneer moved his pregnant wife and six children into an unfinished seventeen-by-twenty-two-foot log cabin that stood on a slight knoll that was an obvious site for a farmstead. With the

9

help of two cousins, he erected the exterior of the cabin in the early winter, using logs hauled from a timber lot at Bevins Grove, two miles to the south. In the timber there and at Illinois Grove, the same distance westward, six or seven cabins had been built by earlier arrivals, but the treeless prairie was empty since it was being held for higher prices by the speculators.

As he began the hard work of converting the tough sod into tillable fields, Jim Howard was happy. Eight days after arrival he wrote to a brother back in Ohio that he avoided "the blues" by a simple procedure, "to think of the hard times our forefathers had in Ohio and then think how much easier it is to begin here than it was for them there."

Genealogists trace this branch of the Howard family to North Carolina, but they do not know which ancestor crossed the Atlantic, presumably from England. Some Howards owned slaves, before and after they married Quakers and joined the Society of Friends. Around 1800, as part of a double protest against slavery and laws that restricted their religion, they migrated to eastern Ohio. That area, south of Steubenville, had undertones of Appalachia and little of the economic promise of the Middle West. Nevertheless, the Howards stayed in Jefferson and Harrison counties for a half century.

Jim Howard led a migration to Iowa, but credit for its inspiration goes to his wife, the former Talitha Ann Covington, the granddaughter of a Hessian mercenary who changed sides during the revolutionary war. Her husband, who had been expelled from the Quaker church because of his fondness for dancing, had a drinking problem. Talitha Ann wanted a change of environment and had cousins at West Branch, a Quaker community in eastern Iowa. According to family legend, several years before the Spirit Lake Massacre she told apprehensive friends, "I fear not the Indians of Iowa half as much as the saloons of Ohio for my sons." There is no reason to doubt her judgment or her influence in getting the family to move to the West Branch vicinity, where they bought an eighty-acre farm, and to Liberty Township two years later. One small great-grandson overheard neighbors relating that the patriarch, homeward bound after taking his first load of wheat to the railhead at Iowa City, literally fell off the wagon.

Howard, who already had borrowed from relatives, did not have enough money to pay a speculator's price for prairie land. Had the Liberty Township quarter section not been available, the family might have been forced to locate in a distant corner of Iowa. Talitha Ann especially was glad that her new home was but five miles beyond Bangor, where the Western Plains Quaker meeting was one of the most important in the state.

In Liberty Township the Howards prospered. Jim bought eighty acres adjoining his farm on the east. Six years after his arrival the log cabin was replaced by a three-room frame house of native oak that for a pioneering family was comparatively palatial. A gregarious Republican, Jim had comrades among the Democratic Irish who rapidly filled up the west side of the township and upset Talitha Ann's hopes that her husband could be isolated from temptation to drink. As a politician holding township and county offices, he won more elections than any of his descendants.

Five of Old Jim's sons reached adulthood and two prospered as city residents. More agriculturally inclined than his brothers, Henry Covington Howard, second in the line, followed in his father's footsteps and became a successful farmer. Thirteen years old when the family reached Liberty Township, he was a plodding but untiring worker in taming the prairie and making a pioneer living. In country schools he advanced as far as McGuffey's *Fifth Reader* and then attended the old Albion Academy one term. "There is no excellence without great labor," began his favorite selection from McGuffey. Solidly built, short of limb and long of body, he wore a short beard and in his middle years was often mistaken for Ulysses S. Grant. Henry Howard liked central Iowa and refused to make another covered wagon journey westward. A political and fiscal conservative who did not drink, he became a respected community leader and helped organize a village bank. Church records do not show that he was ever a member of the Society of Friends.

In 1872, when he was thirty, Henry Howard married Rhoda Jane Adams, who was a year younger, and thereafter insisted that she be known as Jennie. Her father, Joel Adams, whose Quaker piety has not been questioned, did not leave North Carolina until the decade before the Civil War and his youngest daughter had witnessed the slave-auction separation of Negro families. Intellectually the children of Joel and Rachel Davis Adams seem to have been above average. In Iowa Rhoda Jane worked as a hired girl and acquired enough education to teach in a country school. Earlier she had mourned a soldier who was killed at Shiloh. She was both untiring and quick of motion in contributing her full share of the hard labor and thrifty management required in the establishment of a farm and home.

In the Quaker tradition, Jennie Howard believed in the importance of education, especially for her son and two daughters. For her time and station in life, she was an advanced thinker who read newspapers rather than novels. She had an unusual interest in government and elections and she regarded Wall Street as the common enemy of Iowans. Her political opinions were sought by neighboring men. In her home the future president of the American Farm Bureau Federation spent his formative years.

3

Prairie Boyhood

THE second James Raley Howard never forgot an early spring morning of his eighth year when he went with his father into a field to plant potatoes. The frost was barely out of the ground and V-formations of ducks and geese, migrating northward, flew low over the still undrained ponds.

From the fresh furrows a delicate aroma, deliciously fragrant, reached the boy's nostrils and excited his curiosity. His father told him it was the springtime odor given off only by good soil. "Somehow the odor got past my olfactory nerve and into my system," he wrote several decades later. "It became part of my being. At that moment I knew I was born to the soil. In all the years after, the springtime fragrance of new-turned earth has delighted me."

Twice during his adult years, first voluntarily and then in answer to a summons to leadership, he moved from the farm of his boyhood. Each time he returned.

Little Jimmy, as the family called him, was born on March 24, 1873, a few rods east of the southeastern corner of his grandfather's farm. Some neighbors still lived in log cabins, but Jennie Howard gave birth to her first child in a cheaply constructed clapboard house of two small rooms with a lean-to on the north side. The family always called it the shanty. In his final years Jim remembered that he had played in the shanty after it was converted into a wheat bin.

When he was three, the family moved a half mile into one of the best houses in Liberty Township, the three-room house of native oak that the first J. R. Howard had built in 1861 to replace the log cabin of the pioneering days. Henry Howard had gone heavily into debt to buy his father's farm. He wanted the land and he could get it only by borrowing most of the purchase price.

Jim Howard was born several months before the onset of the panic of 1873, a time of business failures and labor unrest that dragged on for five

12

years. On the central Iowa farm the return of better prices did not end the necessity of hard work and frugality, and he never forgot the family's struggles to meet payments on taxes and mortgage.

It was a boyhood of uncomplaining hard work, mixed with adventure. When he was six, Jim was sent on horseback every Saturday afternoon to Bangor to get mail for five or six families. On the return trip, a sack of household articles usually hung from the saddle. At the age of seven he began fieldwork, riding an old Brown planter and jerking a lever that dropped corn into the ground every time old Fan stepped. Henry Howard bought better machinery as technology and his income improved, and at the age of nine his son dropped corn on a cross check mark, so that the field could be cultivated in two directions. That year he began to plow and to load hay. He learned to tie a bundle of grain, doing part of man's work behind a McCormick reaper. Always there were two or three hours of morning and evening chores in and around the straw stable that served as a barn. By Jim's twelfth winter prices had improved. Four cents a pound was being paid for hogs and the mortgage was almost retired. Then the boy was given his first overcoat and overshoes.

"I am thankful for the necessity of work in those early days," he wrote five decades later.

I have little sympathy for idealists who oppose child labor. To be sure there is a wide difference between what I did and what city children had to do in factory sweatshops during the same period, but the boy or girl brought up without plenty of good hard work is missing the best and most useful training for life. There is no enduring excellency in this world that does not have its beginning and end in the sweat of brow and brain. When men avoid work they set aside life's greatest blessing.

For years one of Jim's winter chores was to chop holes in the ice so that cattle could drink the clear water that ran most of the year in the slough east of the farmstead. The Mud Creek Bottom was too boggy—too full of tadpoles, muskrat houses, cattails, and coarse slough grass—for its water to be usable. The house, behind which an orchard and grove had been planted in the log cabin years, stood at the top of the hill, with no water source close at hand, but a shallow well had been dug near the slough. From it water for the house was brought up the hill in barrels. If Jennie emptied the barrels while the men were in the field, as often happened, she would carry up two full pails of water as part of her dinner preparations. She thought she was living in paradise when downspouts finally were placed on the house, a cistern dug, and a chain pump installed.

A half century later Howard recalled pioneer life when he addressed an audience of advertising men in New York City:

I remember very well that, when I was a boy at home, my mother made all our clothing by hand. I remember well when we traded the best horse on the place for a sewing machine, and then we had something that our neighbors didn't have. I remember well how we used to make our tallow candles and churn our butter, and trade our butter and some eggs for the necessities of life at the store. We raised our own potatoes and kept our own orchard. We were in a large way self-sustaining.

If the boyhood involved labor, it also brought outdoor adventure. Returning from a trip to Bangor, he lamented that the balky mule he was riding would not join in a fox hunt. At other times, Bill Dickover, the hired man, taught him that in hunting prairie chickens "you have to shoot where they are going to be, not where they are."

Only the well-to-do traveled in surreys and buggies, and Jim remembered the occasion when his father bought a second spring seat for his lumber wagon, which was the chief means of passenger conveyance for families still faced with mortgage problems. The wagons were strictly utilitarian and could have used shock absorbers had they been invented. Many families had only one spring seat, used by the parents and the youngest child, while the other children bounced on boards.

His first trips had been to Bangor, a village that might have thrived had it attracted a railroad. At its edge, the first generation Howards had retired and Old Jim rived oak shingles, made ax handles, and did other odd jobs in his shop. The patriarch and his first grandchild were great friends. Young Jimmy was nine when the grandfather died at the age of sixty-six, but he long remembered some of the old man's witty sayings, his reading of "Darius Green and the Flying Machine," and his prophecies that someday the boy would fly like the birds and that men would have horseless carriages. The prophecies were never doubted, even though Talitha Ann entered a rebuke, "James, thee should not put such nonsense in Jimmy's little head."

The boy regarded his birthright membership in the Society of Friends as a goodly heritage. To stay with his grandparents, overnight or for several days, was a boyish delight, except when Talitha Ann took him to Fourth Day Meeting, where she sat at the head of the women's side of the old meetinghouse. Sometimes an hour would pass in silence but it seemed like a week. Sometimes Mary Marshall or Josiah Dillon, moved by the spirit, would begin in a sing-song voice, "It seems to me, my beloved brethren . . ." and continue in long exposition. The boy squirmed and waited for the benedictory handshakes of those who sat at the head of the meeting. Later the Iowa Quakers gave up silent meetings, engaged ministers, and introduced preaching and hymn singing in their services. Grandmother Howard always used the plain language, a beautiful form of speech, and even to strangers did not neglect her thees and thous. At home the plain speech was reserved for her and old friends.

Early in his childhood, the boy became aware of the outside world. While playing in front of the house, Little Jimmy watched for covered wagons on the "big road" that bordered the farm and forked at the bottom of the hill opposite Mud Creek. One of early Iowa's main thoroughfares, it had been built by the federal government as a means of reaching the military post at Fort Dodge. The boy learned that if a slow-moving wagon turned westward, its owners were proceeding optimistically through Illinois Grove to a new homestead in Dakota Territory. Wagons that continued southward probably were destined to pass Des Moines and cross the Missouri River somewhere below Omaha.

Jim knew about some of the hardships encountered by cousins and others who had taken westward trails. Liberty Township caught part of the fury of the great Dakota blizzard of January 11, 1883, which shook the house for three days and piled up immense snowdrifts. Earlier he had seen a migrant band of grasshoppers flying northeastward after spreading desolation in Kansas.

Travel began in his eighth year. He was taken along by his grandparents when they visited their third son, Asa, at Yankton, Dakota Territory. The trip kept him within the confines of the prairie country, but the Missouri River gave him a fascinating hint of the outside world, especially the day he counted five steamboats discharging and loading passengers and cargo.

The township was something of a melting pot. East of the farm, toward Bangor, a majority of the people were Quakers. Southward, around a church at Bevins Grove, lived members of the Church of Christ, called Campbellites. They believed in baptism by total immersion, which put winter converts to a severe test.

West of the big road was the Dunn settlement. Among the first neighbors and friends of the Howards were four Irish families who were joined by five cousins in buying land from speculators. All were named Dunn. Other immigrants from Ireland helped establish the third Roman Catholic community in Marshall County. When Jim was five years old the Dunns built St. John's Catholic Church a half mile from the farm and started their cemetery a mile up the road. Originally the parish was ministered to by missionary priests who came on horseback from Des Moines, Ackley, and Iowa City, and later from Marshalltown, State Center, and Eldora.

From Irish playmates a boy could learn humor, independence, and tolerance. It was impossible to be intolerant about differences in religion after Jim's sister Mamie died of diphtheria in the hot summer of 1887 and had to be buried in the Bangor cemetery without waiting for a funeral service. Mary Ann Claffey, one of the Irish neighbors, ignored the possibility of contagion and made the burial dress. Jennie Howard thereafter spoke of her as an angel.

Henry Howard had unusual insight into the problems of child rearing. He understood the attraction of forbidden things and he knew that neighbor boys often would sneak into a haymow with playing cards. Under the strict Quaker code of morals, cards were an almost unpardonable evil, but he believed that children should be allowed some freedom and indulgences at home. One Christmas he brought home a deck of playing cards and gave strict orders that Jim and his sisters—Mamie and Nora—could play at home but must not sneak off. Irish neighbors explained the mysteries of suits and face cards. Jennie Howard was horrified and insisted that the cards be carefully hidden when there was any possibility of visitors. Jim was allowed to attend dances in some homes.

Dr. Zenas Carey of Bangor, who was the chief usher at the birth of the Howard children and a thousand others, ministered to Jim on one other occasion. On a fine spring day the boy played hookey and went fishing in Minerva Creek. Just after noon he went home in physical pain and mental agony, with the fish hook imbedded in his thumb. His father took him to the doctor, who commented that any boy with ambition would play hookey once in a while. Then he pushed the hook so that it emerged an inch from the point of entrance and cut off the shank. His charge was a quarter.

Dr. Carey could not perform a tracheotomy and during Jim's sister Mamie's fatal illness said the only hope was to summon a Dr. Burroughs who lived fourteen miles away on a farm near Albion. Jim Howard remembered the day vividly:

The tension of suspense and fear gave way to the hope that comes from action when father told me to go for Dr. Burroughs in all haste. *No, don't take the roan saddle horse. Ride Jane. She is tougher. Take the old saddle. The skirts are narrower and it won't be as hot on Jane as the good one. Make it as quickly as you can, and if the doctor is in tell him to hurry.*

Jane was a six-year-old bay mare. Her dam was a Texas broncho, tough as ever was made. Her sire was a Clydesdale whose colts had unusual action and endurance. Jane was not a road horse, but on the hottest days could work in the fields without a short breath. She was seldom saddled because her trot was rough and she landed stiff-leggedly with every gallop.

The thermometer stood well over the 100 mark when I started. Not a leaf stirred in the quaking ash tree in the front yard. The shadows on the fence posts pointed west from north, indicating about eleven o'clock.

Tell me not that a horse is a dumb animal, especially not Jane. She sensed every responsibility, and seldom did I speak a word to her. The first mile went slowly. Then she got her wind and the speed gradually increased. We took the downhills at a walk, the uphills at a swift trot, and the level stretches at a gallop. On the level and uphill I stood in the stirrups; downhill I could sit in the saddle.

The loafers in front of the store at Bangor had but a glimpse as we took the diagonal across the public square. When we turned southeast toward Mormon

Ridge the post shadows were still northwest. Five miles were gone. At the north foot of Mormon Ridge we took the Mud Creek Bottom road to the east to save a steep climb. Here we had three miles of level road with a little shade. We crossed the Iowa River at the Indian bridge. Some two hundred Tama Indians lived on the north side, and I wondered whether the Indian who speared muskrats in our marsh every winter was watching me. Nine miles gone and the shadows were straightening.

Five more miles to go, heading always into the coppery haze that seemed to be resting on the horizon just ahead. The road, as always, was two well-worn tracks with a ridge between. The tracks were often a foot deep and in them tumble bugs rolled their dung balls. I don't know how a plow horse could hold the narrow track without a stumble. On, on and on.

The shadows were scarcely past the meridian when I threw the reins over the Burroughs hitching post and with a fearful heart knocked at the door. I anticipated the worst. The doctor would not be back until tomorrow. Should he come then? I could only shake my head and go back to Jane.

The mare was white with foam from nose to tail. Sweat dropped from her flanks with every gasping breath. So long as she could sweat I knew she was safe. For the first mile back I led her. When she was breathing normally I stopped at a well and gave her some water, then pressed home."

Soon after he reached home Mamie died. Self-sacrificing neighbors helped with arrangements for immediate burial at night. Five teams of horses were in the procession to the Bangor cemetery. The brother's recollections continued:

Mamie's death had a sequel a month or two later that became a formative part of my life's experiences. The heat and drought had left scant food and forage for the winter. Father bought the hay from some unbroken land two or three miles to the west. When the last load was on the wagon he noticed that a small bunch, not a half forkful, had been dropped far back across the field. He walked back, carefully gathered it up, and carried it to the wagon. A man who was helping us joked a little about the long walk for so small a wisp of hay. Father said it would make a glass of milk for some child the next winter and that, if it was his child, the walk would not be too long. I knew he was thinking of Mamie.

Some incidents are never forgotten. This one became part of Howard's adult reasoning when a national problem involved the balancing of human needs and farm surpluses. Other incidents turn out to be significant. The boy who had ridden Jane to Albion without ruining her would turn out to be a tough but not destructive competitor.

4

From Country School to University

COUNTRY schools in the late 1800s were as primitive as rural homes. By law, each school district was a two-mile square, covering four sections of land. As a result, children did not need to walk more than a mile to reach the one-room schoolhouse in its approximate center. Terms were short, so that older boys could help with fieldwork. Country youngsters received most of their schooling during the winter months and tax-supported education ended with the eighth grade.

Jim Howard and his two sisters went to the Dunn school, officially designated as District No. 2 of Liberty Township. To reach it they walked almost a mile west, beyond the Mud Creek slough in which boys caught tadpoles in the spring and watched for muskrats in the fall. In the cold winter the bitter wind swept down the flat and piled drifts that could cover fences. Frosted toes and faces were common.

Teachers of that time were inadequately trained, underpaid, and overworked. Even so, some were superior educators, and Jim Howard had the good fortune to be taught mostly by these. There were gaps in his schooling, of course, but he was certain that the basic education he received at No. 2 could not have been equaled elsewhere and that it was more important than his later attendance at two colleges and a university.

His deficiency subjects, he believed, were arithmetic and geography. Although he taught himself to add two columns of figures simultaneously so that he could win ciphering matches, he felt that "it was never properly impressed upon my mind how easily two and two make four and how easily small sums grow into vast totals. I had to find out from personal experience that subtraction is much easier and more common than addition." Maps and charts and geography lessons did not teach him "what a big place the world is and how important every part of it is to every other part."

Charles W. Bacon, one of the teachers, was remembered for the way in which he told grade school children about one of the laws of economics. In one of the recess games at No. 2 the children huddled together while someone outside the group threw a stick, a can, or some other object into the air while shouting, "What goes up must come down, on somebody's head or on the ground." Once the huddle did not scatter in time and one of the children received a hard bump on the head. Bacon quieted the crying youngster, gathered his charges around him, and delivered a homespun lecture. Nothing can go up all the time. The farther it goes up the harder it will hit when it comes down. It is true in school games and it will be true in the business world and in all other human relationships. He concluded by warning that, both now and later, the time to be especially alert is not when things are going up but during the fall.

Several who went to No. 2 achieved success in the adult world. J. C. (Jim) Dunn, who left school just before Jim Howard's first term, became a contractor and owner of the Cleveland Indians baseball team. J. F. (Fred) Reed was a county superintendent of schools and a legislator before he became president of the Minnesota Farm Bureau and a director of the American Farm Bureau Federation.

A significant part of young Howard's education came from literary societies, which he thought were one of the most important means of recreation and instruction devised by country people before the advent of telephones and rural free delivery. Having participated both in Friday afternoon school programs and in meetings of adult literary societies, he felt that they received too little attention from novelists and historians. He recalled that an uncle, who had died before the Adams family reached Iowa, had made a reputation in literary societies as a debater and public speaker.

Teachers at the Dunn school usually closed the week with home talent sessions. Two or three recitations would normally be on the program and a half century later Howard could remember with a fair degree of accuracy such classical and nonclassical selections as "Barbara Fritchie," "Paul Revere's Ride," "Sheridan's Ride," "The Death of Jennie McNeill," "The Goat and the Swing," "Marmion and Douglas," "The Long Lost Breeches," "The Razor Grinder," "Spartacus and the Gladiators," and "Marc Antony's Address." Standard features also included a dialogue or two. A newspaper edited and read aloud by one or two pupils would chronicle school and community happenings, often humorously, and include a poem or two and a short story.

Sometimes the programs would be varied with a spelling match or "ciphering down," a contest of practical mathematics in which sides would be chosen. If he believed he was weak in mathematical theory, Howard at least had a talent for arithmetic. When past middle age, he could, with squinted eyes, do long division and square root problems in his head.

Community literary society meetings held at night in a church or school would draw a packed house, the people coming from miles around. Parliamentary procedure received much attention. Recitations usually duplicated those of school programs. Debates were the outstanding feature, and the literary society served as a forum for the discussion of national issues. Arguments about the tariff took place in thousands of schoolhouses, and youngsters became aware that adults were deeply divided over such questions as the resumption of silver payments, the gold standard, and greenbacks. Not all debates were on serious subjects, but regardless of the topics the advance preparations required a study of available history and literature.

Once the Liberty Northern Light Reading Club was organized by Jim and a few others on a night when the aurora borealis was in full play. That winter he became acquainted with *Pilgrim's Progress, The Lady of the Lake,* and *David Copperfield.*

Essentially a rural people, the Quakers who settled throughout the Middle West believed in education almost as much as they did in their own religion. They sought out the best land and developed communities that centered on their meetinghouses. They founded colleges and because there were no tax-supported high schools, built a number of secondary schools, called academies. Iowa had seven or eight academies, including one at New Providence, a Quaker village in Hardin County, some seven miles north of the farm.

Henry and Jennie Howard did not permit the education of their son and daughter to end with eighth-grade classes in the one-room country school. By Jim's fourteenth year his father had prospered sufficiently to buy a farm a half mile west of New Providence. His stated reason was that he wanted to live near better educational facilities, but he probably was grieving over the death of Mamie. Also, the move was homecoming for Jennie, who had lived near New Providence as a girl. Her sister, Asenath Wildman, still lived nearby. For the next nineteen years the home farm would be operated by tenants, the owner making frequent horse-and-buggy supervisory trips back to Liberty Township.

As a member of the "irregular class," Jim entered the academy in 1888. By his graduation two years later, he had acquired a habit of saving papers of varying importance, including most of his report cards and a diploma signed by the principal and an instructor. The five surviving report cards show that his median grade was 97 and his lowest mark 86, in elocution. He had perfect scores in algebra and U.S. history. He received instruction in such courses as grammar, German, Latin, U.S. and general history, geometry, astronomy, commercial arithmetic, physical geography, natural philosophy, and geology. The course names do not indicate any classes in literature, which became his specialty in college. Throughout his life he saved short essays on such subjects as hygiene, Lincoln, geography, and Shakespeare. During his academy years he adopted the custom of signing his name with his initials—J. R. Howard.

The academy had an influence that spread far beyond the locality. William Wade Hinshaw, a baritone who sang for many years with the Metropolitan Opera Company of New York, was one of the graduates who had sat beneath the old belfry.

Frank O. Lowden, who became governor of Illinois and wanted to be president, owed his success in life to one of the Quakers of New Providence. Lowden did not attend the academy, but in his young years, shortly before the Howards left Liberty Township, he was principal of the two-room village school. He told the story years later when Howard was visiting his Sinnissippi farm. One night after he had swept out the school, Lowden met an elderly Quaker, William F. Andrews, on the street. "Frank, what are thy aspirations in life?" the man asked. The young man replied that sometime he wanted to attend the state university but was afraid he could not earn enough money to do it. Andrews replied, "If that is thy ambition, I'll help thee through." When Lowden was graduated, he owed $1,000. When as a rising Chicago lawyer he married into the Pullman family, he sent a private railroad car to bring Mr. and Mrs. Andrews to the wedding as special guests.

Members of the Society of Friends had dominated New Providence and its trading territory to the extent that in an 1882 township referendum only two voters favored the sale of liquor. Rural settlement began in 1851 and the next year the first church in Hardin County was organized in the Honey Creek neighborhood as one of several offshoots of the Western Plains Meeting at Bangor. Several miles northward, the village of New Providence was platted shortly before a Friends church was established there in 1857. After the Civil War, the Honey Creek Meeting, which had jurisdiction over Quaker affairs in that area, appointed an education committee and raised $3,100 for the academy building. Later a sixteen-room dormitory was built.

Young Howard's first important lesson in geography came in the late summer of his sixteenth year. He had worked for neighbors in the haying and threshing seasons, earning around fifty dollars. A friend who was entering an eastern school asked Jim to ride with him as far as New York City. The railroad advertised a round-trip excursion for twenty-five dollars, which was a great opportunity for a youth who had dreamed of seeing an ocean and mountains. Presumably his parents supplemented his earnings, but by barely enough. During his adult years he frequently recounted his sight-seeing experiences and especially the way he avoided starvation.

Eastbound, the boys rode slow trains that stopped for coffee and sandwiches at low-priced lunch counters. They stopped over at Chicago and Niagara Falls. For several days they tramped lower Manhattan as far as Central Park, paying special attention to the Statue of Liberty, Brooklyn Bridge, and the Brooklyn Navy Yard.

Because he was running out of money, Jim gave up plans to spend a second week in New York. Taking a train that would go through the Catskills by daylight, he carried an overloaded, cloth-covered pasteboard suitcase, known as a telescope, and a sack of three dozen red bananas, something he had never seen before, for which he had paid forty-five cents. He had bought them so that he could have something to take home to his parents. He had a two-dollar bill in his pocket and his mother's kitchen was a thousand miles away.

The train was behind schedule, lunch-counter stops were cancelled, and the boy ate bananas. The next noon he was told that the train would not stop because it was carrying a diner. He ate more bananas, but by two o'clock hunger was overwhelming. His picked up his telescope and the mussed sack of five bananas and went to the diner to inquire about a meal. The price was one dollar and the smiling steward said he could have anything on the menu.

In relays, the waiter brought him ham and eggs with potatoes and gravy, a roast beef dinner, and then frog legs, which Jim had never eaten but which the steward recommended.

The climax of the story was that Jim angered the waiter by not tipping him a quarter. He had never heard of tipping and at the restaurant at Eldora he could get a fifteen-cent meal without having to pay the owner extra.

Howard, who traveled extensively in later years, never ate in a diner without recalling the smiling steward who befriended the hungry country boy.

Jim was the oldest of his generation among the Iowa Howards and his parents were able and anxious to have his formal education continue. Possibilities included Iowa Agricultural College at Ames, a land-grant school mandated to teach agriculture as a science, and the University of Iowa at Iowa City, from which two of the boy's uncles were law school graduates. Iowa also had several smaller colleges that had some degree of church affiliation and were located mainly in smaller towns.

It seems to have been a mistake, but at sixteen the green country boy enrolled as a freshman at Iowa College, later renamed Grinnell College.

Founded by Congregationalists, it was among the elite of midwestern denominational schools. Possibly he went there because of Jennie Howard's ambitions for her son, or possibly because railroad connections were fairly convenient. College records show that he enrolled in the scientific course of study, which normally required first year courses in mathematics, chemistry, French, and English. His first year away from home did not produce lasting friendships or reminiscences. He stayed at Grinnell only one year.

For the next three years, Jim transferred to Penn College, later named William Penn College, a much smaller Quaker school at Oskaloosa. His only explanation for the move was that "I was much more at home among my more commonplace Quaker friends, who after all were my peers. I have always been glad that I chose a small college for my alma mater." Penn had a faculty of fourteen that included the president, several instructors, and the pastor of the Oskaloosa Monthly Meeting. Tuition was twelve dollars a term. Out-of-town students paid three or four dollars weekly to board with private families. The college advertised that the entire expenses for a full year ranged from eighty to two hundred dollars.

He selected the "philosophic" course of study, the option open to those who did not want to become ministers or professors of the classics. Even so, he was required to take such courses as Old Testament and church history, scriptural canons, and Christian evidence. Numerically his grades ranged from 82½ to 98. The highest were in geology and political science, and the latter was the only course that seemed to have a direct bearing on his future career. Nothing in the Penn curriculum pointed its students toward farming.

One of sixteen members of the 1894 graduating class, Howard was deeply involved in academic and campus affairs. He edited the *Penn College Chronicle,* was president of one of the literary societies, debated intercollegiately, and as a junior gave the oration at the 1893 annual exhibition.

He was organizer, captain, and quarterback of Penn's first football team. He was developing a potential for leadership, but according to family legend his main qualification was that he was the only member of the student body who had seen a "rugby" game. The team won one game and lost another. The school paper complained that in the losing game the YMCA team from Des Moines had used ringers. It also regretted that the Penn team did not have a trainer, presumably meaning a coach.

In 1894 he was graduated with a bachelor of arts degree. Penn also offered a master of arts degree, the requirements for which could be met either by an additional year in classrooms or three years of off-campus study, the submission of a thesis, and an examination. No details are available but Howard, by then a teacher in New Providence's tax-supported town school, received the postgraduate degree in 1897.

Then he became professor of English and rhetoric at Guilford College in Greensboro, North Carolina, a Quaker school whose enrollment had dropped to 145. The pay was $500 and board. Presumably it was a happy year. He made a pilgrimage to Yadkin County, where his mother had lived, and reported that old-timers not only remembered Grandfather Joel Adams but spoke of him respectfully as Squire Adams. In later years he told of winning the tennis singles championship of the Carolinas. To their sorrow, undergraduates offered to take the young professor snipe hunting, a form of nocturnal initiation in which the victim was supposed to hold a sack for hours while waiting for birds to be driven into it. He feigned gullibility, outwalked the students through the dark woods, and then, discarding the sack, returned to the campus before they did.

In North Carolina, where his ancestors had lived, he no doubt wished that he could verify a legend, often repeated at family reunions, that an unidentified direct ancestor was the second son of some Duke of Norfolk. Folklore had it that this worthy fellow, refusing to abandon his commoner wife, thumbed his nose at ranking nobility when he was asked to return to England and take over the dukedom after his older brother died. None of the Howards of Jim's generation were genealogists or students of colonial history. In the total absence of proof, the legend is now treated as pleasant fiction.

Anna Pickrell, who had been a fellow student at Penn College, reentered Howard's life when, after one year as a college professor, he returned to New Providence to take his old job as a public school teacher. Anna in 1897 was hired by the academy as instructor in history and literature and the only assistant to Alfred F. Styles, the principal. For a young woman who had attended college only two years to be on the academy faculty was a considerable advancement over her previous jobs as a teacher in one-room schools in her native Mahaska County. Her father, Isaiah Pickrell, was a debt-ridden farmer who lived near New Sharon and later Earlham and who rejected the cheap money philosophy of Democrats in the 1890s. One of his sisters, Sarah Jane, was a member of Penn College's first governing board. Another, Martha, married Cyrus Beede, one of the Quakers who became government Indian agents. On the maternal side, Anna's Hiatt uncles were educators.

During the holiday season of 1900, Howard took a train to Earlham, where Anna and Howard were married on December 27 by the pastor of the Friends church. The only other person present from New Providence was Styles, a close friend of the groom. During the following days they attended a teachers' meeting at Des Moines, visited near Marshalltown at the home of Lenora Howard Moninger, the groom's sister, and were given a reception at New Providence by the senior Howards.

The honeymoon was spent in Chicago, where Howard enrolled at the University of Chicago as a major in English literature. During the winter and spring quarters he took four English and three education courses and rented a small apartment over a grocery store on Fifty-Fifth Street. Anna Howard especially enjoyed the opportunities of the city's cultural attractions. Social life centered around Uncle Asa Howard, who had moved from Yankton to Chicago and was a successful businessman.

At one time Howard must have had an ambition to take more university courses and qualify for a doctor of philosophy degree. On that point the record is silent, but his academic career ended when the couple returned to Iowa in the summer of 1901. That September he signed a contract to act as principal and to teach the upper grades in the town school at Liscomb, in northern Marshall County, with a provision that he could leave at vacation time in March. The former principal had allowed discipline to get out of hand and then used corporal punishment on a wholesale basis. The board, deciding that a new man was needed, asked Howard to take charge. He had no trouble. But he did have a wife to support and he did not intend to spend any more time in classrooms. It was time to change occupations, and he had decided to become a tenant farmer on his father's land.

5

⧳⧳⧳⧳⧳⧳⧳⧳⧳⧳⧳⧳⧳⧳⧳⧳⧳⧳⧳⧳⧳⧳⧳⧳⧳⧳⧳⧳⧳

How to Buy a Farm

JIM HOWARD devoted a dozen of his young adult years to white-collar employment. The only explanation for his delay in becoming a farmer is found in a preliminary draft of an essay on his father's economic views:

I suspect that a love of the soil was born in me, and I know that I have always been delighted with growing things, both crops and livestock, but there was a time of indecision in my earlier years. Certain tendencies toward idealism got hold of me, as I think they do with most young people, but all of us are largely part and parcel of what we meet along the highways which we journey and call life.

The three-year period between the two Penn College degrees was divided between several white-collar jobs, none of great moment, and seasonal work on the farm that provided refuge from unemployment. The young man was confident that his talents were needed by the world and soon would be recognized somewhere, but he entered the job market during the depression of 1893, which began with a bank failure in London and adversely affected businesses around the world. Just before he left college, with little sympathy he saw one branch of Coxey's army of the unemployed rafting down the Des Moines River on its way to a protest demonstration in Washington.

Farm prices had been dropping for some years and he was beginning to "discover that things I had learned would have to be forgotten and other things learned." Having received no job offers, he began to look around, but no one wanted him. In the emergency, he became an educator. He took an examination for a county certificate that would permit him to teach school. Hope that he would become superintendent or principal of some town or city school did not materialize.

The job he landed was the principalship of Ackworth Academy, a Quaker school southeast of Des Moines. In lieu of salary, he had the right to divide tuition fees with another teacher. The income provided little more than expenses and his net material gain for the year was a bicycle. Still, he valued the experience.

He put down roots in New Providence and frequently returned to his parents' home outside the village. Instead of staying in Ackworth a second year, he helped his father with farm work until something better came along. For six months he was a reporter for the *Eldora Herald,* a weekly paper at the small county seat. Then he left journalism to become a teacher at a salary of fifty-five dollars a month, the highest paid by any one-room district in Hardin County. A big frog in a small puddle, he left New Providence only during his one year as a professor at a small college in North Carolina. Unlike thousands of young men from farms and villages, he did not go to Chicago or to one of Iowa's larger cities to compete in the business or professional worlds. The reasons are unclear, unless he was being held in close orbit by the attraction of his grandfather's farm.

Observations during his early years in New Providence led Howard to believe thereafter that the more prosperous and stable towns were apt to have only one church. Multidenominational communities, he said, were liable to become divided over doctrinal beliefs and then over other matters. In his later years he would argue that in one-church villages the merchants were more progressive, the streets and alleys cleaner, and farm produce prices higher.

In a Republican community, young Howard soon won acceptance as a local leader of the dominant party. In his twenty-first summer, after graduation from college, he was named one of Hardin County's delegates to a congressional district convention called to renominate David B. Henderson, a former speaker. Other delegates made the trip by train, but Jim, given an unusually early breakfast by his mother, started out before daylight on his bicycle for Waterloo, some fifty miles to the northeast over dirt roads. He arrived in time for the forenoon session and was surprised to find that he had been made a member of the resolutions committee. In later years he couldn't remember what resolutions were adopted, but he was thrilled to listen and watch as Henderson, who had lost a leg at Shiloh, vigorously paraded the platform during his acceptance speech. Happy that he had taken part in the affairs of the nation, Jim biked back home and arrived about midnight. The trip had cost a total of fifty cents, spent on two meals.

He believed that it was from his mother that he had inherited an unusually keen interest in public affairs. During his school days, Jennie had suggested that he write to Senator William B. Allison of Iowa asking some questions about tariffs. The ultraconservative senator, who was the nation's leading advocate of high protective tariffs, promptly replied and followed with several lengthy letters, always in longhand. Nevertheless, the young man did not become an Allison partisan. He sided with the progressive or insurgent wing against the standpatters led by Joseph W. Blythe, chief solicitor for the Burlington railroad. He personally admired Jonathan P. Dolliver, who was one of the founders of the progressive movement and who became senator in 1910. He also was an adherent of Albert B. Cummins, who unsuccessfully challenged Allison for senator in 1908 but later became governor and senator. Howard disapproved the domination of Iowa politics by railroad attorneys. As a progressive, he supported the reform that let the voters decide nominations at primary elections but in later years he commented privately that the railroad attorneys through their control of political conventions had provided Iowa with senators of greater stature than those nominated by the primaries in the following decades.

In the years before the First World War, Howard developed a political creed based on two principles—that the basic function of government is to maintain equality of opportunity between people and industry and, as a corollary, that every extension of governmental power means a corresponding restriction of freedom, either individual or collective. His restless mind, capable of abstract thinking, was hardly compatible with the unchanging views of conservatism and he considered himself a liberal. He probably voted for the Teddy Roosevelt Bull Moose ticket in 1912 and during his long life he was never known to have voted for a Democrat. In 1896 he heard William Jennings Bryan make a free silver speech, but later he refused, despite his father's urging, to go to Waterloo when Roosevelt campaigned there. The trip didn't seem to be worth the trouble.

In later life Howard described himself as a slow but careful reader who, as a result, did not read extensively. He was charmed by the major poets, whose "imaginations have given me many an inner vision into the mysteries of life." Specifically, in his final years he told of reading and rereading Tennyson's *Idylls of the King,* always with new appreciation. Among novels, he believed that Eggleston's *Hoosier Schoolmaster* had influenced him the most, although he enjoyed any good historical novel, such as Roberts's *Northwest Passage.* Howard considered that his greatest interest had been history,

not the history that records mere events and achievements, but the behind-the-scenes movements which lead up to men and achievements. The Declaration of Independence and the adoption of the American Constitution have not interested me as much as have the men and acts of the 150 years of colonial experiences that led up to the Declaration and the Constitution.

A handsome six-footer, with gray eyes and brown hair, Howard had personality as well as talent. He also had limitations. He appreciated a good joke and he could participate in and if necesary dominate a serious conversation, but he lacked a spontaneous wit and small talk was difficult. He could be understanding, cordial, and sympathetic, as occasion required, but social chatter was not his specialty and he never apologized for the deficiency. Also, he could not sing, probably to his regret.

If the Quakers were pacifistic, they also allowed their members a freedom of conscience. When a fervor of patriotism swept the countryside in 1898, Jim tried to enlist in the Spanish-American War but was rejected because of a temporary infection. The treatment of it ended any possibility that he might become addicted to alcohol. The local doctor suggested that as a health restorative he drink a bottle of malt liquor a day. Jennie Howard disapproved when he brought home a case of beer, so he stored it in the barn. Unable to drink warm beer, he gave up and never tried cooler beverages. The example of his grandfather was never forgotten, and he never approved of the storage or consumption of liquor in his own home. Nor did he use tobacco.

His farm boyhood gave him a rugged physique capable of feats of stamina and strength. He strove to dominate competitive situations, such as his peer group's testing to see who could set one barrel of salt on top of another, end on end. On one occasion, he returned from school to find that a matched team of horses he had helped train had been assigned to the hired man. Jim wanted them back and his father, faced with a dilemma, stipulated that he first must lay-by (cultivate for the last time) a ten-acre patch of corn in one day. He did it, although his legs buckled when he brought the team to the barn in the evening after a twenty-five mile ordeal behind a walking cultivator. To achieve a goal, the young man could push himself to the point of exhaustion.

In the financial distress of the 1890s, Howard began the slow accumulation of money that enabled him to buy a farm in the next decade. It was the result of homespun lessons in practical economics given by his father during the hot and dry summer of 1896, the year William Jennings Bryan ran for president on a platform promising that prosperity would return if the government coined both gold and silver dollars on a sixteen-to-one formula.

Henry Howard would never vote for Bryan. He had no contact with the eastern power structure, but he was not impressed with the economic theories that populists expounded with the fervor of evangelists. He was a conservative who had faith in the future of the United States and who refused to believe that all problems could and should be solved by the federal government. One of his last public appearances was at the New Providence polling place in 1912 when he cast his vote for Taft the stand-patter rather than Roosevelt the progressive.

Jim Howard, who had never taken an economics course in college, had increasing respect for his father's opinions about the forces that caused prices to go up and down. In 1896 they were down, corn dropping to ten cents a bushel and cows with calves at foot selling for nine dollars at public auctions. Bankrupt farmers were being driven into towns to pick up what jobs they could. Neighbors complained bitterly, and the son, who himself had experienced unemployment, listened to parental opinions that he remembered and recorded decades later:

Father often remarked that all the talk about the farmer being down and out was purest bunk. He told the neighbors that he well remembered the depressions of 1858 and 1873. They, too, were bad. He held that every ten or fifteen years it was necessary to go through a process of leveling adjustment. Usually agriculture had ten or fifteen good years, followed by five or eight that were bad. He told them that in every long term of years farming had been and would continue to be just as profitable as any other line of business, but probably not much more profitable. I recall his saying that if there were sure money every year in banking, most of the merchants and manufacturers and farmers and professional men would become bankers. If there was sure money in farming every year, too many of these various tradesmen would become farmers. No line of useful business could permanently be much better than any other.

It had been argued that the returns from agriculture had never yielded production costs to the farmer. I have heard that statement many, many times. Father explained it by saying that no line of business could run very long without returning cost of production. If production costs could not be had in farming, losses would have to be met from capital, and the depletion of capital would soon put an end to the operation. He held this to be true of every line of business. Conditions on the farm had improved greatly in father's time and new capital created on the farm had contributed to every line of national wealth. That was sufficient proof that agriculture had returned costs of production plus a profit. He frequently called attention to the fact that all our factories and railroads and cities were the direct result of profitable agriculture. He held that the political nostrums of any party would hinder rather than help agricultural recovery.

These conversations constituted my principal training and background in the science of economics. I presume a college professor would call it extremely elementary, but father had that practical experience woefully lacking in many of our academic teachers. An ounce of his common sense was worth a carload of finespun theories.

The young teacher, who had saved some money and was earning a little more each month, asked his father what he should do with it. Henry Howard told him that whenever a necessary or useful thing could be bought for less than the cost of production, it was time to buy for certainly it would go higher. Conversely, when anything could be sold for materially more than production costs, it was wise to sell it, for sooner or later it would go lower. Prices, he held, would average a little more than production costs over any term of years.

Jim bought lumber and in his spare time built corncribs. Again taking his father's advice, he bought corn at ten cents a bushel. Sixteen months later he sold it in the crib to a local feeder for forty-five cents a bushel. Simultaneously he bought for eleven dollars each a team of yearling fillies that had cost the seller fifteen dollars in service fees as well as feed for eighteen months. In following years he sold some of their colts for good prices and used others as farm horsepower.

With a few hundred dollars in his pocket, he went back to his father and again received memorable advice:

He told me that practically all wealth comes from the farm or the mine or the forest. Land to him was the most necessary, the most basic thing in the universe. It was the only thing that would not burn up or run away. It could not be carried away. The desire to possess land was one of the outstanding characteristics of the human family. Father pointed out that land prices must depend in large degree upon the price of what it produces. He went back to 1858 and 1873 and said that the recovery of commodity prices had preceded any advance in the price of the land. He argued that with advancing prices of farm products the value of farm lands would soon follow. It was a good time to buy land.

Iowa land was priced too high for a teacher to buy, but there were bargains in the Dakotas. Many discouraged homesteaders, after spending five years in obtaining titles to farms, had mortgaged their holdings and moved out, leaving their possessions to be foreclosed by insurance companies or bankers. On the advice of Asa W. Howard, an uncle who had prospered as a dealer in marginal lands, Jim went to Hand County, South Dakota, and bought three quarter sections for $675. For eleven years the grass returned a little more than the taxes. Then the land for which he had paid $1.40 an acre was sold at $12 and the proceeds turned toward his own farm in Iowa.

In another display of indecision, in the first years of his married life Howard was briefly a farmer and then a banker. After his abbreviated year as school principal at Liscomb, he moved in the spring of 1902 to Liberty Township as the tenant operator of his father's 240-acre farm. Of that stage of his life Howard said little in his incomplete memoirs. His wife gave more details in her autobiography, which she began late in life and abandoned after four penciled pages:

It seemed to be the expectation of Jim's family and especially his father that he would be a farmer and he wanted to see him there. Some of the relatives thought he should. I was not too excited about it because of the condition of the house and all the buildings. It had been rented since 1888 and not much repair work had been done. The house was freshly painted and papered inside, so we made out.

For three crop years Howard tilled his grandfather's original acreage in a stock shares lease and divided the income with his father. They were profitable years, bringing good yields and high prices. Probably they were the best years he experienced as a farmer, for the first decade of the new century was a period of rural prosperity.

If Henry Howard had been instrumental in persuading his son to become his tenant farmer, he also was responsible for ending the relationship. At the end of the third crop year a new bank was organized at New Providence of which his father was a principal incorporator.

"He and the family suggested that we take some stock in the deal and that I become cashier," Jim Howard wrote three years before his death. "I think that I have never said this before, but I have always considered it to be the worst blunder I ever made. I missed some of the best years of American agriculture."

Henry Howard retired to a small tract just east of New Providence and Jim Howard moved onto the farm west of town at the start of his banking career. He soon found that it was unwise to be a banker and a farmer simultaneously, and he bought a substantial house at the edge of town.

Behind the counter of the Providence State Bank, which was housed in a small brick building at the only important downtown intersection, Howard at the age of thirty-two ranked with the principal of the academy and the Quaker minister as one of the community's leading men. He gave personal attention to the needs of the community and as Republican committeeman he was the local contact man for the congressman.

He had no formal training in banking, but he seemed to understand instinctively the principles of keeping money in circulation in a manner that would help the town and countryside and at the same time return a profit to the stockholders. He needed no instruction about ledger balancing and other accounting tasks, and in later life he could add a column of figures in his head faster than they could be punched on an adding machine. He set up a double-entry bookkeeping system for at least one farmer-owned enterprise, and near the end of his life he testified that at one time he could have qualified as a certified public accountant. If so, he was self-taught. The banking years showed that J. R. Howard was a man of many talents.

Not all his enterprises were successful. Then or later, no member of the immediate Howard family succeeded as a merchant, and the bank cashier's sideline investment in a hardware store was a mistake. He was a partner in Bales and Howard, whose 1905 billhead advertised general hardware, machinery, wagons, buggies, paints, oils, mutual and Bell line phones, and poultry feed. The next year, without material loss, he withdrew from the unprofitable business.

He knew the people, their problems, and their potential. Like the other town fathers, he understood that the prosperity of New Providence depended upon the well-being of the country people who were its customers. In a pioneering step, the bank helped small farmers who had a few hogs to sell but lacked marketing facilities. He organized a shipping pool, assembled enough hogs to fill a railroad car, arranged for it to be forwarded to the Chicago stockyards, and then prorated the proceeds. People who sought the bank's services became his lifelong friends. A merchant at neighboring Union remembered that when he borrowed money he also received friendly advice that was worth listening to. For decades Jim Howard was something of a diety to Donald Adams, who as a teenager had assumed responsibility for the care of his widowed mother. The lad wanted to feed cattle during the winter months and came to the bank to borrow money with which to buy them. The cashier gave the only possible answer, that under bank regulations loans could only be made to adults. But since the conversation confirmed his previous opinion of the Adams family, Howard made the loan from his personal funds.

Soon after he returned to New Providence, Howard realized that he would rather work in a cornfield or haymow than at a desk. As a school administrator, he had briefly been principal of the Liscomb town school and presumably he could have advanced to administrative posts in larger school systems. If he had completed requirements for a doctor of philosophy degree, he might have become a low-paid professor at some college. Banking paid more, and he was innovative and community minded. In time the county seat or larger banks might have hired him, but he lacked enough money to buy a sizable block of stock that would have been helpful in attaining a higher position in the financial world. His family was increasing in size, and there is no reason to doubt that he really preferred farming to a white-collar career.

Henry Howard, who was advancing in years, wanted his son to take over his nearby eighty acres and handle it in connection with the bank. That acreage, however, would not justify hiring the help that would be needed. Jim lived in a good house and on seven acres he kept a cow or two and made some money raising pigs, but it wasn't farming.

In September 1906, John Bryant, a real estate dealer at St. Anthony, came into the bank with word that David Rockhill, who had moved from Liberty Township to Washington State a few years earlier, wanted to sell his south quarter section. If anyone knew of a buyer, the price was eighty-one dollars an acre. It adjoined Henry Howard's farm on the north and was an unusually good 160 acres. Rockhill, who did not know that Iowa land prices had recently increased, was selling the land so that he could retire the mortgage on his other two quarters. Howard did some quick mental arithmetic about the marketability of his South Dakota holdings and the increased value of his bank stock. To the surprise of the agent, his wife, and himself, he bought the Rockhill farm on the spur of the moment.

Out of sentiment, Henry Howard insisted on trading farms. He was advancing in years and wanted his son located on the old family holdings. The Rockhill land was a little more fertile, but the buildings were better on the home place. The trade was made, a $5,000 mortgage arranged, and Jim Howard became the third generation owner of the quarter section his grandfather had bought in 1854. More than two years passed, however, before he moved from New Providence. The reason for the delay is not known.

6

Dirt Farmer

FOR Jim Howard, no material possession could be as important as his land. He never lost the appreciation, first realized as an eight-year-old, of the springtime odor of freshly turned soil. One of his rituals, almost an act of communion, was to scoop up a handful of loam from a newly cultivated field and to savor it with skin and nose. To him nothing was as beautiful as a field of red clover in bloom. Neighbors were baffled one Sunday when, at the end of the church service, he told his oldest son to drive the rest of the family home. Then he crossed the road, climbed the fence, and in his best clothes started hiking along the fence rows of neighbors' fields toward his own farm boundary three-quarters of a mile away. When friends asked why, he did not bother to explain that not all men have the same concept of beauty.

About his land he was as sentimental as his grandmother, who always used emphasis in speaking of it as home. Sometime after 1909 he gave it a name she would have liked—Homelands Farm. The name, as registered at the county recorder's office October 13, 1926, applied only to the original quarter section and not to acreage added after 1854.

Three weeks and three days before his thirty-sixth birthday in 1909, on the traditional March 1 moving day for rural families, Howard became a dirt farmer for the second time. Between 1901 and 1904 he had been his father's tenant but now he was owner of the rolling quarter section. Ambitious and in good health, realizing that he would have to work hard to make up for the years spent in town, he was confident of the future.

His chief liability was a shortage of working capital; most of his accumulated savings had gone to pay for the ancestral farm and to buy the basic equipment for a farming operation. He planned to devote the rest of his life to building up the soil, to improving the quality of livestock fed for market, to modernizing buildings, and to buying more land in the interest of providing a better life for his family and himself. The improvements he envisioned would be built for utility rather than display, for he knew that income must exceed outgo if a business was to operate on its own resources. Part of his earned surplus, he planned, could go back into the land as tile ditches, fencing, clover and alfalfa seed, and more and better livestock. Each year he would buy feeder cattle, for Iowa land was too high priced to support a herd of cows large enough to raise the supply of calves needed. The hogs fed for market would be home-grown, since less acreage was needed for a sow that would produce two litters a year. Unlike most of his neighbors, who dealt only in cattle and hogs, when market conditions warranted he would buy sheep. If he diversified to the extent of feeding his corn crop to three kinds of livestock, he would be reasonably certain of a yearly profit. He was not a college-trained farmer, but he intended to learn everything he could from the Extension Service at Iowa State College.

Few families in mid-Iowa lived farther from stores and railroads. On the west side of the farm an ungraded dirt road led southward six miles through Bevins Grove timber to Clemons, the closest shipping point and shopping center. The outside world could be reached through Clemons, which in 1910 had a population of 213. The RFD carrier from its post office stopped daily at the Howard mailbox. Over one of the independent telephone company's multiparty lines, a hand-cranked ring of two longs and a short alerted potential eavesdroppers that someone wanted to carry on a conversation—necessarily loud-voiced—with the Howards. In addition to the railroad station, small stockyard, lumberyard, and livery stable, the village had a one-block retail center that included a couple of general stores, the post office, a hardware store, and now and then a bank. The doctor's office was a block away. Telegrams had to be addressed to Clemons Grove, which was the Minneapolis and St. Louis railroad's official name for the small branch-line station. Passenger trains ran twice a day to Marshalltown and connected with the main line of the Chicago and North Western road, which had frequent and fast service to Chicago. Marshalltown, which was classified as a city, had an imposing courthouse to testify that it was the seat of county government, but it was twenty-two miles from the farm. Only rarely did team and buggy make a journey there.

The original village of Bangor, to which Jim had ridden weekly for mail at the age of six, was dying slowly because railroad tracks had never reached it. At the edge of Bangor lived Henry Howard's only sister, Hannah, who had married Jacob Kinzer and reared a large family. Their oldest son, Roland J. Kinzer, became nationally known as the head of the American Hereford Association.

Under Howard's management at the start were 240 acres, more than most of his neighbors farmed. In addition to owning the basic quarter section, he paid rent to his father for the use of the 80 acres his grandfather had added on the east side. Eventually, he anticipated, he would inherit both the 80 and the Rockhill 160 acres on the north that he had bought and traded to his father. That happened in 1912, when Henry Howard died in his seventy-first year of what doctors diagnosed as a kidney ailment. Jim's sister, Lenora Moninger, who lived eight miles northwest of Marshalltown, was bequeathed the balance of her father's estate. For the present, the Rockhill quarter section would be in the hands of a tenant who paid half of the income from livestock and grain sales. The new owner, a conservative manager, needed to build up his working capital and gave first attention to the home farm. Many improvements were needed but, as far as possible, he planned to make them with his own hands.

Twice during Howard's lifetime the acreage was expanded by purchase of small farms that adjoined Homelands. In 1916 he paid $152.50 an acre for the eighty-acre Liston farm across the road on the west. The new property included part of the Mud Creek slough but was attractive because it had a fine hilltop site for a retirement residence that never was built. In 1925, upon settlement of the Thomas Dunn estate, Howard bought 120 acres to the south for $125 an acre. This transaction had its sentimental side, for Jennie Howard had coveted the Dunn fields because they could be seen from her house. The layout of the Homelands farmstead made it difficult for her to see her own men when they were at work. With the Dunn purchase the farm encompassed 600 contiguous acres of some of the best land in central Iowa.

In addition to the routine of growing crops and feeding livestock, other work needed to be done in 1909. For one thing, tiling would make some of the low-lying land more productive. It is axiomatic that owner-operators keep buildings and fences in better repair than tenant farmers, and the new owner began a program of improvements that continued for much of a decade. Unlike men who give priority to barns and sheds because these structures are directly involved with income production, he began with the house, for he wanted his wife to have as good a home as those of her friends in New Providence.

The 1861 oak house had been enlarged into a white clapboard structure that included four rooms downstairs, three bedrooms over the west wing, and a partial basement, but it lacked many conveniences as well as adequate space. Bill Dickover, the Bangor carpenter who in the early days had been one of the hired men on the farm, came back with his tool chest the first fall to put in an extension measuring twelve by twenty-two feet that provided space for a new kitchen and a bathroom. That winter, without help, Howard fed eighty cattle and more than one hundred hogs, milked six cows, and split the next summer's supply of wood for the cook stove. At night, working by lantern light, he installed the bathroom plumbing and piped water into the kitchen. For a water supply, a galvanized tank was placed in the attic and filled with a hand-operated pump in the basement. With running water in the kitchen and bathroom, the outside privy was abolished. Later a gasoline engine in the enlarged basement provided power for pumping water, washing clothes, and separating milk. About 1914 a hot air furnace was installed.

The house had five gables after the unfinished attic over the dining room was transformed into a dormitory that expanded sleeping space and required that the dining room be enlarged by a bay window. The improvements continued over the years, with an unheated sun room on the front and a two-story woodhouse-storage building attached to the kitchen corner. By that time the house had seven gables. Comfortable and well built, it met the family's needs until it burned down due to an overheated furnace during the winter of 1929. Virtually all the contents were destroyed, but most of the owner's papers were saved from the room he used as an office. Without them, this book could not have been written.

The owner's multiple talents were demonstrated in 1911 after a fire destroyed the barn that his grandfather had built to replace the straw stable. To accommodate the horses and cows that had been in the pasture during the nighttime fire, he arranged makeshift stalls in sheds that were part of a double corncrib built in 1882. Moving quickly because an unusually lush hay crop was almost ready for cutting, he summoned Dickover and at the north edge of the farmstead built a large pole barn, fifty-two by forty-eight feet, in which hay storage began at the ground level and was flanked by sheds for the shelter of feeding cattle.

At a time when poles supported the sides and roofs of most Iowa barns, Howard decided he wanted his main barn to be of balloon-frame construction and to have studding and joists replacing the poles. A floor plan for an unusually efficient group of stalls, grain bins, and work and storage space was thought out while he hauled grain bundles as his contribution to the neighborhood threshing ring. His blueprints were drawn on an envelope when the threshing operation was halted briefly for repairs. Dickover and other carpenters did not understand the mathematics and joinery involved, but Howard ordered lumber for a barn thirty by sixty-two feet with a wing thirty-six by eighteen feet; the high roof was to make room for a second-floor haymow. He cut the sample rafters, studding, and bracing and gave specific instructions to the workmen each day before he went to the field. The material came out even, the barn was square, and a half century later there was no sign of sagging. When tractors replaced horses, the haymow became obsolete and work aisles on the ground floor became shelter for brood sows and growing pigs.

Buildings of native timber that had been erected by his grandfather and father were preserved whenever possible. New construction on which he acted as head carpenter included a combined garage and shop in which he installed a forge and did rough blacksmithing. When Howard was called away from the farm during the early Farm Bureau days, he quickly switched back to overalls and a work shirt upon his return. Once, after a summons to the White House, he came home to find that his part of central Iowa was covered with ice; cattle feeding was handicapped because none of the horses was shod. His first act was to fire up the forge and shoe a team. Jennie Howard was pleased that the trip to Washington had not changed her son's attitude toward manual labor.

In the pretractor era, during the growing and corn picking seasons especially, farmers had to have hired men. Howard began with two young men who in later years said it was an honor to have been asked to work at Homelands, but they soon moved to their own farms. Because single men slept in the house and ate with the family, their presence increased the burdens of housework. Married help usually had greater experience and stability, and so to accommodate them Howard bought a two-story frame house, the original part of which had been the first schoolhouse in the township, and had it moved to a spot near which his grandfather had built the straw stable. In it lived a succession of hired men, most of whom had large families. Later he placed married workers in the Rockhill and Liston houses, with the result that only occasionally did hired help sleep under his roof. Carefully screened in advance, most of the men stayed several years and were competent to carry on the work in the owner's absence. In addition to a monthly check and free rent, each was given a garden plot, firewood, and at butchering time a hog.

In his incomplete autobiography "Making an Iowa Farmer," Howard may have been guilty of faulty self-analysis when he wrote: "I never became a good boss. I never knew how to say to a man, 'Go do that job.' Rather I would say, 'Come, let's do it.' It is a wise man who knows his own limitations and stays within their bounds."

Almost unwillingly, Howard in 1914 bought his first automobile, a Model T Ford that cost $480 plus freight. To him, even a Ford seemed a great extravagance. Previously a few neighbors had bought higher priced cars and there was talk that their farm work suffered because they did not stay at home as much as when they had driven horses. Inexperienced in economics, Jim did not consider cars a necessity and he was afraid that large amounts of money would be transferred to nonproductive uses. He liked to drive fast, within the bounds of safety and with care that engines were not pushed beyond capacity. When he returned from a western trip, part of which was made in a borrowed car, he told of seeing another auto far ahead and wondering whether he could pass it. He did, miles later, by driving steadily at what he considered a safe maximum speed. On another occasion he thought it noteworthy that at night he had driven from Iowa City to the farm, about one hundred miles, without stopping the motor.

The first tractor at Homelands, a second hand Wallis Cub, arrived in 1917 and, despite some operating difficulties, was used steadily for drawbar and belt power. Howard carefully weighed such factors as the cost of gasoline and lubricants against homegrown hay and oats. In the end mechanization was inevitable, and he accepted it as being essential to efficient and profitable production. Testifying in 1927 about the problems and future of agriculture, he said:

We are going ahead to motorize our farms more and more. I have a lot of good horses at home. I love horses, but old as I am I would rather crank up a tractor and work with it all day in the field than fool with horses. The younger men are more keen than I am for the truck and tractor. The result is that in ten years there will be a still greater reduction in the number of horses and a large surplus of corn and oats, unless some other factor changes the situation.

As a banker, Howard had owned one team, but he needed more horsepower to work 240 acres. Instead of attending country auctions, he and Ray Reece, who lived near Union and was one of the North Carolinians who were natural horsemen, combined their talents. The retiring banker and the experienced horse trader went to the Chicago Stock Yards and in one of the Chicago Horse Company's auctions bought a carload of footsore veterans of horse car and dray service. Howard took his share of the deal in horseflesh at less than Iowa prices. The change from city pavement to Iowa loam extended the animals' usefulness by several years. One of them disliked fieldwork but had a long career as Anna Howard's buggy horse. It was a profitable arrangement.

Because two or three mares foaled each year, surplus colts could be sold when they reached peak condition. Howard also attended farm sales and bought yearlings at an age when they were scrawny and unappreciated. Well fed, they grew up to be good horses. Matched as teams, they were sold in an operation that in some years brought a profit of $1,000. At times Howard owned mules. He bragged about the intelligence of a span of mules that he always placed on the outside if a four-abreast hitch was used. Once he ran out of binder twine when he had almost finished cutting a field of oats. Taking a chance, he climbed fence to borrow a ball of twine from a neighbor. Just then the team of four took off on the run for the barn, through two narrow gates and across a bridge. The only damage to the binder was a cutter bar guard broken on a small stump. The gates were no more than six inches wider than the binder and Howard claimed that he could not have driven through the openings at a slow walk without hitting a post.

Instinctively he knew what the soil needed. The Rockhill quarter section, for example, was unusually productive but its northeast field was poorly drained and had a hard and cloddy soil that resulted in below average crop yields. The cure was to sacrifice one crop. One summer he did not cut the mammoth red clover that had been sown with the previous year's crop of oats. That fall the clover was plowed under, with considerable difficulty, as green manure. The character of the field was completely altered and thereafter it was superior in tilth and fertility.

Intuition and patience were demonstrated with one field of wheat. Just before threshing time he built a portable granary and stored the grain while first a crop of red clover and then corn grew around it. In time war broke out in Europe and he sold the wheat at inflated prices.

Corn, the money crop for midwestern farmers, was grown on half the Homelands plowed acreage. To restore the soil, each year half the corn acreage was followed by a small grain planted along with clover. Usually the third crop was oats, in demand for feed for horses, but barley could be substituted or occasionally a field would be planted to wheat. The clover, a legume that restored nitrogen to the soil, grew lushly after the small grain was harvested in midsummer; in the fourth year it was cut for hay and then allowed to continue growing until it was plowed under. This rotation maintained the productiveness of the farm.

Seed corn was carefully selected at Homelands and two high-yielding strains of open pollenated corn were developed—one from Reid's Yellow Dent and the other Silver King—with large symmetrical ears and deep kernels. Howard-grown samples won prizes at local corn shows. To assure a high percentage of germination, several kernels from individual ears were placed in individual compartments in a "rag doll" tester, a long strip of cloth that was kept moist and warm in the kitchen until the kernels had time to germinate. In that manner, the poor ears could be discarded in advance. Howard's oldest son did much of the seed selection in the field. He pleased his father by buying seed at eight dollars per bushel when a farmer several miles away had a sale. He had been instructed to pay as much as three dollars, but decided that the strain on sale was worth the added money. One drawback was that seed selected before frost produced corn that matured earlier than necessary. Another was that the long and brittle stalks of the Howard strains plugged up the mechanism of a new two-row mechanical corn picker, the first in the neighborhood. The machine worked efficiently only after seed from hybrid corn with strong stalks came on the market. At that time Iowa farmers stopped selecting and testing their own seed.

Although he understood soils and crops, Howard was primarily a livestock feeder who made money by selling steers, hogs, and at times sheep fattened in his feedlots. He denied, however, that he had unusual talent. In his incomplete autobiography he wrote:

Success comes merely from the combined results of horse sense and hard work. No man will succeed who does not love his animals sufficiently to sacrifice his personal comfort for their welfare. The saving of a litter of pigs must be more important than a night's sleep. When the thermometer drops to twenty below and a blizzard rages, the comfort of every animal must precede breakfast sausage and buckwheat cakes. The man who continually seeks the line of least resistance had best sell his grain, but he won't amount to much anywhere. Soft-handed endeavors won't bring home the bacon.

Howard recalled that he sold corn on the cash market only once, when a high price of $2.19 a bushel was reached during the First World War. Usually it was necessary to buy grain from neighbors because the Homelands fields did not produce enough to fatten the feeder cattle and hogs that were the main source of income. As a livestock feeder, Howard marketed his corn on the hoof by feeding it in the ear, as ensilage, or by turning animals into the field to forage. In all cases, hogs followed the cattle and salvaged any grain on the ground. A major benefit of the feeding operation was that none of the manure was wasted. Homelands Farm gained steadily in soil fertility and crop production, but its owner never saw a sack of commercial fertilizer until he became president of the American Farm Bureau Federation. Tractor power upset the four-year rotation later by eliminating the demand for oats and reducing the market for clover hay—changes that led to the general use of chemicals.

Since diversification reduced the possibility of financial losses, Howard frequently bought bands of sheep at river markets. The investment was less for aged ewes that could produce one crop of spring lambs and could be clipped for wool. The hogs were homegrown. To upgrade his herd, Howard bought purebred boars and selected the best gilts for breeding. The objective was to produce one litter of pigs for each six or seven acres and to raise one pig for each acre. The count was usually less. Iowa land was too expensive for a farmer to raise his own calves and it was necessary to study the stocker and feeder market, to estimate the forces of supply and demand, and to buy several carloads of animals each year from the range states or Canadian provinces. When the outlook seemed uncertain, it was prudent to buy cheaper animals and hope that a gain in weight would make up for any unfavorable price fluctuations. In bad years the Howard operation avoided disaster and usually made some money. "We never aspired to be a show farm," Howard wrote in the 1936 year-end edition of the *Annalist*.

If we had, we should have failed utterly. But year after year the buldings were improved, fences built, and occasionally more acres added. It was done by a definite plan of cropping and feeding. . . .

Not every carload of cattle or lambs made a profit, but not all eggs were in one basket. There was for more than twenty years some gain at the close of the year. The land gained too in fertility, without buying one pound of fertilizer. The clover and manure did their work.

The former banker understood the uses of money and at all times knew the approximate balance of his checking account. His most important rule for financial stability was that money should not be borrowed unless he had at least two sources of future income from which it could be repaid. He studied markets and seemed to anticipate future trends intuitively.

Borrowing money was a heavy but necessary expense. The purchase of the Liston and Dunn farms was financed by long-term mortgages, and many other expenditures were met by short-term bank notes, which usually were renewed several times before being paid. He had to take out a bank loan to meet the cost of draining wet land, knowing that considerable time would elapse before increased production paid for the tile. When he needed a silo, and then a second one, he borrowed the money knowing that two years would pass before the cost would be repaid by increased cattle feeding profits. Customarily the purchase of feeder cattle required a loan, and during the war he borrowed money to buy Liberty bonds. Most of the borrowings involved the financing of operating expenses and needed improvements that could be paid off with increased production. As a result, some expenditures were deferred, especially if they could not be classed as income producing. In 1909, for example, plans to install an electric light plant had a high priority, but the purchase was delayed nearly a decade.

The electric generating plant was the subject of a speech before an audience of bankers in White Sulphur Springs, West Virginia, in 1922. To meet operating expenses, Howard cropped every acre intensively. In the earlier generation, his mother had the help of one or two hired girls, but his wife found it impossible to obtain domestic help and the nearest laundry was twenty miles away. Anna Howard was overworked with the cooking and washing for the family and extra help. She told her husband she regretted that the purchase of the electric generating plant had been deferred again. His answer was that he would borrow the money at the bank if a plant could be installed promptly.

The next morning, after Howard had been plowing a few hours, a light plant salesman climbed the fence and hopped up behind him on the moving tractor. "I came out to see if you had thought any more about the light plant," he said. Without stopping, Howard asked if it could be put in immediately. The answer was yes. Howard told the salesman to write out the contract while he went another round.

Returning after another trip across the field, Howard signed the document and said, "You take this to the house, and if it is satisfactory with Mrs. Howard she will give you a check for twenty-five dollars. Then you go ahead and put in the plant while I borrow the money."

"It's all right with Mrs. Howard," the man replied. "She telephoned me this morning."

The generating plant's storage batteries were charged by a gasoline engine. The plant cost several hundred dollars and served until a high tension line reached the farm several years later. The electric iron, fan, washer, and other appliances greatly eased Anna Howard's burdens. Her husband said that increased crop production was an indirect result.

The point of the speech was that, as in other cases, the loan of several hundred dollars for two or three months had to be renewed several times before it was paid off. Howard argued that farmers needed an intermediate form of credit.

Before his national Farm Bureau career, Howard spent fourteen years as a dirt farmer. In "Making an Iowa Farmer," he gave this summation of that part of his life: "The years beginning with my earliest recollections and extending up to the World War were probably the happiest the American farmer has ever known. They exceeded all previous centuries in material and mechanical improvements. It was a joy to have lived and worked through them."

7

Liberty Consolidated School

ONE-HALF MILE south of their farm, at a peaceful crossroads that marked the approximate center of four districts with one-room schools, Jim and Anna Howard changed the landscape. In 1914, five years after they left New Providence, Liberty Consolidated School opened its doors in a box-shaped, two-story brick building erected in what had been a pasture. For thirty-seven years, in its four classrooms and auxiliary facilities, nearby children received a state-accredited elementary and high school education. In Iowa's first strictly rural school consolidation, the combined elementary and high school replaced four old-style schools in which only eight grades had been taught.

The Howards, who wanted the best possible education for their children, were primarily responsible for Liberty Consolidated School. Unlike the Quaker pioneers who founded church-affiliated colleges and academies, they worked within the framework of the tax-supported public school system in achieving their goal of duplicating the best facilities of the smaller towns. No cornerstone carried their names, but the building was their monument. Forty years later, looking back over a career that had brought national recognition, they believed that the school probably was their greatest accomplishment. It improved the quality of education in the lower grades and in particular it enabled the children of tenant farmers and hired men to go to high school, and in some cases on to college, instead of having their formal education end with the eighth grade. There were other benefits, of course, but those were the ones that counted.

Liberty Consolidated School also turned out to be something of a training ground for Howard. Because the school was unique, he received recognition from outside his home community and for the first time went to distant places to make public speeches. Later he recalled that given a place on the Farm and Home Week program at Iowa State College, he

45

suffered from stage fright when he faced a crowded auditorium. Nevertheless he went ahead with a carefully prepared argument for fewer but better country schools. When the program ended, he was lectured by an uncle for not standing up straight and for keeping his hands in his pockets. Regardless of the delivery, the speech must have been worthwhile, for the state superintendent of public instruction asked him to repeat it in several other communities that were interested in consolidation. Two years later, when he became involved in the lower levels of the Farm Bureau movement, he was at ease when he made a speech or chaired a meeting.

The story of Liberty Consolidated School begins when Anna and Jim shocked New Providence friends by moving back to the country just as their oldest son was ready to enter the first grade. "Jim came from the country and he got along all right," Anna Howard said loyally, but the couple faced an educational problem, for the one-room schools had gone downhill since Jim as a boy carried his lunch pail to the Dunn School, Liberty No. 2. Now his children would live in the No. 2 district and be exposed to an inferior education during the first eight grades. After that, they couldn't live at home and go to high school. Clemons had a high school and took in tuition students from nearby farms, but six miles was too far for horse-drawn trips before and after school. As a result, arrangements for room and board would have been necessary for the Howard children to go to school at Clemons or New Providence. While more than five hundred Iowa municipalities had high schools, some were limited to two years. Starting in 1896, a few schools had been consolidated. Not until 1911 did the legislature require that the one-room districts be taxed to pay the tuition of children attending high school elsewhere.

The basic trouble was that the small districts did not have enough children and tax revenues to support adequate schools. Both enrollment and the quality of teaching had dropped across the Midwest. Agriculture had prospered, and farms were larger. Surveying the horizon from his farm, Howard could count twenty-one abandoned sites where families had lived during his boyhood. By 1909 only nineteen homesites remained within view. Not only had the number of homesteads been reduced by half, but families were smaller. As a result, enrollment in country schools averaged not much more than ten. In Howard's earlier years from twenty to twenty-five pupils attended No. 2 during the spring and fall and from forty to fifty in the winter.

Meanwhile the young people of ability who had been his first teachers had moved to better careers. Their replacements to a large extent had been city girls who cared nothing for the country, had not received normal school training, and were teaching only to earn some money before marriage. Enthusiasm and interest in schoolwork and social events had diminished along with enrollment. Spelling and ciphering matches and literary society programs had been abandoned because there weren't enough pupils to provide competition, Howard told an audience of Wisconsin teachers in 1921. "We were confronted with a lack of interest in the welfare of education," he said. "Some of the better families had moved to town in order to educate their children."

As the first step from his new base in Liberty township, the former teacher and banker took over the presidency of the three-man school board in the No. 2 district. He could have the job for the asking and be certain that the Dunn School would be taught by the best available teacher. His wife, who had given up teaching in the New Providence academy to get married, became the board's secretary.

To make it possible for some country children to attend town schools, the legislature in 1906 authorized the establishment of consolidated independent districts that had to take in at least sixteen contiguous sections of land. If one-third of the voters signed a petition approved by the county superintendent of schools, separate referenda would be held in rural and town areas. That law had been intended to enable town schools to expand into the countryside, but it could apply to rural areas. On the basis of its statutory formula, the Howards proposed a consolidation of districts 1, 2, 5, and 6, which encompassed a four-square-mile area of farmland in northeastern Liberty township. (Later districts 3 and 4 were added by annexation.) The four districts met a minimum area qualification. In view of the unimproved condition of the roads, four districts were enough. Also, even if a larger district might be theoretically desirable, additional opposition might be courted if an attempt was made to take in more territory.

Jim and Anna were not, of course, the only parents interested in giving their children a high school and college education. For example, Ben and Lulu Parsons needed no sales talk, only an explanation of how consolidation could be achieved. Over Sunday dinners, these families and others discussed the emergence of a public relations problem. The guest list would vary, but the standard topic of conversation was the conviction that one-room schools could be replaced and that consolidation would bring a higher quality of teaching. One argument was that the existing one-room buildings, nearly a half century old, would soon need major repairs or complete replacement. If that was true, the money should be spent on one large building.

Convincing neighbors that school consolidation was desirable required special talents and an unusual background. Members of three churches divided the area involved and Howard had strong ties with all of them. Fortunately he had grown up on the divide between the two largest.

As a boy he had played and gone to school with the children of the Irish families who lived along and beyond the road that bordered the farm on the west. Friendships continued into manhood and he was regarded as unprejudiced. If he wanted to talk about a better school system, at least the Irish would listen. The nearest parochial school was at Marshalltown and the Irish went to mass at St. Anthony. Howard was privately told that while prominent Catholic families wanted their own school they realized that the cost would be too great. In the end most of them lined up for consolidation.

East of the farm lived a concentration of North Carolinians who called themselves Tarheels and whose community gathering place was the small church where the Howard family attended Sunday services. The first North Carolinians, who had arrived—some by way of Indiana—in the middle of the nineteenth century, steadfastly believed in the Quaker virtues of education and temperance. A new migration from Yadkin County had started sometime before 1900. They were hill people who had the energy and initiative to leave their part of Appalachia and contribute to the development of Iowa as an agricultural state. Many of the newer Tarheels became solid citizens and community leaders. They wanted a better life for their children, but at the start only a minority aspired to an education that went beyond the eighth grade, if that far. At the Friends church they were exposed to the doctrine of consolidation.

Majority support for the cause came from the portion of the Bevins Grove Campbellite community within the boundary of the proposed district. The denominational prejudices of the pioneer age had largely vanished, and Howard had a wide acquaintance in the neighborhood.

The original concept, which assumed that local control would be permitted by the authorities at Des Moines, was that better schools could be provided without any increase in taxation and that real estate values would increase. A superior school presumably would attract more experienced teachers, and Howard believed that two or three teachers might possibly do the work of four. An obvious objection was that children living at the edge of the enlarged district would have to travel farther to get to school. It was decided that some additional distance was of small consequence, since a stable could be erected at the school and the more remote families could arrange for neighborly relays. The major objection was that an improved school system would mean higher taxes. Also, in a spirit of provincialism, some did not favor a mingling of neighborhoods and denominations. Others feared that transportation would be too expensive.

Nonetheless, the campaign succeeded and the school opened on schedule. All records dealing with the consolidation have been lost, but in a 1921 speech at a Wisconsin teachers' convention, Howard said that a decisive majority favored the project. He gave no details. Bits of information are contained in the circuit court records of an equity suit filed in 1914, after the school opened. F. E. Northrup of Marshalltown, attorney for the enlarged district, filed an answer saying the plaintiffs, two Cedar Rapids men, had claimed that the school could have been constructed for $8,000, but that the contractor found that the cost would be $15,000. Notice of the suit was filed on B. R. Parsons as president of the board and on Ira Cook as secretary. The defendants' witnesses would have been Howard, Parsons, Charles W. Dunn, William H. Dunn, and Robert R. Ridgway, all members of the consolidated board, and Mrs. Howard, who had been secretary of the board during the transition period. The matter never went to trial.

During the construction period, neighbors contributed teams and time to haul brick and other materials from the Clemons railroad siding. Howard acted as unpaid inspector of the contractor's work. The best of the one-room buildings was moved to the site and remodeled as a residence for teachers. An open-faced stable was erected for horses, and enclosed hacks were purchased for transportation of pupils. In most cases the drivers were upper school students who lived on the outskirts of the district. In 1924 the former St. John's Church was purchased for $600, moved eighty rods onto the school grounds, and converted into a gymnasium and community center. No one complained that the basketball court wasn't large enough for growing boys.

Two classrooms for the six lower grades were on the first floor of the building. The principal and another teacher taught the upper grades on the second floor. Special facilities were provided for the teaching of domestic science, manual training, and agriculture. A folding door permitted use of the two second-floor classrooms as an auditorium.

Limited state aid came under a 1911 law that appropriated $50,000 to consolidated schools that had teachers and equipment for instruction in agriculture, home economics, and manual training. With a four-room building, Liberty Consolidated School was entitled to the top amount, $500 for equipment and $750 annually thereafter for operations. Otherwise revenues came from property taxes.

The school widened the community and helped erase prejudices. Children of Quakers, Catholics, and Campbellites, who played and recited lessons together, developed friendships that continued into adulthood. Perhaps unconsciously, varied elements of the population took pains not to endanger their school and community center by dissension. Not unusual was the action of Leo Dunn, who became the largest farmer in the vicinity. One spring, as the frost went out of the unimproved roads, he used his motorized equipment to carry out emergency grading so that the Catholic church at St. Anthony could be reached on Sunday. Then he turned in the other direction so that Protestants could get to their own church.

The commitment of Jim and Anna Howard to better education far outweighed their sentimental attachment to Liberty Consolidated School, and they heartily supported a new consolidation movement that closed its doors in 1951. Virtually all the rural roads had been graded and graveled, and a long campaign had culminated in laws that eliminated the one-room districts and provided state aid for enlarged districts. In the reorganization, Liberty School was expendable. In the interests of education, efficiency, and economy, the children of northern Liberty Township were bused to Clemons. In three more years Liberty Township became part of a school system that covered the west half of Marshall County, with headquarters at State Center. The Howards had been ahead of their time on the consolidation issue and they lived to see its countrywide acceptance.

There was nothing obsolete about the brick building that stood at the crossroads as a monument to educational progress. Leo Dunn bought the property and used the school as a granary. Decades later the building stood as solid and square as Jim Howard's frame barn.

In several speeches and essays Howard discussed rural education in general and Liberty Consolidated School in particular. In 1919 he told an Iowa Farm Bureau committee that rural Iowa needed better educational facilities, that most high school teachers were not competent to preside over vocational agriculture classes, and that state funds should be appropriated for aid to high schools and the one-room schools. He was supported by Luther V. Carter, a New Providence friend whom he had appointed as one of three members of the committee. Howard commended the work done by Iowa State College but said it couldn't reach enough of the secluded farm population. One of his suggestions was that secondary schools of agriculture should teach some farm business, arithmetic, and agriculture. Federal aid from Smith-Hughes appropriations for vocational agriculture were called inadequate. To emphasize the critical nature of the problem, he said that during the war it was found that many farm people, including the presidents of two school boards, could not read and write. His forward-looking suggestion was that the legislature provide more money for rural education and that it be administered by an agency such as a state board of education.

In its annual report, Carter's committee recommended that Iowa State College and the state normal school establish a three-month winter course on business agriculture, that the Extension Service provide one-week schools on farm business methods and possibly marketing, and that the Farm Bureau cooperate in obtaining Smith-Hughes financing of agricultural and other vocational work.

Seven years after Liberty Consolidated School opened, Howard gave an enthusiastic report on it in his Wisconsin speech. In the one-room districts, the average enrollment had been ten pupils and the average daily attendance 65 percent. After consolidation, without material changes in population, twenty to twenty-five were enrolled from each of the old districts. The average daily attendance approximated 95 percent and had never been as low as 90 percent, and the school year was lengthened from seven to nine months. After consolidation four teachers were employed, and they were more competent and better paid than previous teachers. Manual training, domestic science, and agriculture were taught as part of the high school courses. Advance concerns about transportation with groundless.

Inevitably, taxes were higher for the consolidated school. Howard presented statistics to show that, including the high school and transportation, the consolidated school cost less per day per pupil than the old system. For the preceding year, Howard's school taxes, including the levy for the new building, had been 2.2 mills less than half of the total state, county, township, and road taxes. Two or three decades earlier, the school taxes on the same land were one or two mills higher than half the other taxes. He added that his children had easily made the scholastic and social transition from the rural school to Lake View High School in Chicago.

The number of consolidated schools in Iowa increased from 18 in 1913 to 238 in 1917, by which time 27 were in the open country. Financial problems, chiefly the weight of property taxes, slowed down the trend during the 1920s and at the outset of the Great Depression Howard took a pessimistic view when he surveyed the high cost of educational programs. In "Making an Iowa Farmer," he wrote:

The new schoolhouse was scarcely built before we found we were no longer managing our own school. Local control had largely been superseded and we were under regulations little short of state control. To meet requirements of state standardization, we had to employ five teachers and meet certain other prescribed standards.

It is true that most of these things helped to make the school better, but the tax increase soon became a burden. In other consolidated districts, where building programs were more pretentious, the tax burden was and still is much heavier than ours. But nevertheless our farms became less and less valuable, largely because professional educators, who usually measure economics by the yardstick of salary and not by productive income, have over-promoted development.

It is often stated that such desirable public improvements as paved roads, drainage ditches, new courthouses and improved schools built from tax levies will increase property values. My own observation is that property subject to tax levies usually depreciates. Only those things that actually produce new wealth raise values. There is always a limit to what any traffic will bear.

The Liberty Consolidated School has succeeded. It became the first and is still one of the few strictly rural high schools in the state. The enrollment has always been more than double that of the four original districts. Many pupils have had high school advantages only because of the consolidated school. Many have gone on to college.

All this is commendable but every worthwhile thing is bought with a price. The cost of doubling the enrollment of the district was a quadrupling of taxes. In prosperous years this was not keenly felt, but when farm income dwindled, school expenses did not diminish. Teachers' salaries, janitors' wages and fuel bills were not adjusted on the basis of farm prices. The school became one of the causes of increased mortgages. Tenantry increased in the district. Land became worth less than in adjoining districts where taxes were lower.

All this would not have occurred had the original plan been adhered to. We discussed in the beginning the possibility of lower prices and planned to meet the tax burden. We held and still do that the farm boy and girl should have every reasonable advantage. The public school is America's greatest institution. It cannot continue as such if costs increase faster than do the means of meeting those costs. While human welfare can never be appraised in monetary terms, still every worthwhile thing costs money and tax levies cannot continuously be adjusted upward.

Achievement of a better school system was a triumph for a husband-wife partnership. A modest man, Howard said his wife was responsible for the inception and success of consolidation. Whatever the facts, Anna Howard deserved a sizable share of the credit. In her dedication to education and community improvement, she was her husband's equal. She had not lived as long in the township, but she knew and understood most of the people and set high standards for her own family without claims of superiority.

In a half century of married life, Jim Howard's respect for his wife's judgment and intelligence never wavered. After the school was built and his interest turned to organized agriculture, she continued to be his chief consultant and adviser. As he moved into larger spheres of activity, Anna received a full report when he returned home. He respected her opinion about who could be trusted, who should be watched, and who had a potential that might be valuable. In a few emergency situations, she stood before audiences and read speeches for him.

Howard's memory for names and faces was excellent. He combined it with an active and inquisitive mind that did not slow down when he was resting or recuperating. He assimilated facts and compartmentalized them for future use. He liked people and he enjoyed talking to them, beginning with nearby neighbors and expanding his acquaintances to include merchants in the county seat, farmers in distant townships and counties, and eventually men of consequence in other counties and states.

Up early and working late in the busy seasons, he had little time for books. Livestock and grain market reports received close attention when he hurriedly read the *Marshalltown Times-Republican*, which the RFD carrier brought just before noon, but he did not attempt reading that was not directly connected with farming. On winter evenings, however, he would turn his attention to his favorite literary masterpieces. He loved to read aloud to his children, who remember especially his fondness for Scott's *Lady of the Lake* and the works of Paul Lawrence Dunbar. The books of greatest importance involved his financial records. When he lived in the city and rented his land to two tenants on a partnership basis, he kept full sets of books on both farming operations, but Howard's personal experience was that a man of the soil did not have time to be an accountant.

In New Providence, he joined the Masonic lodge, with Blue Lodge and Royal Arch affiliations. When he moved to the farm he transferred his membership from Eldora to Marshalltown. Some time later, without stating a reason or resigning formally, he dropped out of Masonic work.

His public career culminated in an economic and social crusade, but his religion was both ecumenical and private. He set a public example of conduct based on the Quaker's right to follow his own conscience. Living at the edge of a Catholic neighborhood, he was above all tolerant of the beliefs of others. Perhaps his private religion may best be summarized by his conviction that too many churches can spoil a community. He regarded a strong church as a bastion for good and he didn't want it weakened by denominational bickering. Whichever church it might be he didn't much care.

Except for silent grace at mealtime, by adulthood most vestiges of his Quaker upbringing had disappeared from Howard's outward life. He seldom mentioned what he had been taught about religion at Penn College. If and when he read the Bible, it was outside the family circle. With his wife and children, he attended and supported the Liberty Friends Church that had been built two miles east of the farm in 1904 as another offshoot of the Bangor Monthly Meeting. There the pro-Methodist trappings of Gurneyites had triumphed in a Quaker schism, and preaching and hymn singing took the place of the silent worship of his grandmother's time. For one year Howard was superintendent of the Sunday school.

In Chicago in the early 1920s, Howard attended the Buena Memorial Presbyterian Church because he admired the Reverend Henry Hepburn, who had been recommended by friends. Hepburn's church in the Wilson Avenue district was a half mile from the Howard apartment, while the Friends meetinghouse was far away in the south side. The difference between Presbyterian and Quaker doctrines did not disturb him, possibly because his sister had married a Presbyterian. During the 1920s

Howard listed himself in *Who's Who in America* as a Presbyterian. After he returned to the farm he claimed Quaker affiliation again. In a period when many rural churches succumbed to membership and financial problems and were abandoned, the Liberty church was destroyed by fire in 1941. The congregation then took over the Bevins Grove church no longer used by the Campbellites, but Jim and Anna attended less and less frequently. In their final years they affiliated with the nominally Congregational-Christian church at Clemons, where their funeral services were held.

In guarding their children against racial and religious prejudice, the Howards were vigilant. The Armenian peddler with a strange accent knew that he could get a meal and overnight lodging if he stopped his one-horse van at Anna Howard's hitching post. Since she was not running a hotel, she would not accept pay. And whatever the status of her guests, she provided all with a bed and never pointed the way to the haymow. If Ku Klux Klan agitation had started in the community, the Irish sensed that Howard would have taken a public stand on their side. The Negroes in Marshalltown, few in number and seldom encountered, were more objects of curiosity than intolerance. During the war, German-Americans did not forfeit their status as good people and valuable citizens.

When the United States entered the First World War, the birthright member of the Society of Friends went to the army recruiting office at Marshalltown and offered his services wherever they might be needed. In the selective service enrollment that followed, he did not claim his wife and four children as exemptions. Both recruiting officer and draft board told him that his greatest usefulness would be on his own 480 acres. Without moralizing, the county Farm Bureau president talked freely about his unqualified willingness to support the war effort—perhaps to express indirectly his disapproval of acquaintances whose interest in joining the Quaker church coincided with the possiblity that they might be drafted. Or perhaps he felt that if someone from the farm had to go to war, he could do it with less personal sacrifice than any of the hired men.

Howard identified himself as a pacifist when he addressed the American Legion state convention at Marshalltown twelve years later. Recalling his effort to enlist, he said that a true pacifist believes in an adequate national defense and that, until human nature improves, the United States must have police protection on land and sea to meet any emergencies. He immediately added that "in every age and nation the aftermath of war has fallen with peculiar severity upon the farmer."

He was a prohibitionist, prejudiced against intoxicants and tobacco. Money spent on alcohol, he said, was diverted from the purchase of foodstuffs raised by farmers. When Marshalltown faced a referendum on whether the sale of liquor should be permitted, he wrote an article of several pages (there is no evidence that it was published or delivered as a speech) contending that any loss in rental income from saloon property would be far outbalanced by the trade of people who would drive extra miles to spend their money in a wholesome environment.

On the good roads issue, he naturally sided with the farmer who often had difficulty getting to the nearest village against the city man who wanted to drive longer distances. When D. W. Norris, publisher of the *Times-Republican* urged as early as 1912 that the main highways be paved, Howard was part of the opposition. The two men debated at least once. If memories of Howard relatives can be trusted, Norris displayed superior knowledge of the problem's engineering and financial aspects, while his farmer opponent argued that farm-to-market roads are an economic necessity to rural people.

8

A Picnic at Bevins Grove

ONE of the events that broadened Jim Howard's outlook was a widely attended community picnic in a timbered pasture just south of the Bevins Grove Christian Church, halfway along the road to Clemons. The Campbellite church served as a civic center and, after one of the lyceum courses that brought musical talent and lecturers to the isolated community, Howard and six others contributed nine dollars each to erase a deficit.

For a picnic at the end of the 1912 haying season, the Bevins Grove people appointed committees to arrange for refreshment stands, a ball game, and a program of speaking and music. The mainstays of the program committee were Howard, and Charles R. Ross who belonged to the church. They signed up the Minerva band, which came from a rural community several miles away, and a male quartet from Marshalltown. Howard and Ross agreed that either W. J. Kennedy, the director of extension at Iowa State College, or Frank A. Moscrip, the respected editor of the *Marshalltown Times-Republican*, would be a satisfactory speaker. They hoped that one or both might accept, but they weren't certain that a country picnic would interest a city man.

The more they thought it over, the more they wanted to attract a crowd with a speaker of outstanding reputation. Ross proposed "Uncle Henry" Wallace, the original editor of *Wallaces' Farmer*, a weekly journal that was regarded as the gospel of good farming, clear thinking, and right living. Later his son, Henry C. Wallace, became secretary of agriculture and his grandson, Henry A. Wallace, became vice-president. Howard believed that the logical choice would be George W. Clarke, the Republican nominee for governor, who was reputed to be a fine speaker. Neither Howard nor Ross had ever met Wallace or Clarke. Neither believed that either would come to the picnic.

All four were invited and all four accepted. The occasion was novel, the speakers were top-notchers, and the crisis passed, although Howard learned that it is nearly a crime to overload a program. On the morning of the picnic Kennedy discussed livestock and Moscrip spoke entertainingly on local history and prospects. After the picnic dinner, Clarke talked about state problems while the crowd waited patiently for Wallace.

Uncle Henry's speech would be remembered if only because he wore an alpaca coat over sagging trousers. He advanced to the edge of the platform, threw out his arms, and said, "I like you." Tremendous applause was repeated when he continued, "I like your style." His shirt had rolled up, revealing a broad expanse of bareness.

Calm finally prevailed, and Uncle Henry delivered what Howard believed was probably the best address he ever heard. The advantages of farm life and the need for community development were discussed, but mostly he emphasized the need for economic study to avoid dangers to agriculture that he accurately prophesied. "That address materially affected my career," Howard wrote.

From that day on I began to think along new lines. Our community was not merely part of Liberty Township. Its boundaries expanded continually in my mental processes. I recalled that Newton's law of gravitation stated that every particle of matter in the universe attracts every other particle in definite degree, and I began to see that human relationships of every sort and kind have worldwide horizons. The interest in the common man is the common denominator of every equation.

Automobiles were becoming common, and Howard recalled that possibly three thousand people showed up at Bevins Grove, six times the anticipated crowd. M. A. Hauser of the extension staff later told Howard it was the start of a farmers' picnic movement that spread across the nation.

Five months before he quit banking, Howard became a friend of Perry G. Holden, one of the Midwest's great rural educators. The occasion was a five-day agricultural short course conducted at New Providence by Holden, who was the first director of the Extension Service at Iowa State College. Off-campus short courses, part of efforts to expose farm people to scientific methods, were a major extension activity. Alfred F. Styles, the academy principal, and Zeno H. Doan, the Quaker minister, were rural-minded community workers who knew that the economic and social welfare of the town depended upon the prosperity of the countryside. On their invitation, Holden brought his staff of college experts to New Providence. The bank cashier was the ex officio treasurer of the short course, since Holden required that enrollment fees be charged and at least two hundred farmers and townspeople sign pledges to guarantee payment of local expenses.

Styles turned over his classrooms to Holden and invited nearby farmers to join academy pupils at lectures and demonstrations about grains, livestock, soils, and home economics. Prizes were awarded at a corn show. The best colts, calves, and pigs in the community were displayed for comparison purposes.

Holden, who would be Howard's friend for years, was a scientist who had a national reputation as a popularizer of agricultural education. His great contribution was the stimulation of interest in the selection and testing of seed corn, with the result that yields were greatly increased. He had been a University of Illinois professor, a pioneer in corn breeding, and manager of a seed company before 1902, when he was brought to Iowa Agricultural College as vice-dean. His lectures were so popular that at least once he drew a full house of farmers when he scheduled a short course class at 5:00 A.M. under lantern light. Holden started several demonstration farms and, beginning in 1904, crisscrossed the state with "seed corn gospel trains." In 1905, the year before the Iowa Extension Service was established by law, Holden held his first local short course at Red Oak.

"Possibly he overemphasized the show type of corn and sometimes he overlooked the advantages of early maturity, but his work had excellent results and he created an Iowa corn consciousness," Howard wrote. He also credited Holden with having a keen sense of economic trends. Holden resigned as extension director in 1912 to run for governor as a progressive but lost a close race for the nomination because, Howard believed, he was too far ahead of his time. Holden finished his career as agricultural educator for the International Harvester Company.

During Thanksgiving week of 1916, Howard arranged with Director Ralph K. Bliss of the Iowa Extension Service to hold a three-day short course at Liberty Consolidated School. The extension work had increased in popularity and a full week could not be scheduled, but night lectures and demonstrations permitted the full program to be given in three days. Many farmers attended from outside the Liberty district. When prizes were awarded for individual exhibits, Jim was adjudged to have submitted the best sample of oats and Henry, his oldest son, won sweepstakes for white corn.

From 1914 through 1946 Bliss headed the Iowa Extension Service during two wars and the depression. Howard had known him since the New Providence short course.

Apparently Howard never met James (Tama Jim) Wilson, an Iowan who served sixteen years as secretary of agriculture under presidents McKinley, Roosevelt, and Taft and who died in 1920 at the age of eighty-four. In his earlier years Wilson, who came from a neighboring county, served as speaker of the Iowa House of representatives, as congressman, and as a professor of agriculture who was instrumental in placing instruction at the Iowa experiment station on a practical basis.

Had a local chapter existed near his farm, Howard probably would have been a member of the Patrons of Husbandry, a secret fraternal order known as the Grange. His father and uncles had been members in the 1870s, when some 100,000 Iowa men and women participated in the social and educational programs. In later years, Howard worked closely with the Grange's national officers, but before 1916 he did not belong to any rural organization of general membership. None existed in central Iowa and those he had heard about in other states did not attract his interest.

The Grange grew out of President Andrew Johnson's concern about the condition of agriculture in the post–Civil War South. Its founder was Oliver Hudson Kelly, a government clerk and former Minnesota farmer who had been sent to the South to study farm conditions. He conceived the idea that rural people needed a fraternal order and, with the help of other governmental employees, founded the first chapter in Washington. The Grange spread rapidly across the Midwest after its first rural chapter was organized at Newton, Iowa, in 1868. For a few years the Grange was national in scope. Until the advent of the Farm Bureau, it was the only farm organization with members in most states.

The Grange stood for improved rural living, cooperative buying and selling, and crop diversification. It opposed borrowing on credit, mortgages, and any financial transactions that might lead to prodigal living and bankruptcy. Grangers regarded railroads as essential but joined in a general rural protest against their high tariffs and service monopolies. Although the Grange was nonpolitical, in an era of agricultural discontent its members joined with independent clubs of farmers to win enactment of midwestern Granger laws for state regulation of railroad rates. Iowa's Granger law was enacted in 1874 but before its repeal four years later the United States Supreme Court in an Illinois case upheld the regulation doctrine.

The Grange accomplished much to improve rural conditions but made the mistake of becoming involved in manufacturing. Cooperative stores had been successful, and the Iowa State Grange undertook the manufacture of harvesters. In 1874 about 250 were sold at approximately half of established prices. Elsewhere in the Midwest, Grange officials began to promote implement and vehicle factories, without considering that its officials had inadequate capital and no experience as corporation executives. The financial failure of its harvester factory in 1875 forced the Iowa Grange into bankruptcy. Members resigned, afraid of being held personally responsible for its debts. A quarter century later the Grange movement began a gradual revival and its national and state organizations spoke up for the interests of farmers but represented comparatively few of them.

In his youth Howard had heard of the Farmers' Alliance, which in the wake of the Grange claimed a sizable Iowa membership during the 1880s. Originally a southern movement, the Alliance had southern and northwestern wings that at times disagreed on policy questions. It reached Iowa in 1881, and in its first years seems to have emphasized social and educational programs, although it set up a wire factory in Des Moines that achieved some price reductions. In patent litigation, it was represented by Albert Baird Cummins, a young attorney who later became governor and U.S. senator. The Alliance also was credited with organization of farmers' mutual fire and tornado insurance companies, of which 116 existed in 1889. Before long the Alliance turned political and was of major importance in Kansas and Nebraska. In Kansas "Sockless Jerry" Simpson went to Congress with Alliance backing and Mary Elizabeth Lease, an Alliance organizer, told farmers to "raise less wheat and more hell." During the political wars of 1890 and 1892, Alliance members, other farmer groups, and the Knights of Labor advocated free coinage of silver and merged into the Populist party. Thereafter the Alliance quickly subsided. Like the Grange, it was important only for a decade. It served as a political balance of power at one period but, like other protest movements, suffered the misfortune of having part of its program taken over by the major parties.

For the next quarter century, the Midwest had no important farm organization. Howard knew that the Society of Equity had members in Wisconsin but it did not create a stir in Hardin and Marshall counties. He also had heard of the Farmers' Education and Cooperative Union, a southern movement founded in Texas in 1902 but not chartered in Iowa until 1917.

Farmer-owned and farmer-operated marketing associations made sense to him. Years earlier his father had helped establish the Minerva Valley Cooperative Creamery at Clemons; its attractively packaged butter had been sold through retail outlets. The original investment had been repaid in dividends more than one hundred times. Howard still held the original share of stock and had served his turn on the board of directors. He also had a part in organizing cooperative associations that not only operated grain elevators but sold lumber, coal, feeds, and other rural necessities.

"I knew that not many farmers could amass fortunes," he wrote. "With a turnover only once every twelve months, money must accumulate slowly. Because of this disadvantage, it was more important that at every turn the farmer have the equality of opportunity which is the basic heritage of every American citizen.''

Therefore he could not agree that farmers had no business but production and that they should not be involved in marketing, as boards of trade and other vested interests had contended. Why shouldn't the Minerva Valley creamery join with hundreds of other creameries in a national sales organization? Why shouldn't the cooperative elevators handle their members' products all the way to the terminal markets? He knew of an attempt to establish a cooperative livestock commission agency at the Union Stock Yards in Chicago, but the exchange held that part of the net proceeds could not be returned to the farmer.

It never occurred to Howard that he would have a part in the formation and execution of national programs for cooperative marketing. The years on the farm were more important than he realized.

9

Organizing Marshall County

I N late 1916, two small boys in Liberty Township amused themselves with a game in which they would "play Jim Howard." The beginning was always the same. One would announce, "Here comes Jim Howard." The other, pretending to drive up in a car, would ask, "Where shall we go today?" Then they would take imaginary trips to distant places and talk to strangers. They were imitating the founders of the Marshall County Farm Bureau. Their father, J. Howard Packer, was the right-hand man of J. R. Howard in a campaign to sign up 200 farmers as charter members of a new organization.

Howard was the spark plug, motivating force, and chief organizer of what he called the Marshall County Farm Improvement Association, but which was renamed the Marshall County Farm Bureau. It was his second demonstration of countywide leadership, for in 1914 he had been secretary of a group that attempted to organize the farmers of the county. The failure of the earlier effort is briefly mentioned in his personal papers. An unusual man in many respects, Howard had a sense of history and tried to preserve a record of his career. Sometime around 1932, after he read a file of old documents, he typed and then forgot about a five-page manuscript he entitled, "A Farmer Goes Afield." It contained this paragraph:

I find some minutes of the Marshall County Farmers' Association, of which I was secretary. The list of members included many of the outstanding men of the county. The object of the organization was through cooperative effort to seek reduction in taxes and to work for more effective marketing, lower interest rates and passage of equitable legislation. Other counties were forming similar organizations. There was some talk of merging into a state group and it might have been done except that the World War forced other responsibilities and paved the way for larger group interests.

On Christmas Eve 1953, four weeks before his death, Howard found the manuscript in the back of an overcrowded filing cabinet. To it he pinned a note telling of the circumstances of the discovery. Other parts of the document told of his social and political philosophy and are a source for some of the information in this book.

Neither the minutes nor the membership roster has been located. The context of the long-lost manuscript suggests that he was writing about 1914, the year he bought his first Model T. The fiftieth anniversary history of the Marshall County Farm Bureau does not mention any farm organization activity before 1916.

Howard's permanent involvement with the Farm Bureau movement began in 1916 at a community Thanksgiving dinner at Liberty Consolidated School, a barbecue of pork and lamb that celebrated the successful holding of a short course the three preceding days. After the meal, the men gravitated into one of the classrooms. There they discussed the county agent system that was being adopted by farmers in some Iowa counties.

The short course program had included speeches explaining the objectives and benefits of having a county agent. In the informal gathering of neighbors, Howard added his own sales talk. County agents were agricultural college graduates who served as links between the individual farmer and the agricultural extension staff at Iowa State College, which had the full backing of the U.S. Department of Agriculture. County agents were all-around servicemen who gave demonstrations, answered questions, and passed out information on scientific farming. A county agent in Marshall County would mean improved farms, higher yields of grain, and better prices for livestock. The secret was in cooperation, in convincing farmers to form a county association that would employ and pay part of the cost of an agent. The farmers, the college, and the agent would work together for the common good.

After a thorough discussion, Howard took a notebook from his pocket and on a blank page wrote: "We whose names are subscribed below agree to pay $5 a year for the support of a County Agent in Marshall County." He signed his name and passed the book and pencil to the man in the next seat. When it had been returned to him it bore the signatures of fifteen of the sixteen men present.

The Thanksgiving barbecue launched Howard on a new career as a membership solicitor and as a missionary for rural cooperative efforts. It took him out of his home neighborhood, widened his circle of friends, and propelled him into the front rank of American agricultural leaders.

The fifteen signatures were the first step toward organization of the Marshall County Farm Bureau, but 185 more five-dollar pledges were needed. The state of Iowa encouraged farmers to organize on a county basis under the sponsorship of the Extension Service at the state college, but before Marshall County could qualify for federal funds and for guidance from Iowa State College, the state law required that a minimum of $1,000 in membership dues must be raised by 200 farmers or landowners. Only then could they have the services of a county agent.

The remaining pledges would be harder to obtain, but Howard assumed leadership of a membership drive that soon reached all of the county's eighteen townships. He began with the enthusiastic help of Packer, a distant cousin, who had been one of the fifteen signers. A public-spirited authority on scientific farming who devoted much time to community betterment, Packer later became president of the county Farm Bureau.

An immediate start was vital for the solicitation had to be completed before the coming of spring, when farmers would be busy early and late with another cycle of fieldwork. Also, even if it might be inconvenient, winter was the ideal time for traveling from town to town and farm to farm. Spring rains would make the roads impassable, forming mudholes deeper than Model T axles. It was better to dress warmly, put side curtains on the open car, and start out over ruts that could cut tires to shreds.

In their enthusiasm for the cause, the men thought nothing of a thirty- or forty-mile drive in a Ford roadster while the thermometer registered below zero. If mud was a problem, Howard could leave a team of horses at the Clemons livery stable and take a train to the next group of potential members. If the twice-a-day schedule for branch line passenger trains was inconvenient, he could hitchhike in the caboose or locomotive tender of a freight train. Back home, the dependable hired men did the winter work.

Most townships had cadres of men who believed in cooperation and education and needed only a call to action. Howard and Packer found an early ally in Carey R. Arney, who farmed outside Albion. Within ten days a small group met at Marshalltown to exchange information and give each other pep talks. Extension Director R. K. Bliss, who was eager to have cooperative agencies formed in important counties, assigned Mathias A. Hauser to help with the membership drive. Much of it involved stopping at a farmstead and giving a winter-bound farmer a one-on-one sales talk about the numerous benefits that would come from a five-dollar check.

A milestone was reached December 30 when fourteen men assembled at the courthouse and became charter members of the Farm Improvement Association of Marshall County. Howard was temporary chairman and Merritt Greene, Jr., of Marshalltown, was temporary secretary. Assigned to work with them on a membership committee were Packer, Arney, and J. F. Ingles of Melbourne. At their first 1917 meeting, the former professor of rhetoric was asked to write an article about the county agent system for the *Marhsalltown Times-Republican*. Apparently he didn't have time to do it.

Two or more meetings were held in each township, and in January

Bliss took a personal hand in organizing the county. During a two-week period he spoke once, Hauser seven times, Arney and Packer four each, and Howard twice. In addition to the local meetings, two days were set aside for general solicitation.

Bliss, who stressed the need for immediate action, was the chief speaker at a February 14 meeting at Marshalltown. On the recommendation of a nominating committee, Howard was elected the first president of the Marshall County Farm Improvement Association. C. C. Paul of Laurel was made vice-president and Greene secretary. Nine township directors were named.

Marshall was the twenty-first of Iowa's ninety-nine counties to organize under the farm bureau–county agent system.

In his new sphere of activity, Howard provided active leadership for the association, which always recognized that it was part of the Farm Bureau movement. Not until he had served his two years as president did it become, in the interest of national uniformity, the Marshall County Farm Bureau. He resisted the change, arguing that it did not "seem expressive of the purpose and dignity of the movement." He believed that the average person, unfamiliar with the beginnings of the county agent system, thought of a bureau as a subordinate governmental agency or as a piece of bedroom furniture. He would have been satisfied with any name such as the Marshall County Farmers' Association.

By instinct the county president was a midwestern activist who did not limit himself to the Extension Service tradition that the primary function of his agency was to pass along demonstrations and information transmitted from the state college to the county agent. He believed there were additional reasons, including the economic ones, why farmers should join hands in their own organization.

He respected the Extension Service, some of whose men he had known for eight years, and he worked closely with the educators and scientists on the Iowa State College campus. He considered, however, that the county agent's function should be that of a field manager who carried out policies set by the board of directors. The board, elected on a township basis from around the county, gave him full support and the agenda of early meetings included deliberations about the needs and future of Marshall County agriculture.

"We believed that we knew our county's needs better than authorities at Ames and Washington," he recalled, "and we knew that success or failure of the county agent's work, like all other enterprises, would depend upon intelligent local direction. The average county agent is close enough to his problems to do effective work. When he is given adequate support, his efficiency rating is relatively high."

Since most of the corn grown in the county was fed to cattle and hogs, the directors decided to emphasize a long-range program for the improvement of livestock. Purebred breeding stock, already owned by 126 farmers, would result in higher prices for beef and pork. There was no reason why Marshall County should not be recognized as the livestock as well as the geographical center of the state, but much would depend upon the stature of the county agent to be hired.

After consultation with John W. Coverdale, the state's county agent leader, the job at a $2,500 starting salary went to W. A. Buchanan, thirty-two years old, a native of Kansas who for three years had been on the staff of Iowa State College. A graduate of Oklahoma State College who had studied nutrition at the University of Missouri, he appreciated good livestock and had a great talent for forecasting the development of a calf or pig. "Buck" held the post seven years before resigning to become district manager for an insurance company.

The Farm Bureau made sponsorship of 4-H club work a major part of its program and Buchanan, who was a natural leader of boys and girls, promptly organized a calf club. The county fair board reluctantly allocated twenty-five dollars in prize money for what turned out to be one of its best exhibits. Buchanan insisted that club members have uniformly good calves and that a profit be shown at the end of the year. The county, however, did not produce enough calves that met his standards. D. S. Collins of Liscomb, the first truck owner among the county's farmers, made major contributions to the cause. Collins and Buchanan would drive as far as 150 miles searching for desirable calves. Those they bought were offered to club members at cost, and Collins kept the rest for his feedlot. Uniformity was rewarded at the state fair, and Marshall County consistently made a good showing for groups of ten animals, a special class, as well as in the judging of individual calves. Several men, including Collins, bought purebred heifers for their own farms. The financial deflation of the 1920s slowed down but did not stop the livestock improvement campaign, and in 1928 a twelve-year-old boy, Clarence Goecke of State Center, exhibited the champion steer at the International Stock Show in Chicago.

The solicitation of 200 five-dollar memberships did not insure solvency for the county unit. The board of supervisors allowed Buchanan to use the grand jury room in the courthouse for his headquarters, but the county had a reputation for political and fiscal conservatism. By a two-to-one vote, the board turned down a request that it contribute $2,500 to support the county agent work. Allocations of Smith-Lever funds were inadequate. The directors sent a committee to remind the Marshalltown club that it had promised the equivalent of 150 memberships, and Buchanan was instructed to be on the lookout for prospects. The directors talked almost constantly about the need for additional members. When a canvass was made in June 1918, Coverdale was asked to send two or three men to help. Small items caused serious problems. For office furniture, the board at first authorized expenditures of $250. A year later, when the stenographer asked for a filing cabinet, a special committee was appointed to see if one could be obtained. In 1918, the supervisors agreed to appropriate $1,500 for the men's division of Farm Bureau work, but the financial emergencies persisted. Board minutes show that the treasurer frequently was authorized to borrow money at the bank to pay bills that ranged from $212 to $437 a month, including part of Buchanan's salary.

The work soon became coeducational. Buchanan's agenda for the September 29, 1917, meeting included the possibility of obtaining government aid to add a "lady county agent" to the staff. Two months later the president was authorized to sign an agreement with the Extension Service that a home demonstration leader would have Farm Bureau sponsorship to work with rural women and girls, even if the supervisors balked at paying part of the cost. The position went to Mrs. Mary K. Gregg of Sioux City, who reported for duty the next February. Howard later said that because of her impressive work a women's committee was established by the American Farm Bureau Federation.

Finances were not the only problem; attendance at board meetings was irregular. Impassable roads forced cancellation of an early spring business session. The president and others occasionally stayed at home when emergencies arose during the cultivating and haying seasons and at one time he was out of action with an attack of mumps, to which he supposedly had been immune since childhood. Directors were urged to mail proxies if they were going to be absent.

Howard's two years as county president overlapped the First World War, during which the Farm Bureau movement and county agent system expanded in the name of home front patriotism. The allied nations faced a shortage of foodstuffs, the new U.S. army had to be fed, and there was a great food-will-win-the-war mobilization of rural resources. Congress passed emergency laws and President Wilson placed Herbert Hoover at the head of the U.S. Food Administration, a superagency whose goals were to increase production and conservation. Fortunately, the machinery for reaching farm communities was largely in place. The Department of Agriculture had its cooperative arrangement with the land-grant colleges, and the extension services already were working with farm bureaus and county agents in many of the important counties. Washington ordered the establishment of emergency county crop improvement committees throughout the land and the appointment of a cooperator in each of the four-square-mile country school districts. Detailed plans for the organization of county farm bureaus were distributed through the northern and western states.

In Iowa, farm bureaus had been established in twenty-four of the ninety-nine counties before April 6, 1917, when war was declared. In the rest of the state a heavy load was carried by Coverdale and Murl McDonald, the assistant county agent leader. In the unorganized counties they set up temporary war emergency crop associations and appointed not only the officers but, to fill the county agent role, emergency agricultural agents. Retired farmers were in demand as school district cooperators. The system worked. Not only did production increase, but farmers saw the value of organized cooperation with the Extension Service. Within eleven months there were 100 farm bureaus in Iowa, and Pottawattamie County had two. On a nationwide basis, the organization of some fifteen hundred county farm bureaus with one million members was reported by Alfred C. True, who had charge of the extension work for the U.S. Department of Agriculture.

The U.S. Food Administration asked Iowa to increase pork production and wheat acreage by 25 percent, to promote war gardens, to encourage the canning and drying of food, and to establish labor bureaus. Although some fifty thousand farmers, one-third of those between twenty-one and thirty-one years, were called into service, the goals were met and during the war Iowa produced more foodstuffs than in any two previous years. Without a formal statewide organization, the county farm bureaus worked together to stabilize seed corn prices during a time of scarcity and to set uniform wages for corn pickers.

Buchanan, who became county agent ten days after war was declared, and Mrs. Gregg were the local leaders in a national campaign that asked farmers and city people to observe wheatless and meatless days. Among other activities, the county agent urged farmers to grow more wheat and to raise sorghum as a substitute for sugar. The Farm Bureau involved itself in the economics of production, and Howard, at the head of a committeee of three, went before the county Council of Defense to ask that the maximum pay for corn shucking, which had been set at seven and eight cents a bushel, be reduced a penny. Because of early frosts the preceding September, the seed corn situation in particular was critical in the spring of 1918 and county farm bureaus took united action to distribute the supply at stabilized prices. The Extension Service pushed drives for early testing and for locating old corn. As a result the 1918 crop was above average. Farmers were learning to work together, and the wartime accomplishments showed the value of cooperation. Sentiment increased for completing the organization of county farm bureaus and for establishing a statewide organization.

Always short of manpower, the expanding Extension Service assumed that a man who had successfully organized his own county would be an effective recruiter elsewhere. Howard volunteered and was assigned by Coverdale to membership solicitation in Tama and Benton counties, which are east of Marshall. With the title of assistant emergency demonstration leader, he worked there the last three weeks of 1917 and four days of the following month. By February, farm bureaus were operating in both counties. The Extension Service provided him with copies of letters by Secretary of Agriculture David F. Houston and Governor William L. Harding of Iowa emphasizing the importance of wartime food production. Houston specifically endorsed the county agent system as being greatly useful in the development of the nation's agricultural resources. Howard's expenses for railroad fares, meals, and lodging approximated fifteen dollars a week and were paid by the federal government. His highest meal charge was fifty cents and only once did he pay as much as one dollar for a hotel room.

Reelection as county president came February 4, 1918. Howard then became a political candidate for the only time in his life. On March 27 the *Marshalltown Times-Republican* announced that the president of the county crop improvement association was a candidate for the Republican nomination for state representative from the single-county district. He ran as "one of the leaders in progressive movements for farm and country life." The voters were reminded that he had taken the first step in organizing the county association and had led the movement that organized the only rural consolidated school in the county. His credentials also included six years as a director of the Minerva Valley Creamery Association, "which is known throughout the state as one of the foremost cooperative creamery concerns in Iowa." The announcement also gave details of his education in three colleges, his career as a teacher, including a year as professor of English literature in North Carolina, and the three years as bank cashier.

Howard had hoped to be the first county official elected from Liberty Township in thirty years, but his qualifications were not enough. Some family members recall that an attack of mumps interrupted campaigning. In any event, at the June 3 primary Howard polled 45 percent of the vote, which wasn't a bad showing for an isolated farmer. Ray P. Scott, a Marshalltown man who won the primary, thereafter had a long career in the legislature.

Beyond question, Howard's defeat was fortunate. Election to the legislature could have had the effect of barring him from the presidency of the Iowa Farm Bureau Federation. At the founding convention at the end of 1918, the delegates were warned that the organization should stay out of politics. Specifically, they did not want to emulate the Non-Partisan League, some of whose officials had been elected to state office in North Dakota. In his memoirs Howard said nothing about his candidacy, but it is possible that when he announced he had no thought of being state Farm Bureau president. His goal at that time could have been a career as a county president who would be agriculture's spokesman in the legislature. Joint service as state representative and state Farm Bureau president would have been difficult, for he would have been tied up with state business at Des Moines when the federation's executive board was making its first decisions.

The American Farm Bureau Federation early adopted a policy against political partisanship. To this day its officers do not run for public office and it refrains from endorsing candidates. At the same time it seeks support on a partisan basis from both Republicans and Democrats. It is strongly political in that it recommends legislation, presents testimony before congressional committees, and urges its members to bring influence to bear upon the legislative and executive branches of government. In that way it provides the vehicle through which farm families can affect legislation and make their opinions known.

10

❦❦❦❦❦❦❦❦❦❦❦❦❦❦❦❦❦❦❦❦❦❦❦❦❦❦

Farm Bureaus and County Agents

THE name Farm Bureau originated with the Binghamton, New York, Chamber of Commerce, a dynamic organization that set up separate departments or bureaus to handle municipal problems. When officials in Washington expressed concern about the large number of abandoned farms in upstate New York, the chamber of commerce created a farm bureau.

When the chamber solicited advice and finances, the Lackawanna Railroad offered to help establish a demonstration farm, but the U.S. Department of Agriculture had a better idea. On its suggestion, in 1911 the Extension Service at Cornell University assigned John H. Barron, a college-trained man, to demonstrate useful farm practices such as orchard pruning and pasture liming. Under authorization of the New York legislature, the Broome County Board of Supervisors in 1912 appropriated $1,000 to help pay Barron's salary and expenses. Other funds came from the railroad, the chamber of commerce, and the Department of Agriculture. The Extension Service supervised the work. Some of the more progressive farmers objected to the chamber of commerce connection and in 1913 organized the Broome County Farm Bureau. Barron was the county agent, the man who had the backing of local farmers and who represented the Extension Service and officials in Washington in an effort to show country people how to be better farmers.

By that time the Farm Bureau movement, under various names, had spread across the North from state to state and county to county. Educational in its original concept, the godchild of the U.S. Department of Agriculture and the land-grant colleges, it merged with the county agent system and in less than a decade was ready to be organized into the country's most important farm organization.

The Farm Bureau name was new, but in the previous decade the system of assigning agricultural educators to work on a countywide basis has been launched in the sharecropper South by the Department of Agriculture. In 1903, when a severe infestation of boll weevils from Mexico

71

caused a crisis among Texas cotton growers, the county agent system was founded by Seaman A. Knapp, the department's special agent for southern states. He recruited thirty trained demonstrators and sent them in the role of itinerant educators to show that cotton could be grown despite the eastward-moving weevils. The demonstrators prevailed upon more progressive farmers, known as cooperators, to set aside ten-acre tracts on which they followed instructions to burn plant residues, plow deeply and cultivate often, fertilize, and use early-maturing seed. On the demonstration plots, yields were spectacular.

In 1906, Smith County in northeastern Texas allocated money to pay for its own demonstrator, W. C. Stallings. He became the first man whose work corresponded with that of the county agents who came later. Within a few years several hundred demonstrators were on duty in southern states. Money came from the federal Department of Agriculture, state and county governments, and local private sources, but John D. Rockefeller's oil millions paid the bulk of the cost of the farmers' cooperative demonstration work. Concerned about southern agriculture, Rockefeller had established the General Education Board just in time to finance a mammoth adult education campaign in the cotton country.

Knapp was a New Yorker who reached the South by way of Iowa, where he was a farmer and a Methodist minister in Benton County, superintendent of the Iowa School for the Blind, publisher of the *Western Stock Journal and Farmer* at Cedar Rapids, organizer and first president of the Iowa Improved Stock Breeders Association, and professor of agriculture and manager of the farm at Iowa Agricultural College. There he drafted a bill that led to the federal Hatch Act of 1887, which created state agricultural experiment stations. He served two years as president of the state college at Ames, but resigned in 1886 to take charge of an experiment in the colonization of northern farmers around Lake Charles, Louisiana. Under their example, southerners adopted more modern practices. One of Knapp's achievements was the development of the rice industry in the United States and for several years he was president of a rice growers' association. Appointed by Agriculture Secretary James (Tama Jim) Wilson as the department's special agent, he toured Japan, China, and the Philippines to investigate rice varieties, growing, and milling. He had just returned from a survey of agriculture in Puerto Rico when, at the age of seventy, he formed the county agent system.

In part because Knapp had a prejudice against the land-grant colleges, the Farm Bureau movement developed along sectional lines. Neither Knapp nor the extension services in most Dixieland states (Alabama and Tennessee were exceptions) encouraged the sponsorship of demonstrators by countywide organizations of farmers. When northern farm bureaus began to set up state federations and talk of a national organization, the southerners had to play catch-up ball.

On the other hand, the agriculture department's office in charge of educational work in northern and western states had a self-help philosophy and advocated the creation of county groups that provided local leadership for and paid part of the cost of extension activities. Almost spontaneously, the idea of having a trained expert working with local people became common. Businessmen provided much of the original impetus but soon stepped aside to let farmers have local control, as had happened at Broome County.

Pennsylvania had the first county agent in the North. A. B. Ross, a corporation lawyer in Cleveland, Ohio, gave up his practice because of ill health and, on his doctor's advice, traveled by horse and buggy along the back roads of his native Bedford County. Preaching modern farming methods, he collected and passed along information about legumes, fruits, and corn. He went to Washington to solicit help and on March 20, 1911, was given a small salary, mail franking privileges, and the title of county agent. Ross was a free lance who worked directly with the federal government and did not have an organized group of farmers to support his activities. The Pennsylvania Extension Service, unlike the agencies of the Midwest, did not help set up local farm bureaus.

The pioneer among midwestern county agents was Samuel L. Jordan, who in April 1912 took a leave of absence from his job as farm institute lecturer for the Missouri Board of Agriculture and became farm adviser in Pettis County under the sponsorship of a boosters' club at Sedalia. As a result, Pettis County claims to have had the first Farm Bureau. While working with the Extension Service and the U.S. Department of Agriculture, Pettis County put local sponsorship under a group of farmers.

The first man to do county agent work in the West was Luther M. Winsor, an irrigation specialist who in 1911 was assigned by Utah State College to work in the Uinta Basin, where irrigation companies had been organized as early as 1905.

At first there was little uniformity about terminology and sponsorship. The men on duty in the counties were known variously as agents, advisers, demonstrators, and experts. Only a handful were hired without the backing of the extension officials at the land-grant colleges. Many of the first agents were financed in part by city people who wanted their rural customers to be more prosperous. Often the money came from a variety of sources, including the federal government. Always the placement of men in the North and West had the encouragement of William J. Spillman, a former professor at Washington State College who supervised cooperative programs and farm experiment stations for the agriculture department's Bureau of Plant Industry. Gradually local control passed to farmers', farm improvement, or crop improvement associations or clubs. Eventually all these groups met federal and extension service standards and, on the Broome County example, used the Farm Bureau name, which was favored by officials in Washington. It has been durable, distinctive, and pervasive.

Men who worked in large city offices were responsible for part of the spread of the farm bureau–county agent system across the North and West about 1912. Programs to improve agriculture were promoted by railroads, farm implement companies, associations of bankers, and the fertilizer industry. Railroads and banks, for example, provided the money that made possible the early placement of a county agent in Bottineau County, North Dakota. Concern about the poor quality and low yields of wheat, corn, oats, and barley led the Chicago Board of Trade to hire a field man, Bert Ball, who assisted state extension directors with farmers' institutes, calf and colt shows, short courses, and corn trains. He became secretary of the National Crop Improvement Committee, which was backed by other grain exchanges and a number of business concerns.

Julius Rosenwald, the philanthropist head of Sears Roebuck and Company, joined the cause and at Ball's urging donated $100,000 to encourage the formation of crop improvement associations. He offered $1,000 each to the first 100 counties in which farmers would organize, raise from $2,000 to $5,000 locally, and hire an agent for at least two years. Dubuque County, Iowa, rejected the grant on the theory that money from a corporation would be tainted, but Rosenwald was responsible for the founding of farm bureaus in the Midwest and one in Arkansas.

Financing problems were chronic. Other states followed the example of the New York legislature and authorized counties to appropriate money that would support extension work. In 1913 the Iowa legislature approved formation of "county corporations for the improvement of agriculture, animal husbandry and horticulture," without specifying their name. The optional law provided for a county tax that would yield not more than $5,000 a year to support the local extension activities. A later amendment required the contribution each year of $1,000 in gifts and membership dues from not less than 200 farmers and landowners. Any name was permitted, but the county organization had to cooperate with the state college. With its requirement for a membership base and minimum dues, the law became the legal framework for the spread of farm bureaus into all Iowa counties.

Before the Civil War, some states showed concern about the welfare of rural people by sponsoring agricultural societies. State fairs, which were the next step, focused their attention on superior crops and livestock and were followed by county fairs that could be attended by more people. The land-grant colleges, which grew out of the Morrill Act signed by Abraham Lincoln in 1862, soon reached beyond their campuses and organized farmers' institutes that emphasized lectures and demonstrations and established two principles—that people should be encouraged to help themselves and that the state should support educational work among farm groups. In many communities institutes were held one or two days a year, and the farmers bought tickets as a means of financing the cost of sending college men to small towns. To promote better-germinating and higher-yielding corn, the Sioux County, Iowa, Board of Supervisors in 1903 appropriated money for a farmers' institute. It set a national precedent for county financial support of a local group that was cooperating with the state college in an educational campaign. On that principle the Farm Bureau movement was founded later.

Satisfied with the husbandry of their forefathers, many rural residents rejected opportunities to listen to young college graduates, but others believed their income could be increased if they knew more about drainage, improved seed, and livestock feeding. Some sought help only when they were afflicted with such tribulations as hog cholera, soft corn, and smutty oats. To meet a consistent demand, the land-grant colleges and extension services early in the twentieth century experimented with several procedures for the off-campus education of isolated farmers who in most cases had attended only one-room schools.

The experimental farms at the state colleges were copied in many counties but were difficult to reach in the era of horse-drawn vehicles and dirt roads. Many communities sponsored such events as calf and colt shows or encouraged boys and girls with corn growing projects that were forerunners of the 4-H movement that sprang up in much of the country after 1912. In Iowa about 1903 Perry G. Holden organized corn trains, whose service was advertised in advance, that stopped at stations long enough for interested farmers to climb aboard and hear a lecture-demonstration or study an exhibit. Railroads furnished the trains for several years, and most of Iowa was covered either by the corn trains or by the week-long short courses held in county seats and smaller towns.

The earlier extension procedures reached only a small number of the country dwellers and were available only a few days a year, if that often. When a new system was needed, educators saw the advantage of having an expert stationed in a county on a full-time basis. The more progressive farmers, a group that included some of the renters and smaller landowners, had become acquainted with each other and had learned about their mutual problems. Usually they were willing to become Farm Bureau members.

A considerable boost for Farm Bureau work came in 1914 when Congress passed the Smith-Lever Act that set up the Cooperative Extension Service in Agriculture and Home Economics and provided for joint federal-state financing. The land-grant colleges had been receiving federal money for resident students and research work, but the Association of American Agricultural Colleges and Experiment Stations contended that off-campus education also was needed. The new law extended federal finances to colleges that cooperated closely with the U.S. Department of Agriculture. Also, federal aid had to be matched by the state legislature or by contributions "provided by the state, county, college, local authority or individual contributions from within the state." Money raised by local farmers to support county agent work came within that category.

In the northern states, the men who directed most of the extension services believed that they had no option but to help create and work hand in hand with the county associations. On the Iowa State campus, Holden at one time attempted to organize a Grange chapter as a conduit for educational work. The National Grange and the Farmers' Union were the oldest of the existing farm organizations, but their strength was rather inconsequential. Furthermore, the Grange was ineligible for participation in extension activities because it was a secret order that did not admit all rural people into membership. The Farmers' Union was largely regional, operating out of Texas, and it did not reach the Midwest until the formation of local farm bureaus had begun. More than its competitors, it had a reputation for political radicalism. Another drawback, so far as the extension people were concerned, was that it seemed to be less interested in education than in marketing cooperatives and credit associations.

Midwesterners and Yankees rather quickly adopted divergent views about the proper function of a farm bureau. In New York and New England, where the movement started, the county associations believed their primary objective was to further rural education. Many of them charged a dollar or less a year for membership and found it adequate to support the local work of the Extension Service. In the Midwest, on the other hand, Farm Bureau members believed that the educational work of the county agent was not enough. Agriculture had off-the-farm problems involving marketing, transportation, and government, among other things. Since no other wide-based rural agency of general membership was paying attention to economics and legislation, the Farm Bureau made the best of the opportunities for added service. West of the Allegheny Mountains the members envisioned activities that justified a five-dollar membership.

The Farm Bureau spoke for all farmers, but only a minority were members. It met the need for a rural organization of wide scope and in state after state it was larger and more active than the alternate bodies. It offered an opportunity for people to join hands in helping themselves. Among rural residents, however, a high percentage were nonintellectuals who did not want anything new and did not believe that a young college graduate could teach them anything worth knowing. Barring an economic crisis and an evangelistic recruiting campaign, they were not inclined to be joiners. To a large extent, those who joined the Farm Bureau came from the more progressive and more prosperous class.

Across the Midwest there were many complaints that were not being met by the Farmers' Union cooperatives. The farmer-owned elevator movement needed strengthening. Freight rates were high, trains slow, and service indifferent at stockyards. The Farm Bureau, which developed in a period of prosperity, was nonpartisan and had strong leaders from both parties. They didn't intend to copy the tactics of the radical groups that hadn't worked in the past. They wanted to accomplish many things and they were willing to spend a long period of time in understanding and solving the problems.

The first effort to federate the farm bureaus in Iowa took place in 1917 under the sponsorship of the Extension Service and the personal direction of John W. Coverdale, the county agent leader. On Farm Bureau Day at the state fair, fifteen or sixteen county presidents met with Coverdale and set up a temporary committee headed by F. D. Steen of Muscatine County, who had been an active leader in wartime conservation work. A German-American, Steen spoke with an accent that impaired his statewide effectiveness. As a result, Coverdale was forced to mark time for a year and call on new leadership.

When Howard and Coverdale first became acquainted is not known, but sentiment continued to build up for a state farm bureau. Howard probably was among a larger group that met with Coverdale at the 1918 fair. R. K. Bliss in his *A History of Cooperative Agriculture and Home Economics Extension in Iowa* (1960), which was written after his retirement as extension director at Ames, omits details about the next steps but said that Farm Bureau directors in Polk County voted for a state federation and that Marshall County followed. He credits Frank Justice of Polk County and Howard with writing to other county presidents and urging the cause of federation.

The abbreviated minutes of the Marshall County Farm Bureau make no mention of the movement for a state organization before November 30, 1918, when Coverdale addressed a board meeting. Polled by Howard, the directors unanimously supported federation.

Correspondence and other records have not been located, but a committee of Howard, Justice, and Adam Middleton of Eagle Grove, Wright County, was appointed to work with Coverdale in calling a statewide meeting. Three decades later Howard said that Bliss and Coverdale appointed the committee because they wanted to avoid further delays but that they did not attempt to dictate to it. Coverdale remembered that Justice was not a fluent speaker and that Middleton was a "rough and ready Abe Lincoln type of fellow who didn't have quite the quality of leadership that Howard did.''

Coverdale planned that the county presidents would meet at Des Moines in early December, after the corn picking season, but the influenza epidemic that swept the country at the end of the war interfered. When a severe outbreak occurred in Des Moines, he switched the site first to Ames and later, for the same reason, to Marshalltown. The choice was logical, for it was in the center of the state and had passenger service on three railroads.

Bliss's history notes that county farm improvement associations adopted the name Farm Bureau on a suggestion by the U.S. Department of Agriculture that was approved by the Extension Service. He credited the Farm Bureaus with having given ''such effective help to extension work in this difficult period that they became an important part of state extension educational activities and history.''

Howard and other midwesterners were leading the Farm Bureau movement into new fields of action that had nothing to do with the original goal of education, but the Department of Agriculture and the state extension services did not object. Their officials knew that Congress would cut back the wartime emergency appropriations. Faced with deficits, officials in Washington and Ames would continue to work closely with the Farm Bureau for two reasons. Personnel cuts could be avoided by putting extension workers in new county agent jobs. As more farm bureaus were organized, more of the extension expenses could be paid from county funds. Bliss wrote that funds provided by the farm bureaus prevented any serious decline in county extension work.

11

State President

SEVEN weeks after the armistice that ended World War I, the Iowa Farm Bureau Federation was founded in Marshalltown, Iowa, December 27, 1918, by county leaders who believed that through organization and cooperation they could solve the rural problems that promised to be troublesome in peacetime. So that agriculture could have a spokesman, they laid a solid foundation at an auspicious time for what was then and is still the state's largest organization of farmers.

Unlike the rural movements of the previous century, the state Farm Bureau was not the outgrowth of an emotional and single-issue crusade of temporary duration. Early agrarian parties had sprung up in periods of depression but when prices rose lost their incentive to organize. As a result, for a quarter of a century no truly statewide organization of farmers had existed in Iowa. To fill the need, the Farm Bureau federation was launched in a period of comparative prosperity by men who were building for the future. They wanted changes made in the fields of marketing, transportation, and finance, and they wanted someone with a clear and respected voice to represent rural Iowa. Farmers needed a spokesman who could talk face-to-face with government officials and corporation executives. The Farm Bureaus had been successful on a county basis. The important test would be whether they could provide state and national leadership.

The Iowa federation was founded by a convention in the courthouse at Marshalltown. Seventy-two counties sent delegates and ten others were represented by proxies. One source said the total attendance was 130. Pretty much as a matter of unanimous consent, J. R. Howard was named chairman of the convention. He delivered a keynote address and he presided while the delegates debated and adopted a constitution tailored to his ideas. Late in the day, when the time came to choose the men who would lead the federation, the state presidency went to Howard, again pretty much as a matter of unanimous consent. In his memoirs he said that the delegates elected him only out of politeness because they were meeting in his home county seat.

John W. Coverdale recalled that Howard "conducted the meeting very easily" and that men from other counties regarded him as the logical president. The county agent leader, who assumed the sideline job of seeing that committees met on schedule, said he did not concern himself with the election of federation officers. Of Howard's qualifications, in an oral history interview, Coverdale said: "He was a successful farmer, practical, but not a fancy farmer. The neighbors thought well of him. He was a good church man. He was a good clean man. He didn't seek political office, locally or countywide. He had a good family and he hadn't made enemies."

The keynote address made it clear that Howard envisioned an activist organization with goals far beyond the Extension Service's educational programs transmitted through the county agents. For too long, he said, farmers had concentrated on production of crops and livestock and hadn't considered marketing and other problems. The time had come to unite in an organization that, among other programs, would look after farm business interests, such as dealings with packers and railroads. In the cities, business and professional men had their own organizations. It was vital that farmers follow their example and join in an organization that would formulate and voice effectively the rural attitude on a large number of issues. Unless the county Farm Bureaus united into a state federation, he said, they would not make their voices heard in the discussion of the large public questions that were arising as the world demobilized and turned to peacetime pursuits.

He added that he had no grudge against the railroad, manufacturing, and commercial interests of the cities. The new leader of Iowa farmers made it clear that he was neither a Populist nor a demagogue, and that his willingness to seek a common ground with urban organizations, to agree on a formula for cooperating with them for the general good, would prevail during his Farm Bureau career. But he asserted the primacy of agriculture:

I never go into a store in a big city or town but I think of the fact that all industries and all business enterprises are dealing with the products of the farm, the forest and the mine. Mother Earth is the source of all wealth and it is the farmer who is the essential factor in converting the stores of plant food in the soil into serviceable commodities for humanity.

Several speakers urged that the federation avoid political radicalism and proceed in a conservative and nonpartisan manner. Any attempt to follow the example of the socialistic Non-Partisan League in North Dakota would inevitably be divisive, they warned, adding that the organization should scrupulously refrain from endorsing candidates for office.

The objectives of the Iowa Farm Bureau Federation, as stated in the constitution adopted during an afternoon session, was to "effectively organize, advance and improve, in every way possible, the agricultural interests of the great commonwealth of Iowa, economically, educationally and socially, through the united efforts of the County Farm Bureaus of the state."

Years later, when he was recalling the genesis of the Iowa Farm Bureau, Howard noted that he had written the constitution of the Marshall County Farm Bureau and that it was the model for the constitutions of the Iowa and national federations. The Iowa constitution was written by Coverdale, after consultation with the arrangements committee, and was brought from Ames to Marshalltown for final approval by Howard and others before it was submitted to the convention. Howard appointed to the convention's constitution committee three of the strongest county leaders—Adam Middleton of Eagle Grove, E. H. Cunningham, of Cresco, and J. E. Craven of Kellogg. Craven was the federation's first treasurer and within a few years Cunningham was a member of the Federal Reserve Board. When Howard was elected state president, Middleton and Frank Justice of Berwick served under him as vice-president.

Much of the debate involved money. The majority held that the benefits of Farm Bureau membership would exceed annual dues, and therefore, the federation should be financially independent. As a result, the delegates accepted a per capita system under which the state organization received fifty cents out of each five-dollar membership paid to a county Farm Bureau. There were an estimated forty thousand members in the state and it was hoped that $20,000 would be sufficient to open an office, hire a competent secretary, and begin the compilation of information needed by farmers. To hold spending to a minimum, the constitution provided that state officers, committeemen, and directors would serve without pay but would be reimbursed for expenses while attending meetings. Since the county units had found it difficult to meet expenses, several delegates proposed that the federation request financial help from state or local governments. The subsidy question never came to a vote.

Despite changes in nomenclature and detail, the basic framework of the Iowa Farm Bureau is still in effect. The constitution provided that a board of directors, one man from each county, would set policy when they met at annual conventions. Management functions would be in the hands of an executive committee that would meet at least twice a year. Directors from each congressional district would elect an executive committeeman. (Later the names were changed, the directors became voting delegates, and the executive committee became a board of directors.) The executive committee had responsibility for electing the officers—a president, three vice-presidents, and a treasurer. The state leader of county agents and the director of agricultural extension were ex officio members of the committee without voting rights. County farm bureaus were required to cooperate with Iowa State College and the U.S. Department of Agriculture.

In caucuses held on congressional district lines, Howard, Middleton, Justice, and Craven were elected members of the executive committee. The other members were William Kitch of Mount Pleasant, Charles F. Coverdale of Delmar, L. S. Fisher of Edgewood, J. H. Lyman of Corning, W. W. Latta of Logan, S. A. Barber of Kanawha, and Oscar Heline of Marcus. Charles F. Coverdale was a brother of the county agent leader.

After the convention adjourned, the executive committee elected Howard the first president of the Iowa Farm Bureau Federation. For the second time he had responsibility for translating a constitutional blueprint into an organization that would be an effective representative of rural people.

The day's work was commended by the farm journals whose opinions mattered most to the federation. Among others, both *Wallaces' Farmer* and the *Iowa Homestead* approved the manner in which the county farm bureaus had joined forces. The *Homestead* called it "the most conservative and at the same time most progressive meeting of farmers we ever had the pleasure of attending." The editors of *Wallaces' Farmer* commended the constitution and said the convention was "one of the most sensible efforts toward organization of farmers that has yet been made." The delegates had avoided discussion of politics and had not indicated any interest in the government-ownership policies that had given a radical reputation to the Nonpartisan League in North Dakota. The most emotional resolution, adopted unanimously, called for repeal of the daylight savings law that had been enacted as a wartime measure.

Jim Howard liked his unpaid job as state president, which probably required only one day a week of his time on the average. That was fortunate, for on Homelands Farm he had assumed personal management of all of his 480 acres. The tenant on the Rockhill quarter section had been replaced with a hired man who drew monthly wages plus fringe benefits but did not share in the profits. Now the year-round work force consisted of three hired men, all married. Maximum flexibility was possible, for they could be concentrated on one operation or spread over the acreage. The owner was the boss and no one had the status of foreman, but the men had been selected for loyalty as well as for competence. They understood what had to be done from day to day and week to week, and Jim made a point of keeping them informed about priorities. If a man asked what should be done the rest of the day, he was apt to get a semihumorous answer listing tasks that would keep him busy for more than a week. As a result, the owner could be away for several days at a time.

In 1919 the main task at Homelands Farm was an extensive upgrading of the Rockhill property. Anna Howard's brother, William Pickrell, who had long experience as a lumber camp carpenter, came for a visit and stayed to take day-by-day supervision of the building of a barn, the remodeling of the house, and other improvements. Meanwhile there were tile ditches to be dug and fences to be rebuilt. All were matters of expense that Howard could not neglect.

Even on a part-time basis, the state presidency stretched his horizons. He presided at frequent meetings of the executive committee, attended sessions of four special committees, and accepted full responsibility for studying what needed to be done and for assessing the effectiveness of current programs. As head of the largest, if still untried, agricultural organization in the state, he rated among the important men of Iowa. His acquaintance broadened, and he never considered that his responsibilities were limited to the state of Iowa. As head man in one of the leading farm states, he had opportunity to be influential nationally as his connections extended to the Farm Bureau hierarchies in the Corn Belt and the East.

Apparently he did not make many speeches in 1919. Those he did make seem to have been extemporaneous, although he may have prepared an outline of what he intended to say. Faced with new challenges and opportunities, his active mind assimilated and analyzed information that could be called upon when he addressed audiences. Always the potential subject matter included the conviction that farm people should join forces in a broad-based organization that did not accept geographical restrictions and would not take extremist or limited positions. He was the official spokesman for Iowa agriculture and part of his job was to explain farm problems to city people. He sensed that many situations were surprisingly complex and he believed that their ramifications should be analyzed before intelligent action could be taken. He believed that more progress would be made if he conferred with the heads of other industries, including the unpopular terminal markets and packing companies, than if he denounced them with demagogic rhetoric. To his mind, the president of a farm organization should have the same stature as the head of an association of businessmen. He had high ambitions for his federation, and his ultimate goal was that a national organization of cooperating farmers would collaborate with other organizations for the national welfare.

There is no indication that Howard gave thought to how long he might have remained as state Farm Bureau president. Had another man headed the national federation, Howard no doubt would have served on

its executive committee. As national president, he insisted on retiring after three years. Whether he would have favored limited tenure for state
presidents is not known.

Soon after the Iowa federation was organized, Howard unwittingly
and undeservedly acquired a lifetime enemy in the *Iowa Homestead,* the
oldest and one of the largest of the seven farm magazines published in
the state. Founded in 1862, it had been purchased in 1885 by James M.
Pierce, who previously had published three weekly newspapers in south-
western Iowa. For ten years his editor was the first Henry Wallace, a Scottish Calvinist who had been a pastor and a dirt farmer. The two men
disagreed over *Homestead* policies, Wallace protesting that they were
more concerned with the business office than the welfare of agriculture.
Wallace soon launched his own journal, *Wallaces' Farmer,* which in its
editorial page preached agrarianism and Christian idealism. About 1913
Pierce began practicing the personal journalism that had gone out of style
during the preceding century.

Howard's memoirs include a dissertation on farm journals and their
emphasis on circulation and advertising. While they helped the cause of
education by printing information taken from government bulletins,
generally each regarded itself as agriculture's preordained spokesman on
all matters, including politics and legislation. Since advertisers wanted a
large subscription list, each journal employed traveling solicitors who
often offered valuable merchandise premiums or accepted poultry or
produce as payment.

The *Homestead's* favorite whipping boy was the Greater Iowa Association, a chamber-of-commerce type of organization headed by G. Wat-
son French of Davenport. Rural readers had little interest in the association, but in issue after issue, Pierce claimed that French had not ac-
counted for a typewriter purchased with state funds for a display at the
1915 San Francisco World's Fair.

When the Iowa Farm Bureau was organized, Howard and his colleagues failed to pay deference to Pierce. They did confer with Henry C.
Wallace, the second generation editor of *Wallaces' Farmer,* who did not
give his blessing to the federation. The *Homestead* commended the Farm
Bureau in its first issue after the Marshalltown convention, but within a
week it proclaimed that the federation was a tool of French and the
Greater Iowa Association. Concerned about the charge, Coverdale called
a special meeting of Farm Bureau leaders. Their records showed that
French had not been in Marshalltown and no one could understand what
Pierce was writing about. Cunningham, a red-faced Irishman who had
been speaker of the Iowa House and who knew more than his colleagues

about the political infighting that went on in Des Moines, insisted that the charge must be answered.

Totally inexperienced in such matters, Howard delegated to Cunningham the writing and issuance of an answer to Pierce. It took the form of a letter over the state president's signature that was released to the daily press:

We consider its publication by the *Homestead* without a thorough understanding of the facts or consultation with the executive committee of the Iowa Farm Bureau Federation to be unfair and an injustice not only to the state federation but the entire county agent work of Iowa and misleading to the general public.

The executive board which was chosen to perfect the organization of the state federation absolutely refuses to be a party to any private or public controversy. We refuse to tear down, attack or seek to destroy any beneficial organization.

Our proposition is rather to cooperate with all organizations working toward permanent agricultural good, fostering better agricultural education and an increased production and distribution, maintenance of soil fertility, and development of Iowa citizenship. We are ready to cooperate along these lines, not only with agricultural associations, but with the agricultural press and commercial organizations. But we refuse to go outside these lines of activities or to adopt any partisan politics or measures.

The answer was prominently printed and well received. Howard stood by Cunningham. The next issue of the *Homestead* bemoaned the "illegitimate parenthood" of the federation, but Pierce received an unfavorable reaction from his farm constituency. He pulled in his horns and announced that the Farm Bureau's skirts had been cleared.

Dante M. Pierce, who soon inherited the editorship, nevertheless kept up a prolonged vendetta against Howard, who wrote that he had "replaced French as the scapegoat of Iowa agriculture." Two *Homestead* editors privately told Howard they were instructed to "kill me off," by fair means or foul. "Practically every statement or address was garbled by omissions, or punctuation or transposition of phrases or sentences to change my meaning," Howard wrote in his memoirs. "It wasn't always pleasant, but I doubt if in the long run it was harmful. In fact, I think it benefited both me and the federation."

Wallaces' Farmer on October 8, 1920, came to the defense of Howard, who as president of the American Farm Bureau Federation had made a speech in Des Moines on the railroad problem. It noted that Howard had been under attack by the "Iowa Hatestead," which had been against the Farm Bureau since its inception. The Wallace publication said that Howard was levelheaded and forward-looking and added that "during the war the publisher of the Hatestead was put off the state council of defense."

Howard's memoirs included an anecdote involving the *Prairie Farmer*, a Chicago-based journal published by Burridge D. Butler and edited by Clifford V. Gregory, an active Farm Bureau supporter. Butler once invited Howard to lunch at the Union League Club. Businessmen stopped by their table to chat with the publisher, who made comments that were in conflict with positions taken by Gregory's editorial page. When Howard inquired about the discrepancies, Butler answered that he allowed Gregory some freedom but nevertheless frequently ordered him not to take stands that would be detrimental to business interests such as the Board of Trade. In 1937 Gregory resigned to join *Wallaces' Farmer*, which by that time had taken over the *Iowa Homestead*.

12

꧁꧁꧁꧁꧁꧁꧁꧁꧁꧁꧁꧁꧁꧁꧁꧁꧁꧁꧁꧁꧁꧁꧁꧁

John W. Coverdale, Right-hand Man

ORTUNATELY for the Farm Bureau movement, one
of the great men of organized agriculture became the secretary
and chief executive officer of the Iowa Farm Bureau Federation.
John Walter Coverdale, hired in late February 1919 at $5,000 a
year, had been county agent leader in Iowa and was familiar
with the Farm Bureau's personalities, problems, and opportunities. More
than any other man in the state, he was competent to make day-to-day
decisions for the new organization. Howard and his board members still
did not comprehend the amount of work they would face and they offered Coverdale the option of being part-time secretary, if arrangements
could be made with the Extension Service, but they could not.

The oldest of four children of Elijah Anthony and Sara Jane Jepson
Coverdale, John Coverdale was born April 4, 1883, on a 540-acre farm in
Bloomfield Township, Clinton County. There his grandfathers, an Eng-
lish butcher and a Danish ship carpenter, had settled before the Civil
War. An uncle, Franklin Coverdale, was credited with introducing sweet
clover into the midwestern crop rotation. "My father's farm was more or
less an experiment station and almost a livestock commercial plant,"
John Coverdale wrote in his autobiography.

Usually we had 200 or more cattle, 250 to 300 hogs and from 30 to 100 heavy
draft horses on feed. Father was a great lover of horses and had the reputation of
being largely responsible for the building up of a draft horse industry in that section of Clinton County. While I was a small boy, father decided that our horses
were not of the right type and he organized a cooperative horse company. It
bought Speculation, a Shire stallion that had just been imported from England
by the Dunhams of Bushnell, Illinois. Later an imported Percheron stallion was
bought by the company and still later a Belgian stallion by the name of Bedigion.
The offspring of those stallions became the foundation of a widely-known draft
horse area that soon became famous in logging camps, in heavy dray service in
the cities and in the potato section of Maine. In the fall of 1904, father had the

honor of selling in the horse auction at the Chicago Stockyards a Belgian crossroan gelding for $475. It was the highest price ever paid for a work horse up to that date.

In that environment, the boy became an expert on livestock and live-stock feeding. He also learned carpentry after a tornado, which killed twenty-six persons elsewhere, demolished the Coverdale farmstead, killed 48 cattle, 7 horses, more than 100 hogs, and scattered 20,000 bushels of corn across the countryside. The next summer, at the age of sixteen, he worked in the neighborhood as a dollar-a-day carpenter. To go to high school, he drove each day to Delmar, six miles away, and did morning and evening chores at home.

In 1902 he entered Iowa State College, which had an enrollment of about 900. There he paid $2.50 a week for room and board, participated in intramural debates, and in his spare time earned spending money by working at the college farm for fifteen cents an hour. As a judge of livestock, he was a member of the college teams that competed at the St. Louis World's Fair and the Kansas City Royal Livestock Show. He failed in the great ambition of animal husbandry students and did not make the judging team that went to the International Livestock Exposition at Chicago. After two and a half years he left college. He had neglected the fields of mathematics and science, but he was going to be a farmer and he had taken most of the courses offered in animal husbandry and farm crops.

Back in Clinton County, he married Elsie Grindrod and became a farmer for six years. He established small herds of Aberdeen Angus cattle and Poland China hogs. Neighbors admired his Reid's Yellow Dent corn, and he built a seed house and developed a commercial seed business in corn and oats. He attended the two-week winter short course at Ames. He exhibited livestock, poultry, and grain at fairs and shows. He won Iowa championships in 1909 for oats and in 1910 for breeding corn, a special class of a parent ear and five of its offspring.

From the start, young Coverdale's interests were larger than his farm. While still in college he had been sent to several county fairs to be a judge. When he was twenty-three he made the first of many talks at farmers' institutes. The next year he was secretary of the Clinton County Farmers' Institute and helped organize an eastern Iowa association, of which he was secretary, that saved expenses by scheduling speakers from one institute to another. He organized short courses and colt shows, judged farm and corn shows, and was vice-president of the Iowa Corn Growers Association.

The state Board of Agriculture in 1907 appointed him assistant superintendent for the state fair, a post he held until 1919. He instituted exhibits for individual farms and county Farm Bureaus. Shows for 4-H clubs were established and 4-H calf auctions started. Beginning in 1914, the state fair program included a Farm Bureau day. The fair provided a special section of its campground and a large tent where members talked over their problems.

Inevitably Coverdale became involved in extension work. In the spring of 1912, the Clinton Commercial Club and the county superintendent of schools raised $1,000 to match a contribution from Julius Rosenwald to counties that organized a crop improvement association. It wasn't enough to hire a topflight county agent, and Coverdale and two hog raisers, Warren Walrod and Elmer Forrest, were asked to solicit their neighbors for memberships of ten dollars a year. Coverdale soon signed up fifty Bloomfield Township farmers. The others had similar success and Forrest became president of the first county Farm Bureau in Iowa. M. L. Mosher, an agronomist on the state college staff, became the first county agent in the state.

At the age of twenty-nine, Coverdale became a white-collar worker. While he was judging corn at the Sioux City Fair, W. J. Kennedy, a livestock specialist who briefly headed the Extension Service in Iowa, offered him the opportunity to join the state college staff, take charge of the county agent program, and organize more farm bureaus. He held a sale, rented his farm to his hired man, and moved to Ames first as an assistant to Dean C. F. Curtiss of the College of Agriculture and then as the Extension Service's county agent leader. For the U.S. Department of Agriculture he was a dollar-a-year man who was called to Washington for training and conferences on educational work. Coverdale wouldn't have taken the job, he revealed later, if he had known of a high-level campus feud. Perry G. Holden, the extension director, had wanted the post to go to Henry A. Wallace, the third generation of the Des Moines publishing family who became a plant scientist, secretary of agriculture, and vicepresident. As a result, for years there was a strain in Henry C. Wallace's relations with Coverdale.

Coverdale made a lasting contribution to the Farm Bureau structure when he drew up the bylaws of the Clinton and Scott county improvement associations, the first in Iowa. He had unusual talent as an organizer and encouraged farmers in other counties to join hands in the cooperative movement. During the war, Iowa became the second state (New Hampshire was the first) to have a farm bureau and county agent in every county. Within a year he was the closest associate of J. R. Howard in laying the foundations of the Iowa and national federations.

The inexperienced farmers began to build an organization that in time duplicated the resources and facilities of statewide associations of city men. The beginning was spartan, and the first office was a room in the Masonic Building in Ames. If they found it necessary, Howard and Coverdale were authorized to hire a stenographer. Everyone knew that rural problems would require the collection and close study of a great deal of information, but at the Marshalltown convention the delegates either believed that the Farm Bureau would not need or could not afford a staff of experts. As a substitute, the constitution provided for four special committees, each composed of three farmers, to serve as specialists. Appointed in January 1919, the members were:

—*Marketing and transportation*—Charles W. Hunt, Logan; Adam L. Middleton, Eagle Grove; and J. I. Nichols, West Liberty.
—*Education*—Luther V. Carter, New Providence; George M. Fox, Dallas Center; and A. L. Bishop, Bedford.
—*Legislation and representation*—L. C. Willits, Mount Pleasant; E. C. Cunningham, Cresco; and J. E. Craven, Kellogg.
—*Organization*—W. P. Dawson, Aurelia; I. N. Taylor, Oskaloosa; and C. E. Arney, Albion.

The committees contained some unusually capable members, and within a year Hunt would be president, Fox vice-president, and Cunningham secretary of the state federation. Carter, a Quaker who later became speaker of the Iowa House of Representatives, and Arney were long-time friends of Howard.

The Farm Bureau had not expected to be concerned with transoceanic shipping, but heads of midwestern federations were called to Washington by Edward N. Hurley, chairman of the U.S. Shipping Board. The question of the hour, which Howard would not attempt to answer without study and consultation, involved the future of the nation's merchant marine. Later Howard developed controversial opinions on the issue. Since it was his first trip to the national capital, he took time out to look over agencies that represented agriculture and to make preliminary judgments about the possible establishment of a Farm Bureau office in Washington.

Farm Bureau officials from Illinois, Missouri, and Nebraska and editors of four farm papers attended an Iowa executive committee meeting in April to which Senator Albert B. Cummins, the top congressional expert on railroad legislation, had been invited. His speech gave Howard an introductory lesson in the complexities of returning to private ownership the railroads that had been taken over by the government in wartime. It also provided an opportunity for discussion of the merchant marine issue. As the educational process continued, an authority on southern agriculture spoke at a later meeting.

Because the county Farm Bureaus needed money, Howard soon made his debut as a lobbyist. Accompanied by Bliss and others, he testified before a joint meeting of the legislature's agricultural committees in support of a bill, enacted ten days after its introduction, requiring that county boards of supervisors appropriate tax revenues for the educational work of county agents. Since 1913, tax support had been optional. The new law divided counties into two categories and set a maximum grant of $5,000 for those of more than 25,000 population and $3,000 in smaller counties. Within those limits, the counties were required to match the dues paid by Farm Bureau members. The new legislation didn't use the Farm Bureau name, but the tax funds could go only to associations that cooperated with the Extension Service and the federal Department of Agriculture.

In his testimony, Howard supported the "county agent bill" on the ground that the educational work benefited nonmembers of farm bureaus. He held it was consistent with the theory that all who reap the benefits of government should contribute to its costs. Moreover, he held that the benefits vastly exceeded the county appropriations. Although the county funds could be spent only on educational work, the law was criticized later on the grounds that the Farm Bureau was being subsidized. Nearly three decades later, Howard went to the Marshall County Farm Bureau office and inspected the treasurer's annual reports. He found that the county appropriations were properly carried as a separate ledger account and that not a cent had been added to membership accounts or spent for organization, publicity, or legislation.

The Farm Bureau also supported higher appropriations to match Smith-Hughes funds and a law for tuberculin testing of dairy herds. During Howard's term as president, most of the lobbying was done by Cunningham and Willits.

To demonstrate that a membership was worth five dollars, Howard and his colleagues took such early steps as circulating 18,000 petitions for repeal of daylight savings time. Special counsel was engaged to present farm interests while a special commission revised the Iowa code, an unspectacular project that the state president regarded as important.

The work of the Farm Bureau could no more be confined to the state of Iowa than it could to the county of Marshall. Almost at once federation officials were crossing the state line to investigate marketing conditions and to confer with their opposite numbers in other states. No wonder that sentiment spread for a national federation.

Coverdale made a trip to Washington to assist Secretary of Agriculture David F. Houston in setting up a study of the cost of producing farm products. An article of rural faith was that owners of fields, barns, horses, and machinery were as much entitled to a return on their invested capital as were the owners of factories and banks. If a farmer worked longer and harder than a city laborer, should he not receive equivalent pay for his time? It was an old question, and when Theodore Roosevelt appointed a Country Life commission in 1908, he expressed the belief that in economic and social progress rural people had not kept pace with city dwellers. The agitation for prices that would at least equal the cost of production came up repeatedly at meetings, without a ready answer. To begin with, no one was certain what costs might be, especially on different farms in different regions. Howard and his colleagues wanted their decisions to be based on facts and the executive committee voted to help the state college with the distribution at cost of farm record books.

Howard not only believed that individual farmers should join in cooperative ventures but he also encouraged the Farm Bureau to work with other farmer organizations, including the Farmers Union. He thought that the Farm Bureau was best equipped to be the rural organization of general membership but he saw no reason why it should be all-inclusive. The scattered Iowa farmers who kept flocks of sheep and marketed the wool as individuals had a special problem that could be solved by uniform grading and cooperative marketing. The Farm Bureau helped them set up the Iowa Fleece Wool Growers Association and noted approvingly that 1 million pounds of wool were marketed at satisfactory prices.

The Farm Bureau worked closely with the Corn Belt Meat Producers' Association which had been founded by Henry C. Wallace. The Association, of which Wallace was secretary, did not have a large membership but was effective particularly in the field of freight rates. Wallace, who would become secretary of agriculture in the Harding administration, had been a farmer in Adair County and a professor of dairying at Iowa State until the death of his father. The rare combination of practical experience and scientific knowledge made him a superior editor and Howard regarded him as the best of the farm paper men. Howard had attended two or three of the Corn Belt Meat Producers' conventions and in particular remembered a speech by Gifford Pinchot when he was chief forester.

The marketing and transportation committee headed by C. W. Hunt actively pressed complaints about freight trains, terminal markets, and meat packers. As the respresentative of Iowa pork producers, Hunt attended a meeting at Kansas City to talk about setting up a midwestern committee that at regular intervals would meet with packing officials. Wallace, who had called the meeting as spokesman for Iowa beef interests, objected to a permanent organization on the ground that in a conference with packers the farmers could not hold their own. He broke up the conference by walking out and taking the important Kansas Farmers Union delegation with him. As a result, nothing was done until 1921 when the National Livestock and Meat Board was formed in Chicago with the encouragement of the American Farm Bureau Federation. By that time Howard had played a key role in enactment of the Packer and Stockyards Act.

Later Farm Bureau men from Iowa, Illinois, and Indiana met in Chicago with representatives of packers, stockyards, and the Federal Trade Commission to discuss regulation of the packing industry. Never impetuous, the Iowa federation refused to take a specific stand without knowing how farmers would be affected.

In the late summer, Coverdale demonstrated his superior talents as an organizer. He took personal charge of a membership campaign that kept the socialistic Non-Partisan League from invading Iowa and at the same time raised a special reserve fund that made the Iowa Farm Bureau unique for its solvency.

Governor William L. Harding, a conservative Republican who made a point of maintaining good relations with the Farm Bureau, warned Coverdale and Howard that plans for a membership drive should not be delayed. The governor had information that solicitors for the Non-Partisan League were working southward through Minnesota and had made arrangements for drivers and cars to take them from farm to farm in northern Iowa. Had that happened, both the fledgling Farm Bureau and the established Republican party would have faced strong competition.

One warning was enough, for Howard was familiar with the programs and problems of the Non-Partisan League. It had been organized in 1915 by North Dakota spring wheat growers in a protest against the domination of their market by the Minneapolis Chamber of Commerce. A terminal market similar to the Chicago Board of Trade, the chamber controlled country elevators and was accused by farmers of adopting regulations that depressed prices of a special type of wheat produced only in the Dakotas and Minnesota. Dominating North Dakota politics, the grain trade also selected and elected governors and legislators who would play ball with the big city interests.

In a revolt against the monopoly, 87 percent of North Dakota voters in 1914 favored establishment of a state-owned terminal elevator, but the conservative state administration refused to support enabling legislation. In a monumental public relations error, an old guard politician advised the farmers to "go home and slop the hogs." Out of that meeting the league was born. Instead of forming a third party, it took over the Republican primary and elected Lynn J. Frazier governor. In 1918 it gained full control of the legislature and, along with tax reforms, created a state-owned elevator, warehouse, flour mill, and bank.

Howard frequently said that if he had lived in North Dakota he would have been a member of the league. He admired the spirit of the men who refused to be subservient to business interests, but he did not approve socialistic programs and he felt that the new officials in North Dakota lacked business experience and were overlooking the best interests of their state. He was aware of the dissension that soon resulted in the recall of Frazier and other officials. (Before many years, the Non-Partisan League lost its clout and was succeeded by the Farmer-Labor party, which was successful in a coalition with Democrats in Minnesota.)

As a third generation Republican, Howard did not want league politics established in his state. He also believed that the Corn Belt had a more diversified agriculture and more complex problems than the wheat region, and he thought that Iowa farmers should be represented by an organization similar to the Farm Bureau.

The league could be kept out of Iowa if the northern counties were Farm Bureau strongholds, and Coverdale already was starting up the machinery that made it possible. At a meeting during Farm Bureau day at the state fair, he explained his plan to increase the state membership by 100,000 and to raise a special fund that would enable the federation to expand its work. Somewhat skeptical, the executive committee left the matter in his hands. Membership drives were expensive and the Iowa federation was short of money.

Coverdale was so confident of his ability to stage a successful campaign that he gambled $20,000 of his own money on the outcome. He personally guaranteed to pay membership solicitors $10 a day or $250 a month, plus expenses. The drive began September 22 in Hardin County. With extension service assistance, he recruited sixteen of the more successful county presidents and assigned each to work one week in a township. A local committee provided each solicitor with a driver-guide who introduced him to nonmembers. Each farmer received a personal invitation to sign a perpetual agreement that authorized his bank to pay the Farm Bureau five dollars yearly. In addition, he was asked to contribute to a reserve fund that would guarantee future success of the Farm Bureau movement in Iowa. Times were prosperous, farmers had high hopes for the new organization, and the solicitation paid off. In the first week in Hardin County, 1,140 members contributed $5 each plus $2,200 for the special fund. That covered the expenses of the drive and Coverdale did not have to make good on his guarantee.

A key element of the campaign was that the solicitors were well paid. Ten dollars a day was a top wage in 1919, attractive to ambitious men who were glad to get an off-season income. The campaign managers had their pick of farmers talented as salesmen. Those hired were willing to work long hours in the hope that a good showing would bring them future assignments.

The campaign pyramided. The solicitors had new driver-guides each day and were instructed to indoctrinate the most promising for membership work in other counties. As a result, during the second week thirty-two solicitors in other counties signed up members, collected money, and trained additional men who were deployed into other parts of the state. In his report on 1919 accomplishments, Coverdale said that Farm Bureau membership had grown from 30,600 on July 1 to 104,388 at the end of the year and that $350,000 was contributed to the reserve fund. The campaign continued during the early months of 1920.

For the only time during his six years as a Farm Bureau president, Howard had a treasury that was unquestionably solvent. Recruitment of an office staff began with the hiring of the state fair's publicity man, who began publication of the *Farm Bureau Messenger.* When the American Farm Bureau Federation was organized that winter, expense accounts and other bills were picked up by the Iowa federation. Iowa soon was sending solicitors to help in neighboring states. Among other federations, Ohio and Michigan adopted Coverdale-type membership drives.

After his term as governor ended, Harding told Howard that if it had not been for Coverdale's aggressive campaign Iowa would have been taken over by the Non-Partisan League. The governor overstated his case. At its peak, the league undoubtedly hoped to spread into Iowa, but it soon disintegrated and ceased to be a force in Minnesota and South Dakota.

Nothing on record indicates that the Farm Bureau leaders were concerned with competition from the Farmers Union, which also was new in Iowa. On the national scene, Howard worked closely with Farmers Union leaders in the cause of cooperative marketing. As was his custom, he maintained friendly personal relationships, despite policy disagreements, with such men as Charles S. Barrett of Georgia, whose long career as Farmers Union national president began in 1906, and John Simpson of Oklahoma. The Howard papers do not mention Milo Reno, whose colorful career as Iowa Farmers Union president began in 1921.

Howard's chief criticism of many past and present farm groups was that they often became involved in politics, lacked solid financing, and were apt to be inconsistent on policies. He believed that the Farmers Union did not merit public confidence because it had been "rather radical" and unstable. That point came up April 6, 1951, when he was interviewed at his farm home by Kenneth Langer of the Iowa Farm Bureau Federation and Joe M. Bohlen of the Iowa State College faculty. One of the topics was the Extension Service's decision to cooperate with the Farm Bureau, rather than the Farmers Union or the Grange, in its educational programs. Howard in a long anecdote told of Coverdale being in the audience of a Farmers Union convention that was well attended by businessmen and educators. Barrett presided and the agenda included the old complaint that prices at the farm were too low. From the audience he appointed commodity committees and instructed them to report back at the afternoon session with definite cost-of-production figures. Because no sheep raisers were in the room, he appointed a sheep buyer for a major packing company as a one-man committee. When the wheat committee reported that costs were three dollars a bushel, Barrett announced that thereafter they would receive three dollars a bushel for wheat, without saying how. When someone said that price was a little high, Barrett had the committee go over its figures, which on the spot were reduced to two dollars. Even with modern computers, Farm Bureau and Department of Agriculture economists have never been able to determine cost-of-production data that would apply from farm to farm to say nothing of from state to state.

13

Lobbying in Washington

FARM BUREAU officials soon began to ride trains to Washington. In the summer of 1919, Howard was a member of the first delegation that went to the White House and asked the president to consider agriculture's problems. Then, acting alone, he had success in convincing some members of the House of Representatives that they should change their votes. As far as the record shows, that made him the Farm Bureau's first congressional lobbyist. His example was quickly followed and within a few months state federations began to station men in Washington during sessions of Congress.

After the war, inflated prices were a problem that put farmers on the defensive. Many politicians and publications complained about the high cost of living (shortened in headlines to HCL) and demanded that something be done. Government officials joined in the agitation and helped spread a belief that the solution would be to cut prices, beginning with the original producer. The farmer thus became the scapegoat, with no one to defend him unless it was going to be the newly formed state farm bureaus, for no one in Washington seemed to be speaking up for agriculture.

When Coverdale and officials from other midwestern states met at Chicago on June 18 and 19, 1919, a counter offensive was advocated by David O. Thompson, secretary of the Illinois Agricultural Association. He proposed that a delegation be sent to Washington to see what could be done. Howard, who believed that the Iowa Farm Bureau must be active in the national capital as well as Des Moines, approved the project. In a Washington hotel he met Thompson and three other state presidents—Oscar E. Bradfute of Ohio, John G. Brown of Indiana, and T. C. Crocker of Nebraska.

Totally inexperienced in the operation of the Washington power structure, they spent a day or more discussing strategy and working over a statement that Thompson had drafted. On his inspiration, the five men went to a hotel dining room and ordered the two-dollar dinner, an average price. Before eating they carefully estimated the amount of meat, flour, potatoes, and other ingredients. The next morning at a market they found that the producers had received seventeen cents for the raw materials. Therefore, farm prices had little to do with the high cost of living, for the dinner would have cost $1.83 if the food had been donated.

Still wondering what to do, the farmers—with Bradfute as their spokesman—asked for an appointment with David F. Houston, the secretary of agriculture, and were surprised when they got it promptly. A rumor that Houston was opposed to rural interests proved untrue. While publicly supporting administration policies, he was privately sympathetic and had told President Wilson that farmers should not be blamed for the cost of living. Houston asked the five men to go to the White House with their story and made an appointment for the next day. None had dreamed that their mission to Washington could culminate in a meeting with the president.

Woodrow Wilson and the White House made a lasting impression on Howard, who had never seen a president. Many times in private conversations and before Iowa audiences Howard, the Iowa farmer, described the interior of the presidential residence and told of the brief wait before the immaculately dressed Wilson entered the Blue Room exactly on time, greeted each man courteously, and listened attentively to their argument about prices and living costs. Any difference of opinion was preceded in a rich baritone by the words, "May I suggest so and so?" There was no disagreement as to details and Wilson listened closely to the story of Thompson's dinner.

The president closed the matter by saying that living costs must come down, that a start had to be made somewhere, and that he knew of no better place to start than at the beginning of production.

"We knew then that the President of the United States in this matter was not our friend," Howard wrote in his memoirs. At the end of the conference, which lasted an hour, Wilson said it was the first time in seven years that he had been called upon by a delegation of farmers. He added that many editors, bankers, manufacturers, and economists had claimed to speak for rural America.

In another new experience, when the group left the White House Howard participated in his first national press conference. To a dozen newsmen, Thompson handed the statement signed by the five men. In rather bombastic language it said the HCL issue had been befogged by political quackery and, threatening a production strike, made it clear that any price cuts would have to be accepted also by industry, labor, wholesalers, and retailers. It expressed doubt that price cuts at the farm would bring the desired results. Presumably Howard had little part in writing the statement. He would have used a calmer tone and would have resorted more to logic in discussing economics. The next day in a train trip across Saskatchewan, where she had visited a brother, Anna Howard found a newspaper account of the White House visit. She had not known that her husband had made another trip to the East Coast.

The unexpected audience with President Wilson was followed by an opportunity to influence the legislative branch of the federal government. The other members of the midwestern committee went home, but Howard had unfinished business that involved Congress and 67,000 signers of Farm Bureau petitions for the repeal of daylight savings time. If he really believed that agriculture should have a stronger voice in the halls of government, he felt obligated to become a lobbyist and stay in Washington several more days. It would be a new experience, since he knew little about Congress, but the president of the Iowa Farm Bureau was a self-starter who could act on his own initiative when faced with challenges.

Like other rural people, he did not like the federal law that since March 30, 1918, had required all clocks to be turned an hour ahead during seven midyear months. To farmers, who couldn't start working in their fields until the sun evaporated the dew, it was tinkering with a natural law that caused them to work an hour later than city residents. At its first meeting the Iowa executive committee had voted to circulate repeal petitions. On the suggestion of Howard's committee, several other state farm bureaus took the same action.

Congress had passed a repeal bill that for nine days had been on Wilson's desk. It would become law automatically the next day if not vetoed. As the White House meeting ended, Howard expressed hope that the repealer would be signed. The president replied that he recognized the farmer interests, that the problem was one of the most perplexing he had faced, and that at the moment he did not know what action he would take.

Howard made his own position clear: "Mr. President, your decision, it seems to me, will depend upon whether you consider the interests of agriculture to be of greater importance to the nation than the interests of industry," he said. "If the agricultural interests are of first importance, you must sign the bill. If industry is of greater importance, you might be justified in vetoing it."

"You are exactly right," the president replied. "That will be the basis for the determination of my action."

Howard, who saw the president on a later occasion, considered him to be one of the great presidents.

Without waiting for the veto to be announced, Howard began learning how to find his way in the halls of Congress. He joined forces with Charles A. Lyman of the National Board of Farm Organizations and S. M. Loomis of the National Grange. Help came from two congressmen—Christian W. Ramseyer of Iowa and Edward J. King of Illinois. They provided a house roll call on passage of the repealer bill and suggested that Howard talk to men who had voted against it. The next two days were hard physical work as he tramped the intricate maze of corridors of the House Office Building. Fourteen congressmen promised to reverse their stands and vote to override Wilson's veto. Only eight changes would be needed in the House of Representatives.

With the roster in hand, Howard had a front row gallery seat when the House met. The situation was unusually tense and everyone of the fourteen congressmen made good on his promise.

"Probably it was the first time the farmers scored on an important issue," Howard wrote years later in a marginal notation when he read Coverdale's account of the early Farm Bureau days. He never asked for personal credit, on the daylight time issue or other matters, but had he not stayed in Washington as a fledgling lobbyist, the veto probably would have been upheld.

Howard, who as American Farm Bureau president was personally acquainted with four presidents, became familiar with the interior of the White House. His memoirs describe how President Wilson wanted to mobilize farm sentiment for American membership in the League of Nations. Gray Silver, the Farm Bureau's Washington representative, had telegraphed to Howard that President Wilson wanted to see the two of them as soon as possible.

The President . . . wanted to know of us what was the attitude of farmers toward the treaty and the league. We told him that so far as we knew no group of farmers had ever committed themselves on the subject and we presumed that they were as much divided as were all other groups of American citizenry.

Then he told us that the farmers' stake in the treaty and the league was greater than that of any other group or individual. He pointed out to us very clearly that we were a surplus producing nation and that our market for the surplus had always been in the industrial centers of Europe. He stated that as a result of the war European industry was practically annihilated.

Not only had the physical plants of industry been destroyed in many sections, but capital itself was badly depleted as well as the morale of the people. Unless America helped rehabilitate European industry, Europe could not buy our farm surpluses. But the people of Europe must have food from some source. What they were unable to acquire from other nations, they must produce themselves.

He pointed out to us that there were large areas of adaptable agricultural lands in Europe which were not in production. Some of these, he told us, were in large tracts, but mostly they were in small areas adaptable for acreage farming or gardening. I distinctly recall his statement that every garden would strike a certain toll from our export markets.

He pointed out also that there was always a surplus population in most European countries desiring to emigrate permanently or temporarily to the United States. Up to the turn of the century most of these people joined the ranks of American agriculture, but for the last two or three decades they were more inclined to settle in our industrial centers.

During the war we had set up immigration barriers which largely prevented the surplus European population from reaching our shores. The result was that they would be forced to emigrate to other countries such as South Africa, South America, western Canada or Australia, regions which were agricultural rather than industrial. This would add to the agricultural production of those countries and, hence, add materially to the market competition of our surpluses.

After that exposition, the president asked the Farm Bureau officials to prepare a list of twenty-five or fifty outstanding farmers. He wanted to invite them to a meeting that, because of his poor health, was never held. Consequently, the list was not prepared.

14

"He Was at Ithaca"

I N his final years, when recalling the beginnings of the Farm Bureau movement, Howard suggested that his epitaph state simply and proudly, "He Was at Ithaca." There, on the campus of Cornell University, February 12–13, 1919, he was one of a small group of men from twelve states who laid the foundation for the organization nine months later of the American Farm Bureau Federation. The Ithaca conference was a first step toward the establishment of a truly national farm organization, the first since the National Grange a half century earlier. Howard had been there at the beginning.

At Ithaca, a month and a half after his election as Iowa president, Howard was recognized as one of the strong men in the emerging leadership. He spoke up for the midwestern belief that the U.S. Department of Agriculture and the extension services were overemphasizing production and had done nothing to solve the problems of marketing and distribution. He told easterners that educational programs weren't enough and that attention must be paid to economic questions. He urged that the work of the national organization not be delayed. On the latter point, the other twenty delegates agreed and voted to hold a convention in Chicago in November. As a result of his leadership at Ithaca, when the program for the Chicago meeting was arranged, Howard was assigned the role of keynote speaker for the midwestern point of view.

The agitation for a nationwide federation came from the grass roots and the initiative had been taken by men from the Northeast who believed that education should be the Farm Bureau's primary function but who in an emergency had not hesitated to call on the government for help. In November 1917 a group of county Farm Bureau presidents from New York and New England went to Washington to tell high government officials of their fears that truck and fruit crops could not be grown and harvested if esssential laborers were drafted into military service. As a result, wartime policies were revised. Before the group returned home, four county presidents from New York met with L. R. Simons of the

States Relations Service (which later became the Extension Service) of the Department of Agriculture to talk about the need for a national organization that would deal with the government on questions of agricultural policy. After a long discussion, E. V. Titus, a Long Island potato farmer, said a national Farm Bureau, with state federations as members units, was needed. Simons agreed and predicted that it would be the next development. He consulted with other department officials and wrote to Titus that the movement should be sponsored by some committee or organization, preferably by the New York state federation. He added that the national agency, once in business, should employ a "high-class manager."

The New Yorkers acted promptly. A committee headed by Frank R. Smith of Springfield Center, who later served in the New York assembly, corresponded with Farm Bureau men from other states. Smith mailed the invitations to the Ithaca conference during the third annual meeting of the New York federation.

Howard, who had unnecessarily been instructed by the Iowa executive committee to be an advocate of nationwide federation, found general agreement when he reached the College of Agriculture and exchanged introductions and points of view with delegates from Illinois, Massachusetts, Michigan, Missouri, New Hampshire, New York, Ohio, Vermont, and West Virginia, which had state federations, and Delaware and Pennsylvania, which were represented by county presidents. When he opened the meeting, Silas L. Strivings, the New York president, said that a national organization could not be created at Ithaca because not enough states were on hand.

The official delegate from the New York federation was D. V. Farley. The men from other states were: William G. Eckhardt, Clifford V. Gregory, and J. C. Sailor, Illinois; Fred W. Burnham and Ernest H. Gilbert, Massachusetts; C. A. Bingham, Dr. Eben Mumford, and E. G. Potts, Michigan; Chester H. Gray, Missouri; George A. Hill, New Hampshire; Oscar E. Bradfute and Harry G. Beals, Ohio; E. B. Cornwall and L. K. Osgood, Vermont; and Nat T. Frame and J. R. McLaughlin, West Virginia.

Gray, the second delegate from west of the Mississippi River, was president of the oldest state Farm Bureau and at thirty-five was one of the youngest men at the Ithaca meeting. A group of county agents had organized a Missouri federation in March 1915. Gray, who wanted a broad-based membership, took over as state president in 1918. Previously his talents had been devoted to organizing a national farmers' association about 1912 at Kansas City and the National Marketing Association, a subsidiary that attempted to buy and sell cooperatively. Gray, who envisioned a more militant organization that would concern itself with economic problems, was impressed with the potential of the Farm Bureau. A successful organizer of county units, he arrived in Ithaca with a proposed national constitution in his pocket. Many of his ideas were incorporated in the Farm Bureau's plan of organization. Gray served on the American Farm Bureau Federation's first executive committee and for fifteen years was its Washington representative.

When the Ithaca meeting was thrown open for discussion, Howard made a strong speech in favor of Farm Bureau involvement in economic and governmental matters at county, state, and national levels. He wanted a federation that would be free from partisan influence and would develop its economic potential on a nationwide and even worldwide basis. Speaking to men from Washington and the land-grant colleges who were in the audience, he added that the extension services, operating through county agents, had failed to touch problems of vital importance.

In his memoirs, he did not mention his own role at Ithaca but said that the best speech was by Gregory, editor of *Prairie Farmer,* a Chicago-based journal. A graduate of Iowa State College and owner of a farm in DuPage County, Gregory had been a founder and early vice-president of the Illinois Agricultural Association. He did not object to the goals of education, provided that increased crop and livestock production was needed. Forecasting future trouble with surpluses, he said that the second blade of grass should not be grown if it was not needed. Gregory believed that the marketing system needed to be improved and, taking issue with easterners, argued that agricultural economics must be studied and interpreted for the advantage of the individual farmer.

Between sessions, Howard's opinion of Gregory's speech was asked by Dr. C. B. Smith of the U.S. Department of Agriculture, who had spoken earlier. The Iowan gave it high approval. Smith replied that his own speech had stressed the great need for education and that Gregory did not seem to understand that economics was but one branch of education. Howard recalled that Smith's speech, which carefully outlined the agriculture department's widespread work, was a typical department address that "lacked the punch that appeals to farmers."

Easterners and midwesterners did not agree on the emphasis that should be placed on education and economics, but all wanted to belong to a national Farm Bureau and they were willing to let the final decisions be made at a later meeting to be attended by men from more states. Gregory, Gray, Bradfute of Ohio, Cornwall of Vermont, and Smith of New York were appointed to a committee on organization. On the second day, under Bradfute's chairmanship, the committee recommended that a conference be held in Chicago on November 12 and 13 to organize a national Farm Bureau. Without dissent, a call for delegates was issued and Bradfute's committee was placed in charge of permanent arrangements. Gregory, who believed that only actual farmers should handle the details of permanent organization, stepped aside and was replaced by Sailor, the Illinois vice-president. A motion was made to enlarge the committee so that a place could be made for Howard. It was defeated, at Howard's request, on the grounds that a large committee would be unwieldy.

During the summer, midwesterners began to worry because they had heard nothing from Bradfute about arrangements for the November convention. When, on the invitation of the Illinois Agricultural Association, men from Indiana, Iowa, Nebraska, Kentucky, Minnesota, and Michigan held a regional conference in Chicago on July 28 and 29, Sailor reported that as far as he knew Bradfute had done nothing about such fundamentals as the drafting of a tentative constitution. They decided not to wait for Bradfute to move. For leadership they turned to Coverdale, who represented Iowa at the meeting, and gave him responsibility for reaching a Corn Belt consensus on the major constitutional controversies—the name, objective, and financing of a national federation and the methods of selecting a board of directors. The group planned another regional conference at which they would draft their own version of a constitution. Then they would ask for a meeting with Bradfute.

When Coverdale reported to him, Howard had an alternative suggestion. He acknowledged that Bradfute was "a bit lethargic," but he did not want the large convention in November to be preceded by a public controversy. To his mind, it would be advantageous if the seven-state group did not meet a second time. He had complete faith in Coverdale's ability to fulfill any assignment and he remembered that the Iowa secretary had been an Aberdeen-Angus breeder. He sent Coverdale to visit Bradfute at his Meadow Brook farm outside Xenia, Ohio. After the Iowan had admired Bradfute's black cattle and after the two men had discussed the livestock business, they began talking about a constitution for the proposed national federation. Three days later, Coverdale had their ideas on paper. Bradfute called a meeting of his committee on arrangement. The midwestern leaders were satisfied with the report they received from Coverdale and they never held a second meeting.

Happy with the results, Howard and Coverdale kept silent about the manner in which they had stirred Bradfute into action. Recalling it more than three decades later, they disagreed on only one point. Howard remembered that Coverdale had made a special trip to Ohio. Coverdale said he had stopped there on an eastern journey. When he read Coverdale's "Early Days" memoirs of the Iowa and American federations, Howard made this marginal notation:

This committee was not getting action and it was to speed it up that you went to see Bradfute. It was you who wrote the constitution and by-laws (as you had the

Iowa federation) which were adopted by the LaSalle meeting in November. In the largest sense, you are the daddy of both the Iowa and AFBF. Neither constitution has been changed greatly through the years. The credit is yours and it should be so stated.

There was no assurance that the widely scattered state federations would be able to agree on the framework of a national Farm Bureau. On the controversial topic of the primacy of education, southerners and westerners were inclined to side with the Northeast against the Corn Belt. Some midwesterners held a third point of view, that regional federations would be preferable. Among them was Henry C. Wallace, the second generation of the Des Moines publishing family. Some of the Illinois leaders also were reportedly willing to forget about the rest of the country and organize on a sectional basis. Inside the Iowa Farm Bureau, Howard and his associates stood solidly for a nationwide organization. They anticipated differences of opinion, but they wanted agriculture to speak with one voice. They did not want divergent views to be expressed at Washington and elsewhere by four or more regional organizations of farmers.

In March, when he was called to Washington for a merchant marine conference, Howard made the trip with Wallace, who took time to introduce him to some of the men a state Farm Bureau president should know. On the eastbound train and in Washington, the two Iowans argued about organized agriculture's future. The editor, who doubted the ability of U.S. farmers to take a stand on anything, had previously suggested that the midwestern states form a Corn Belt federation instead of becoming part of a national organization. The Midwest wanted higher prices for wheat and oats, he pointed out, while the eastern states, which did not produce their own dairy feed, wanted to purchase grain as cheaply as possible. He contended that the two regions lacked common interests and that a national federation would generate conflicts rather than unity.

Howard took the opposite view. He answered that all regions operate under the same economic laws and have many common problems. Cooperation should be nationwide and in no region should farmers seek advantages by opposing the welfare of farmers in other states. He contended that labor, taxes, interest, and other production costs are essentially the same in New Jersey or California as they are in Iowa and that in general farmers sell on the same market regardless of their state of residence. Later he wrote:

I fully agreed that the economic differences between Iowa and other states were correctly stated by Wallace and that the split which was evident at Ithaca between the economic viewpoint of the West and the educational viewpoint of the East might be hard to reconcile. Yet the East had problems where they needed help.

For some years we had attended a little Quaker meeting where the pastor was one of those unvarnished pioneer farmer-preachers now all too nearly extinct. Henry Hickman in every prayer and sermon used a single word to convey the context of his message—oneness. From Henry Hickman's preaching came my answer to Wallace—oneness.

The common interest of American agriculture far outweighs sectional or individual differences, unless basic principles are at stake. It is always better to seek common denominators than to increase divisors and reduce quotients.

The vision of Ithaca was that of a united farm people—oneness.

15

The Founding Convention

NE V E R had farmers from so many states met in convention. Leaders of a movement less than ten years old, the men who assembled in Chicago on November 12–14, 1919, were upper-middle-class landowners, forward-looking, hard-headed, and bipartisan, convinced that agriculture long had needed national leadership and hopeful that they could establish a Farm Bureau federation that would provide it, then and in future years, for the good of rural America. Most were strangers who came from distant states and who practiced divergent types of husbandry according to the peculiarities of their soils and climates. Although they had a single goal, the Yankees wanted to concentrate their efforts on education whereas the midwesterners wanted to be activists in the economic and governmental areas. The possibility of establishing the nation's first coast-to-coast organization attracted a crowd that included a delegation from the Department of Agriculture, officials of land-grant colleges, and observers from corporations and associations concerned with foods and fibers. Among them were skeptics who wondered whether a deadlock might develop or whether some state might bolt the convention and start organizing a regional federation. The difficult situation bore some parallel to the constitutional convention 132 years earlier that had survived a summer of dissension in Philadelphia. One difference was that the farmers in Chicago planned to meet for only two days. It wasn't enough; they needed three days to do the job, but they did it.

Howard had arrived early, after a side trip to Louisville where he presided over the birth of the Kentucky Farm Bureau Federation. At the LaSalle Hotel he backstopped the committee on arrangements and, keeping his ears open for trouble, gave pep talks about nationalism as men from other states gathered around him. Iowa's thirty-man delegation was second only to that of the host state of Illinois and on the afternoon before the convention Howard called a meeting of his executive committee (only one man was absent) and transacted important business. Vice-

President Adam L. Middleton was authorized to inspect the Canadian grain elevator system. The annual meeting in January was to be asked to increase dues to ten dollars, which would allow fifty cents to go to the national office. With Extension Director R. K. Bliss and Missouri President Chester H. Gray participating, most of the time was spent on a section-by-section discussion of the proposed national constitution that Bradfute and Coverdale had drafted. Howard was authorized to cast the Iowa vote at the national convention, but when the executive committee met the next day in an emergency, Middleton presided. Too busy to attend, Howard was involved with more important business.

Farm Bureaus were represented from coast to coast and from Canada to Mexico. Some of the federations were little more than paper organizations, however, and most of the newer ones were weak in membership and short on finances. Participation in the convention required optimism, devotion to the cause, and a vision of the future. On the first day, voting privileges—one vote to a state—were granted to thirty-one states: California, Colorado, Connecticut, Delaware, Georgia, Illinois, Indiana, Iowa, Kansas, Kentucky, Maryland, Massachusetts, Michigan, Minnesota, Mississippi, Missouri, Montana, Nebraska, New Hampshire, New Jersey, New York, North Carolina, Ohio, Oklahoma, South Dakota, Tennessee, Texas, Utah, Virginia, Vermont, and West Virginia. The credentials committee later qualified Arkansas, Rhode Island, and South Carolina. In the impending power struggle, only North Dakota and Wisconsin were missing from the Middle West and Pennsylvania and Maine from the East. Despite a delayed start in organizing the southern states, only Alabama and Florida failed to qualify for attendance at the founding convention. The large gaps were in the Plains and West Coast regions.

Speculation about election of officers centered on the respected heads of two of the stronger state federations. The midwestern candidate, a farmer who looked like a banker, was Oscar Edwin Bradfute of Ohio, who as chairman of the arrangements committee was the convention's presiding officer. Born in 1862, he had graduated from Indiana University and then returned to the Ohio farm his grandfather had purchased from the government. In partnership with his father, he had established a major herd of Aberdeen Angus cattle bred for size and quality without regard for pedigree fads. Bradfute was a member of a committee of nine that organized the International Stock Show at Chicago in 1899, and he served continuously on its board of directors until he died. A prominent stock judge, he had been president of the American Aberdeen-Angus Association and the Ohio Livestock Breeders' Association. He also was prominent in educational circles. In 1905 he was appointed a trustee of Ohio State University, a position he held for twenty years. Earlier he had been a trustee of the Ohio experiment station for five years. A Presbyterian elder, he had been a college and theological seminary trustee. President Wilson had recently appointed him to a special industrial commission that attempted to pacify postwar disputes between capital and labor.

The choice of the easterners who wanted to emphasize the educational work of the extension services was Silas L. Strivings of Castile, New York. Tall and scholarly in appearance, he had headed the New York State Farm Bureau Federation since it was founded in 1917 and had been instrumental in calling the February conference at Ithaca where the groundwork had been laid for the Chicago meeting. Like Howard, Strivings had been an educator. A normal-school graduate, he had been Wyoming County superintendent of schools for six years and a high school principal for eight years. He inherited a farm from an aged couple he had cared for, owned a herd of Jersey cattle, and had the best pear orchard in his county. He had helped organize a cooperative fruit growers' association and a cooperative creamery. He had been prominent in the Grange as master, purchasing agent, and, in later years, state master. Howard, who considered him the best public speaker among the first generation of Farm Bureau leaders, had brought Strivings to Des Moines to speak at a state fair meeting three months earlier.

Keynote speeches by Strivings and Howard followed an address of welcome by Harvey J. Sconce, president of the Illinois Agricultural Association. At the moment the Iowa federation might have more members, but the Illinois association had the strongest program among state farm bureaus. It charged the highest dues, fifteen dollars, paid most of the county agent salaries, and, had it wished, could have operated independently of the Extension Service at Urbana.

Howard took a middle-of-the-road position and asked that regionalism be rejected. He argued that all states have basic interests and that they must unite on the fundamentals that apply to all. His broad vision called for the Farm Bureau to cooperate rather than compete with other rural organizations and he specifically commended the National Grange.

The Iowa president inaccurately prophesied that food production would decrease during the next few years, since he believed that no more large tracts of land could be brought under cultivation and no more laborsaving machines were being invented that would increase production. All farmers have a patriotic duty, he continued, to prevent decreases in food production. Any short-term advantage in prices in time "would mean discontented men and national disorder which might disrupt the fabric of our civil being." The speaker added that "therefore stable production of food from a patriotic standpoint seems to be a matter of important and careful concern."

Farmers have never regarded themselves as blood brothers of city laborers, and the speaker drew applause when he demanded that factory, railroad, and mine employees "render an honest day's work for an honest day's pay.'' At the time coal miners had just gone out on strike. Howard also expressed concern about a national "tendency toward Bolshevism and anarchy" and said that radicalism was the great enemy of the farmers' constructive work. Other convention speakers also expressed concern about a wave of radicalism that coincided with the Russian revolution. Howard continued:

Scientists tell us that every particle of matter in the universe, whether of the earth, moon or sun, has an influence upon every other particle, and that even the most distant stars affect the earth in its orbit. I perceive a similar situation with regard to the commercial affairs of the nation. The welfare of every man in the country, whether he be manufacturer, railroad man or laborer, has to do with the welfare of every other man in the country.

The coal strike, the steel strike, or the local street car strike affects my business as a farmer. Hence we must act in the broad spirit of sympathy, not with criticism, in dealing with these elements. It is necessary to our national life to have railroads, mines and factories, to have wholesalers and distributors, as well as farmers, and it behooves us to get together in a broad way and with a broad vision.

Arguments about the proposed constitution consumed possibly half of the three-day meeting. Since "Farm Bureau" had become a household term in rural areas of the United States, the delegates finally agreed upon American Farm Bureau Federation as their new organization's name. Busy in another room, Howard did not try to make an issue of his private belief that it was not the best possible name. His first choice would have been some such name as American Agricultural Association, but to his mind the convention had more vital controversies to settle.

A prolonged dispute over representation on governing boards recalled the 1878 constitutional debate over the makeup of the United States Congress. At Chicago the small states, agriculturally speaking, were pitted against those with large areas of fertile soil and hence more farmers. The eastern contingent wanted each state to have one member on the proposed board of directors that would set policy at future conventions. The midwesterners liked the draft proposal that allowed states to have an additional director for every 20,000 Farm Bureau members. The Corn Belt states, which had the largest membership but a minority of the votes cast at the founding convention, were allowed to have their way, in part because of fear that some state might walk out.

The Midwest then lost a fight over the makeup of the executive committee that would meet with federation officers and make management decisions. The draft proposal, patterned after the Iowa constitution, called for a twelve-man executive committee with three members each allocated geographically to the Midwest, East, South, and West. Men from the central region complained that the states with the largest membership, which would contribute the bulk of the federation's revenues, would be in the minority. The other regions served notice that they did not want to belong to an organization that would be dominated by one area. The Iowa doctrine of Farm Bureau nationalism prevailed and, to prevent a crisis, the large states gave in.

More trouble was caused by the questions of how much financial support the states should give the national federation. The original draft called for each state to pay 20 percent of its membership fees plus a $1,000 initiation fee to the American Farm Bureau. Some small states protested that they could not afford that support and those that emphasized educational work did not conceive that the national organization would need that much money. Coverdale took the floor to argue that a much larger financial program would be necessary if the delegates took home a broad vision of future activity. The final compromise was that the national organization would receive 10 percent of dues received by the states, with special provision for some small states. The American Farm Bureau Federation would not have much money, but at least it would exist.

On its third day, the convention finally adopted the constitution. There had been changes in the amount of dues and number of directors, but the basic document was that drafted in advance by Bradfute and Coverdale.

The spotlight then turned on Howard for several hours. After his keynote speech he had reminded Bradfute that a resolutions committee was needed. In reply, he was appointed its chairman and as a result had been off the floor during most of the constitutional debate. Nevertheless, he had appeared briefly several times before the delegates. Once he pointed out that a motion for the previous question could extricate the delegates from what seemed to be a hopeless parliamentary snarl. Again he obtained approval for telegrams of goodwill to President Wilson, ill in the White House, and to the National Grange, in convention at Grand Rapids, Michigan.

The first resolution, pledging continued support of the extension services and the county agent system, assured the northeastern delegates that educational programs would never be diminished by business enterprises and legislative activity. It was followed by declarations that landowners were entitled to a fair profit based upon the cost of production, including a wage allowance for their own labor and that of their families. Espousing the Howard doctrine of the interdependence of U.S. institutions, the resolutions asked that farmers be treated as equals of business and labor but did not demand more than a fair share. In future years, Howard would negotiate a legislative agreement with meat packers under terms of a one-sentence provision: ''We recommend such regulation of all purveyors of food stuffs, including packers, wholesale grocers, commission men and all similar industries, in such manner as will be just and fair to producers and consumers as well as to the industries.'' Also of future importance to him were planks demanding early return of railroads to private ownership and asserting that farmers should have the right to engage in cooperative marketing, regardless of antitrust laws. The report laid the foundation for the federation's development as a stable and nonpartisan organization that attracted a large membership in all states and deserved the attention and respect of the top levels of government, business, and finance.

With his responsibilities out of the way, Howard complimented Bradfute at lunch for his tact and fairness. In advance of the final session, he added congratulations for Bradfute's election as president, which he felt was certain and well deserved. In response, the Ohioan said he had in mind suggesting that Howard be secretary of the American Farm Bureau Federation. It was a new thought to the Iowan, who replied that he had more than enough work to do at home but that they could talk about it sometime.

The two men said goodbye. The weather had been bad in central Iowa and Howard was anxious to return to Homelands. The week had been strenuous and he went to his room to rest until train time.

Other delegates had started to leave Chicago, and Bradfute, who wisely had allowed divergent points of view to be argued at length, now hurried through the afternoon agenda. He ruled that nominations would be made by announcement of name, without speeches. A New Yorker nominated Strivings and an Ohio delegate did the same for the presiding officer. Then Bradfute magnanimously sacrificed his own chance by announcing in one sentence that votes also could be cast for Howard.

When the written ballots were counted, the result was six for Strivings, four for Bradfute, and fifteen for Howard.

No evidence suggests that Howard had considered himself a potential candidate or had courted support. To the end of his days he insisted that he never understood why he was elected over Bradfute and Strivings. Coverdale in a 1963 interview said that the Iowa delegation had not caucused in advance of the convention. "I doubt if anybody in Iowa, when they went to the meeting, had an idea that Howard would be president," he said. The Iowa secretary said he sat in the back of the room during the convention and was not aware of any politicking.

An analysis of the vote indicates that Strivings had solid backing from New York, New England, and New Jersey. While he could have headed an educational Farm Bureau, he seemed to lack the initiative needed to deal with the broader fields of work envisioned by many at the convention. He served one year as vice-president of the American Farm Bureau and soon dropped out of the national picture. Why Bradfute received support from only four states is not clear. He was placed on the

executive committee as a consolation prize and the next year succeeded
Strivings as vice-president. Bradfute loyally supported the Howard administration during its three years and then became the federation's second president. In two more years he was defeated for reelection. The
votes of half of the midwestern states and presumably all of the South
and West went to Howard. While Bradfute had restricted himself to the
role of impartial presiding officer during the three-day convention, Howard had demonstrated initiative, performed well as keynoter and resolutions chairman, and gave the delegates reason to believe that he would be
an active leader who combined a broad vision of the federation's potential with a prospect of keeping agriculture's diverse elements working in
harness. The convention was not deadlocked, and had Howard not been
in the field, Bradfute presumably would have been an easy winner.

Like Jefferson, Howard did not refuse the office he did not seek. In a
completely extemporaneous speech, he accepted the presidency, thanked
the delegates, and hinted at his personal problems. His three sons were
still in school, too young to shoulder the responsibilities of the farm. He
had no idea what could be done about his personal life but something
could be worked out. Applause followed a promise that he would work
"not an eight-hour day and a five-day basis, but I will put in full farmer
time." He warned that achievements would not be immediate and said
that mistakes must be avoided during the years that would be needed to
put the federation on an established basis. Meanwhile the new organization must deserve the support of the farmer back home. "My heart is in
this movement and I will put my best efforts into the work," he concluded.

The chair then announced that Strivings had been elected vice-president over Gray Silver of West Virginia. Bradfute, who showed no sign of
regret that he had lost the election to the man he himself had placed in
nomination, conferred with the new leader while delegates held regional
caucuses in corners of the room to select the twelve members of the executive committee that would function as a board of directors, the name
it was given in later years. The original members were:

—*Eastern group*—E. B. Cornwall, Middlebury, Vermont; E. F. Richardson,
Millis, Massachusetts; and H. E. Taylor, Freehold, New Jersey
—*Southern group*—Gray Silver, Martinsburg, West Virginia; James W.
Morgan, Athens, Georgia; and George Bishop, Cordell, Oklahoma
—*Middle West group*—O. E. Bradfute, Xenia, Ohio; Harvey J. Sconce,
Sidell, Illinois; and Chester H. Gray, Nevada, Missouri
—*Far West group*—W. H. Walker, Willows, California; W. G. Jamison,
LaVeta, Colorado; and John F. Burton, Garland, Utah

Technically, Howard was president of a temporary federation that would hold another convention in the same hotel on March 3 and 4. Because some delegates were unhappy about certain compromises adopted, no attempt had been made to implement the constitution. In effect, the dissatisfied were allowed a recess of three and one-half months, during which time the state federations would vote on ratification of the national constitution. Unless ten states voted to ratify, the American Farm Bureau Federation would not exist.

As the convention adjourned, Howard called a meeting of the executive committee in his room at eight o'clock. There he asked Coverdale to take notes. Little business could be transacted before the second convention. Gratified that they had done their job well, the officers and committeemen were confident that their own states, which would be more than enough, would support ratification. The necessity of a membership drive in the South was discussed and vague hope was expressed that the Department of Agriculture might be of help. Howard was instructed to go to Washington and support pending farm legislation as best he could in conformity with the resolutions he had helped draft. If necessary, he could serve as a speakers' bureau. Until the committee met again in March, Howard was authorized to call on any executive member for any service. Temporary headquarters would be in Coverdale's office in Ames.

In its next issue the *Farm Bureau Messenger* told the Iowa membership:

The honor came to Mr. Howard unsought and unsolicited. Those who know him intimately cling to the belief that while he is duly appreciative of the recognition, he had no desire to be singled out to shoulder the responsibility or the prominence and publicity that are necessary to such a position.

The prestige of holding the foremost elected position among American farmers was less than the personal sacrifice Howard had to make. As national president he would have to leave Homelands, for the second time in his adult life, if he was to give the promised "full farmer time" to the new position. His style of living would change and he would be a white-collar executive with an office in a large city. Probably it would be in Chicago, three hundred miles from Homelands and reachable by overnight Pullman from Marshalltown. He knew that he could return to the farm occasionally—with luck, for most weekends—but he also knew that he would have to travel to other cities and that at times he might not see his family for several weeks. The only logical action would be to move them to Chicago and find the best possible tenant farmer for his acreage.

He helped with the last days of the 1919 corn harvest, knowing that in 1920 and for an uncertain future he would not participate in plowing and planting his fields, cultivating and harvesting his crops, and feeding the steers and hogs in his feedlots. The solution, worked out by summer, provided for his 480 acres to be operated by two tenant farmers. Roe Hiatt moved into the main house at Homelands and farmed 320 acres under a Howard and Hiatt partnership. He came from the Hartland neighborhood where Lenora Howard Moninger lived and was a level-headed farmer whose grown sons would serve as hired men. John Blattel, a hired man who lived in the Rockhill house, was highly regarded by Jim. A native of the Ozarks, he took over the Rockhill quarter section under another partnership. Their contracts could be terminated any March 1 if the owner returned as on-the-scene-boss of his farms.

By spring, headquarters were located in Chicago and, when he was not on the road, Howard lived in the original Palmer House on State Street. The break from Homelands came in the late summer, when the family of six piled into a Buick touring car at four in the morning and, by hard driving, reached Chicago after dark. For his wife and children it was the start of an adventure, but Howard left his home unwillingly. Despite the rush to get away, without saying anything he took time for a farewell walk through a feedlot.

The new home in Chicago was a furnished apartment at 745 Irving Park Boulevard, two blocks from Lake Michigan and five miles from the Loop. Howard's sons enrolled in Lake View High School and his daughter in the nearest elementary school. The apartment lease ran for ten months, the length of the Chicago school year. During the summer the family returned to Homelands and lived in the house formerly occupied by the hired man. In the autumn they returned to apartment life, always in the same high school district. That arrangement was followed during Howard's tenure as Farm Bureau president. In the city he kept two sets of partnership accounts. He followed market trends and usually was at the stockyards when the fat cattle he half-owned were consigned to market. At times he arranged to be at the South St. Paul or Omaha markets when it was time to buy the next year's supply of feeder cattle. Always he tried to visit Homelands at least briefly every month or two.

During the interval between the two conventions, words of commendation came from important places. *Successful Farming,* a monthly published at Des Moines, editorially urged in January 1920 that all farmers become Farm Bureau members and support the national federation:

It is built on a solid foundation and its growth has been in the normal and natural way—from the bottom up; it is democratic and thoroughly representative in its form of organization; it has enlisted the support of the most substantial farmers; it has thus far selected efficient and sane leaders; it is thoroughly American in its policies; there is a vital need for such an organization and much work for it to do.

The support of *Successful Farming* was gratifying, since its publisher E. T. Meredith on February 20 was appointed secretary of agriculture by President Wilson.

Led by Indiana, state Farm Bureau conventions one by one ratified the national constitution. Howard, who would travel extensively during the next three years, attended all the midwestern conventions that could be scheduled. His speeches explained the objectives of the new organization and laid a foundation for the membership drives that would be necessary. Meanwhile he expanded his acquaintance with state and local leaders and made certain that nothing went wrong with the ratification campaign. In the Northeast, Strivings did the same work.

Howard was present at Peoria on January 13 when Illinois became the tenth state to ratify and thus guaranteed that the American Farm Bureau Federation would exist legally. Participation of the virile Illinois Agricultural Association was vital, and Howard, as the chief speaker at the convention, pledged that marketing would be of first importance. He made it clear that the Farm Bureau had a vital interest in national legislation but would not become directly involved in politics.

At their annual convention, Iowa Farm Bureau members celebrated a year of achievement. In his last appearance as state president, Howard outlined unfinished business and demonstrated a belief that cooperation should be practiced by farm organizations as well as by individual farmers. His special guests were men from the Farmers Union, Grange, and Society of Equity, who pledged cooperation with the Farm Bureau. The correspondent of the *Prairie Farmer* was impressed with the new president of the American Farm Bureau Federation: "He has done things. He can guide deliberations and do it in splendid form and good spirit. Iowa farmers have unbounded confidence in him." Over his protests, Howard was reelected state president. Just in case something went wrong at the ratification meeting, Iowa wanted him back.

Late in March, with regrets and good wishes, the Iowa executive committee accepted the resignations of Howard and Coverdale. Able successors took over their work. Charles W. Hunt of Logan, who had headed the Iowa delegation when Howard was off the floor, became the new president and E. H. Cunningham of Cresco took over as secretary.

16

Starting Up the
American Farm Bureau Federation

AS president of the American Farm Bureau Federation, Howard began at the top. Other men with farm backgrounds occupied executive suites of business corporations and national associations, but they had spent years working their way up the ladder of leadership. The AFBF, however, did not have the luxury of apprenticeships, training programs, and a hierarchy. Howard, elected by men who had known him only a few days, was president of a federation that existed only on paper, without an office or a staff. It did have a program, as expressed in the resolutions his committee had drafted, that somehow had to be implemented. He was conscious that the task of creating and putting into motion the machinery of the interstate organization was much more complex than his work a year earlier as Iowa Farm Bureau president. He knew he would be held responsible for the success or failure of the much needed agrarian organization, which had a great potential but which could fall on its face if he moved too slowly or acted impetuously, or made serious policy or administrative blunders, or failed to establish and maintain sectional harmony.

Within a few months the federation had offices in Chicago and Washington and was functioning under the leadership of three strong men who respected, understood, and trusted each other. Working in harness, Howard, John W. Coverdale, and Gray Silver made a reality of the dream of a strong and effective organization of farmers. Six-footers with rugged constitutions and attractive personalities, they were three of a kind—intellectual conservatives who thought alike and had the same ideas about how the Farm Bureau's goals should be achieved.

Rising to the challenges, Howard accepted the responsibilities and made the final decisions as president and executive officer. Coverdale, who in the Iowa federation had been executive officer as well as secretary, became secretary of the AFBF and was based in its Chicago headquarters. Howard, whose unsuspected executive talents included an ability to delegate authority, used Coverdale as a strong right arm, a backstop, and a private counselor. In their old age neither could recall a matter on which they had disagreed. By March, when the delegates returned to Chicago for the ratification convention, the president had arranged for Coverdale to be unopposed for the secretaryship.

Silver, the West Virginian who was the only member of the executive committee with political experience, was the obvious choice to head the Washington office. He had made his reputation as a wily lobbyist who could influence congressional committees and administrative agencies, but he also was a student of agriculture and government who contributed more than his share to the decision making process. When relations with the federal government were at issue before the executive committee, the president and the Washington representative dominated the discussions. As AFBF president, Howard frequently went to the capital to testify before committees and confer with officials, but the operation of the Washington office was left to Silver, who in turn recognized that the major decisions had to have the concurrence of Howard.

The livestock feeder from central Iowa who was the federation's first president had a high opinion of the original executive committee, whose backgrounds were as diverse as U.S. agriculture. "I have never ceased to appreciate their loyalty and helpfulness," he wrote after his retirement. "They were all farmers and they knew the farmers' needs. The common denominators of life were their first concern. They realized that large divisors make small quotients."

When he addressed the twentieth annual AFBF convention, Coverdale recalled: "The early program of the Farm Bureau was to feel its way by the trial and error method. It did not have the backlog of years of study and research. It set up departments to find out something about the problems it was set up to solve." Some changes were made each year in the committee membership, and before the ratification convention Howard Leonard had replaced Harvey Sconce as the Illinois representative.

The ratification convention held on March 3 and 4, 1920, was a success. Twenty-eight states unanimously accepted the November constitution and became charter members of the American Farm Bureau Federation. Those with active state organizations but varying membership bases were: Arizona, California, Colorado, Idaho, Illinois, Indiana, Iowa, Kansas, Kentucky, Maryland, Massachusetts, Michigan, Minnesota, Missouri, Nebraska, New Hampshire, New York, Ohio, South Dakota, Utah, Vermont, West Virginia, and Wyoming. They were admitted with forty-nine voting delegates, of whom twenty-six came from the Midwest. The other five states—Connecticut, Georgia, New Jersey, Oklahoma, and Texas— in effect were paper organizations without membership plans.

By acclamation, Howard was elected president of the permanent organization. His brief acceptance speech again emphasized the necessity of maximum food production. Coverdale was named secretary. A new set of resolutions defined in detail the Farm Bureau position on problems to be faced in the 1920s. The delegates stood for the Constitution, national stability, collective bargaining rights for farmers, tariff reform, arbitration of labor disputes, simplified income tax returns, good roads, improved health conditions, and an international agricultural conference. They were concerned about a trend toward shorter working hours for city men at a time when increased production was needed.

By resolution, the convention instructed the executive committee to set up a business organization directed by trained experts that would operate in six fields—transportation, exports, marketing, statistics, legislation, and cooperative marketing. Henry C. Wallace, who in a year would become secretary of agriculture with the endorsement of the Farm Bureau and the Grange, at the November convention had urged that the AFBF hire the best-qualified men in the country to manage its efforts to improve the business of farming. Wallace, who privately believed that the Grange was impotent and the Farmers Union irresponsible, wanted the Farm Bureau to succeed. "This federation must not degenerate into an educational or social institution," he said. "It must be made the most powerful business institution in the country."

At the ratification convention Wallace again was on the program. He warned that the Farm Bureau would court disaster if it advocated unworkable programs for farm relief or if it passively adopted innocuous resolutions. The committee met for several hours at the LaSalle Hotel, continued its discussions on a Pullman train, and completed its business in the Hotel Harrington in Washington on March 5 and 8. Secretary Meredith had invited the leaders of the new organization to Washington so that they could become acquainted with the personnel and facilities of the agriculture department. Along with the business sessions, the agenda included introductions to officials and talks by men in and out of government who had expert knowledge and worthwhile opinions about the complex facets of problems that involved farming. Howard had a full schedule as he met with congressional leaders and called at the Justice Department, the Railroad Administration, and the Interstate Commerce Commission. He was both representing the Farm Bureau and learning about government and economics.

Committee action was taken to locate the general office in Chicago and a legislative office in Washington. Silver was made Washington representative. The board voted a $15,000 salary for Howard and $12,000

James Raley Howard I (1814–1881) and his namesake grandson (1873–1954), the first national Farm Bureau president.

Talitha Ann Covington Howard, grandmother of JRH

Rhoda Jane ("Jennie") Howard, mother of JRH

Henry Covington Howard, father of JRH

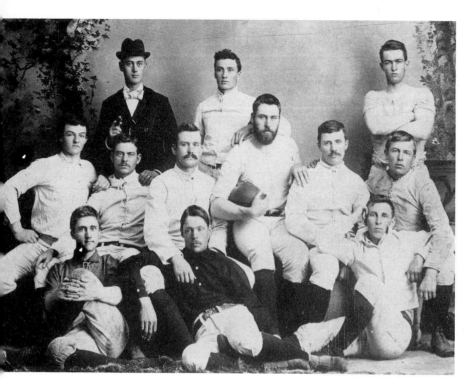

Penn College football team,
early 1890, JRH seated at left.

JRH, graduation from Penn
College, Oskaloosa, Iowa,
1894.

Anna Pickrell, 1900, shortly before her marriage to JRH.

JRH, 1901

Home in Liberty Township, JRH in overalls standing at fence.

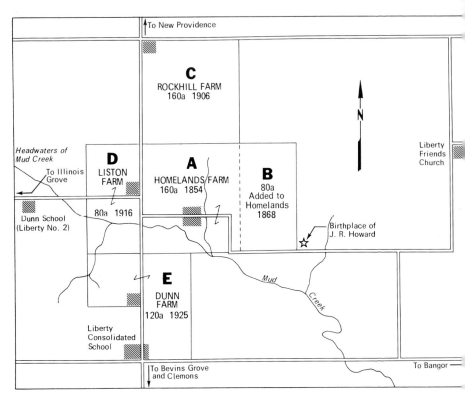

HOMELANDS FARM: *the 480 acres owned by J. R. Howard while he was Farm Bureau president. Original quarter section (A) was bought by his grandfather, who enlarged it by 80 acres (B). Howard bought the Rockhill farm (C) and traded it for (A). Upon the death of his father in 1912, he owned 400 acres by purchase and inheritance. The year he organized the Marshall County Farm Bureau he also bought the Liston farm (D). The later purchase of the Dunn farm (E) increased his acreage to 600.*

Liberty Township Consolidated School, ca. 1915. (Courtesy Albert Dunn)

James Raley Howard, first president of the American Farm Bureau Federation, 1919–1923. (Courtesy Kile, *Three Decades*)

Executive Committee, AFBF, 1921. From left to right: *James W. Morton, John F. Burton, J. R. Howard, Howard Leonard, O. E. Bradfute, H. E. Taylor, Gray Silver, J. T. Orr, Dr. W. H. Walker, Chester H. Gray, E. B. Cornwall, John G. Brown, Dr. A. C. True, E. F. Richardson, J. S. Crenshaw, W. G. Jamison.* (Courtesy Kile, *Three Decades*)

John W. Coverdale, first secretary, AFBF

Gray Silver, first Washington, D.C., representative, AFBF

Oscar E. Bradfute, second president, AFBF

JRH with Allan B. Kline, president AFBF, and Edward A. O'Neal, former president AFBF, 1947 AFBF convention.

JRH and Anna, ca. 1950

each for Coverdale and Silver. Special field agents needed for membership work would get at least $5,000.

The $15,000 presidential salary was both a vote of confidence in Howard and a signal that the AFBF had elitist status. No other farm organization, as far as was known, paid its head anything close to that amount. By comparison with the top executives of comparable business and professional groups, the Farm Bureau president should have received from $40,000 upward, but the rural membership had an ingrained sense of the equality of mankind and found it hard to believe any farmer could be worth even $1000 a month, regardless of responsibilities, talents, and the expense of city life.

By May, Howard and Coverdale had an office in the Chicago Loop. They hired a stenographer and rented two rooms on the twelfth floor of the Mallers Building at 5 South Wabash Avenue. At the time it seemed spacious, but overcrowding became chronic. They expected to sublet space when they moved to a second floor office that was three times as large. The next January, during testimony before a congressional committee, Howard estimated that the federation had twenty employees in Chicago. As soon as he found a manager for his West Virginia farm, Silver rented an office at 1411 Pennsylvania Avenue in Washington. His first staff consisted of O. M. Kile and three secretaries. Howard in Chicago meanwhile learned that elevated trains running outside his window made an infernal racket, and no one complained when the AFBF office moved on March 1 to larger, quieter, and expandable space in the Garland Building at 58 East Washington Street.

The federation's high hopes soon were tempered with strict economy. In his March convention pep talk, Howard had boasted of more than one million members, and a report by the resolutions committee said that the Farm Bureau had 1,060,000 members in twenty-eight charter states. If accurate, those figures would have included women and children. Memberships, however, were paid only by heads of families, and only fifty cents was allocated to the national office. Incipient trouble was kept under control at the ratification meeting when Howard Leonard, the new president of the Illinois Agricultural Association, protested that the central western states had 65 percent of the membership and contributed 85 percent of the income but had only 25 percent of the representation on the governing board. Men from other regions refused to change the sectional formula, however, and the midwesterners, loyal to the one-big-federation concept, did not press their complaint, although private grumbling continued.

When Coverdale made his report for the five months ending December 1, 1920, he counted 826,816 members in thirty-seven affiliated states, plus 85,000 in eight other states ready to affiliate. If that report was accurate, not all the dues reached the Chicago office. In some cases, state federations were admitted on payment of a nominal fee. Some of the strongest states often were several months late in paying up, in most cases because they needed the money as much as the national organization did. The budgeting job was made more difficult by the arrival of a rural depression in 1920. For the abbreviated year revenues had been estimated at $196,925, but only $137,344 came into the treasury. Nevertheless economizing left a balance of $33,338.

Coverdale supervised a continuing membership drive that concentrated on the more anemic states. Howard, Silver, and others joined salaried solicitors in helping state organizations get on their feet.

When the AFBF met in convention at Atlanta on November 21, 1921, Coverdale reported that forty-six states had federations "with a total membership, with the water squeezed out, of 772,634 members." The great problem was income, which according to a certified public accountant's report totaled $241,442.28 for 1921 and $248,140.90 for 1922.

The 1921 membership of the American Farm Bureau Federation was placed at 466,421 by Gladys Baker in *The County Agent* some thirty years later. Using data obtained from AFBF headquarters, she said the membership was 363,481 in 1922 and 392,580 in 1923. A low of 163,246 was reported for 1933, in the depth of the depression, and the million membership mark was not recorded until 1946, when the total was 1,128,259.

Throughout his presidency, Howard referred to himself as the representative of a million or more farmers. If the Farm Bureau did not receive membership dues from that many farmers, at least he was certain that he spoke for them. The Farm Bureau was the largest and most influential of farm organizations, past or present, and to claim one million members was a figure of speech showing its importance.

The federation's only income came from the fifty-cent portion of the local dues. Membership was optional and many farmers thought that the annual fee, which averaged about ten dollars a year, was an avoidable expense. Competing organizations charged only fifty cents or a dollar a year. The Farm Bureau was unique, however, in having ambitious programs that required financing at the county, state, and national levels. Unlike the hard-working leadership, many rural residents did not consider that the immediate and potential benefits of Farm Bureau membership exceeded the dues. Since the Farm Bureau was not a mass movement, membership solicitation was an important item in AFBF budgeting. Howard and his colleagues could not afford to do all the things they wanted to do, but they were determined to show that large dividends could be earned by a coast-to-coast organization.

The Farm Bureau dominated the agrarian scene even during the first months when its mailing address was Coverdale's office at Ames. Despite the initial difficulties, its far-flung membership, financial resources, and potential for leadership could not be matched by any other farm organization. Of its major rivals, the ritualistic Grange had passed its prime and the Farmers Union membership had declined to the lowest point in two decades, to about 140,000 members at the end of the war. The Grange had fragmented when the Pennsylvania state agency and some lesser units withdrew from the national body because of policy differences. The Farmers Union had similar troubles. The American Society of Equity was important chiefly in Wisconsin, where it counted 40,000 members. An offshoot organization, the Farmers' Equity Union, specialized in cooperative buying and selling agencies and operated at the Denver, Kansas City, and South St. Paul markets. Equity Union creameries did business primarily in Nebraska. Agencies such as the Gleaners were localized and miniscule.

The Farm Bureau set up an office in Washington only after a careful survey of the situation there. Howard's first thought was that a partnership arrangement might be made with the National Grange, whose leaders were generally in agreement with Farm Bureau policies and whose Washington representative, T. C. Atkeson, for a year had done skillful work on a small budget. The Grange, however, would have been an unsatisfactory teammate since it was not national in scope.

Another possible partner was the National Board of Farm Organizations, a loose federation to which Howard had been introduced in 1919 by Henry C. Wallace. At that time he was impressed with the stature of Judge John D. Miller of the National Milk Producers Association and Charles W. Holman of the National Dairy Council. The National Farmers Union was a leader in the National Board, which had opened a Washington office in 1917 without creating much of a stir. Its legislative program—for cooperative marketing, farmer representation on government boards, government control of packing, and regulation of terminal grain markets—was similar to the programs of the Farm Bureau and Grange. Howard wrote:

The National Board had bought the old John Wanamaker property, expecting to make it an agricultural headquarters in Washington. I think they gladly would have taken us into membership and, indeed, the matter was taken under advisement. It was rejected primarily because the AFBF would have had no more voice in its proceedings than any of their other groups and some seemingly were not of much force. I recall one such group was the Jewish Farmers of America. The National Board seemed to be working on the theory, as did many others, that the sole solution of agricultural difficulties lay in legislation.

Late in the 1920s the National Board went out of business.

Only the Washington State Grange supported the Farmers' National

Council, whose leaders, George P. Hampton and Benjamin C. Marsh, advocated government ownership of railroads and cooperation with labor and thus were out of step with the other farm groups.

Howard estimated that several hundred organizations in the capital claimed to be looking out for the interests of the U.S. farmer. One was the U.S. Chamber of Commerce, whose secretary mildly suggested that it had facilities to do the Farm Bureau's Washington work.

As part of the staff to be hired, the Farm Bureau needed a general counsel and a transportation expert who would oppose the railroads in complicated rate cases before the Interstate Commerce Commission and state regulatory agencies. The Federation filled both jobs with one man— Clifford Thorne, a native of Washington, Iowa, who practiced law in Chicago and was a specialist in railroad rates.

The transportation situation was critical. Between the two Chicago conventions the railroads had been returned to private ownership and Congress had enacted the Esch-Cummins law for their regulation by the government. All farm organizations had opposed continued government operation, but in its temporary status the AFBF had not had time to take a position on the regulatory law, which contained a controversial provision intended to guarantee that the carriers could make a profit on their invested capital. Freight rates were a major expense to farmers, who feared that higher tariffs would be inevitable, perhaps permanent, and that freight train service, which had been roundly criticized during the war, would deteriorate further. The railroad brotherhoods had asked for higher wages and the carriers for a compensatory rate increase.

Thorne was a protégé of Henry C. Wallace's Corn Belt Meat Producers' Association, which wanted both railroads and meat packers to be regulated. Over a long period of years he had won most of the rate cases that he had brought with the backing of the Meat Producers and the National Farmers' Grain Dealers Association, which was composed of farmer-owned country elevators. With one speech, he rallied the Farmers' Grain Dealers of Illinois into a fight against the Esch-Cummins guarantee clause. He needed the backing and financing that could come only from the Farm Bureau in a new battle involving railroad valuations. Railroad financial interests wanted high valuations that would justify rate increases.

During its sessions in Washington, the executive committee for three hours listened to Thorne contend that the case could be won only with voluminous, detailed, and accurate statistics. The board then voted to retain him and allocated $10,000 for his use. A close check was kept to see that the Farm Bureau was getting its money's worth, and three months later Thorne was appointed general counsel of the federation and made head of its transportation department. A battery of statisticians compiled data that Thorne used in filing a brief contending that the railroads were overvalued by several billion dollars, that their current income and expenditures were not a fair basis upon which to compute future profits, and that allowance had not been made for future increases in business. Thorne then was the first opposition witness. Instead of the dull summarizations by experts, which were traditional in rate cases, Thorne summoned a parade of farmers and elevator managers who were self-conscious when they testified before the commission but fervent in relating from their personal experiences that severe hardships would follow if freight rates were increased.

The $10,000 investment paid high dividends when the Interstate Commerce Commission lowered by $1.7 billion, or approximately ten percent, the valuation requested by the carriers. Thorne estimated that it meant a net savings of thirty dollars a year for every farmer in the United States.

The Farm Bureau attorney was back in action immediately after the commission held on August 25, 1920, that the railroads could raise their tariffs to compensate for a general wage increase granted by the Railway Labor Board. The increases were 40 percent east of the Mississippi River, 35 percent between the Mississippi and the Rocky Mountains, and 25 percent west of the mountains. Seeking lower rates for some of the commodities hardest hit, Thorne obtained a 20-percent or $10-million reduction for livestock shipments from the range country and, in another case, he won a reduction averaging 16 percent on hay and grain shipments.

Except for a few livestock and grain dealers' associations, the Farm Bureau was the only farm organization opposing the rate increases.

Howard, the former cashier of the Providence State Bank, soon became acquainted with big city bankers and financiers with whom he held conferences in New York, Chicago, and elsewhere. The top Federal Reserve officials; presidents of major metropolitan banks; the secretaries of commerce and agriculture in the Wilson cabinet; Herbert Hoover, then a private citizen; and Julius H. Barnes, president of the Chamber of Commerce of the United States, attended a meeting in Chicago in 1920. Howard recalled that they discussed a proposal to organize under the Webb-Pomerene Act a $100 million corporation to aid in the disposal abroad of farm surpluses:

After the farm situation had been discussed at length from every angle, someone suggested that a farmer was present and that it might be well to hear from him. I merely told them that I considered very helpful their interest in farm markets. So far as the organization of the proposed export corporation was concerned, I was not in a position to make any statement since it had never been discussed by any farm group. I proposed to appoint immediately a special committee and report at the next meeting.

Then I added that in my lifetime I had traded horses a good many times and that I had never made a trade after which I did not discover a lot of things about the horse that I had not seen before the swap. Most of the men present thoroughly understood this since, like most other important people, they had lived on the farm in their earlier years, but whether or not they were farm born they had followed careers based on horse-swapping principles.

W. S. Shearer, then president of the Idaho State Farm Bureau Federation, happened to be in the Chicago office. A commercial lettuce grower, he then was on his way East to establish market outlets. He returned with a report that the metropolitan bankers were primarily interested in liquidating stocks of canned meats, vegetables, and other farm products on which they had made collateral loans and found themselves stuck. If they had any interest in the corn in the farmers' cribs and the cotton in his [*sic*] warehouses, it was merely nominal.

I so notified the chairman of the organization committee of the proposed finance corporation. Whether or not our action was responsible, the movement failed to materialize.

A new problem arose in the federation's first months. Howard learned that eastern industrial interests wanted to replace the wartime excess profits tax with a tax on sales. To start the campaign, a study of the revenue situation was being made by the National Industrial Conference Board. The Farm Bureau expected that the board would recommend that a large part of the cost of national government be shifted from corporations to producers, especially farmers. Other agrarian organizations were doing nothing.

Howard was always willing to meet with and if possible work with his opposite numbers in the world of big business. He asked that agriculture's importance be recognized by appointment of a farmer to the conference board's committee on federal taxation. When the request was granted in April, he gave the appointment to one of the most active men in the New York Farm Bureau, H. C. McKenzie of Walton, chairman of its taxation committee.

McKenzie at the start was a minority of one, but he recruited support of economists and university professors in arguing that farm profits were so small that a general sales tax could not be passed on to the consumer and that, therefore, confiscation of capital would result. With the assistance of Thomas S. Adams of Yale University he filed a brief that laid down the AFBF's principles. It held that the chief burden of taxation should be paid from income and profits, not from capital; that all people should make some contribution toward the support of government through luxury taxes, the tariff and, if necessary, through consumption taxes on a limited number of articles; and that, as far as possible, taxes should be levied progressively so as to promote the redistribution of wealth rather than its concentration.

Howard warned his board members that they should be ready for a major tax fight at the next session of Congress. McKenzie predicted that a 1 percent federal levy on sales would produce two billion dollars a year and that farmers would pay half of it.

By the fall of 1920, however, the conference board accepted McKenzie's position and recommended an increase in the flat tax on corporations. Without any help of consequence, the Farm Bureau had won a major battle. The president had grasped an opportunity to work from within the board. Having appointed the right man to do the job, he then backed him fully, if without fanfare.

McKenzie scored a second time when the conference board disapproved of the Nolan bill, introduced in Congress by an iron molder from San Francisco with the backing of the American Federation of Labor. A single tax proposal, it would have levied a direct federal tax of 1 percent on all real estate valued at $10,000 or more. The Farm Bureau took a popular stand by ordering a referendum on the Nolan bill. In 545 counties in 19 states, the vote was 2,261 to 363,601. The referenda technique had two advantages: it showed the farmers that the AFBF was on its toes, and it demonstrated to Congress that a land tax would be unpopular.

At the annual convention held in Indianapolis in November 1920, Howard said that he considered that McKenzie had "done a greater piece of work for American agriculture during the past year than has been performed by any other individual." Because the federation's early press relations were at a primitive stage, most members had not been informed that the Farm Bureau was active in the tax field.

The AFBF opposed a bonus for war veterans, for fear that it might be financed by a sales levy. Other revenue issues arose, and a tax office headed by McKenzie was established. The New Yorker replaced Strivings on the executive committee and was an unsuccessful aspirant for the vice-presidency at the Indianapolis convention. From the Midwest, both Howard Leonard of Illinois and John G. Brown of Indiana were candidates, but the delegates avoided a deadlock by giving the post to Oscar E. Bradfute of Ohio.

In his presidential speech at Indianapolis, Howard said: "The character of the men who daily come into our Chicago office is all the evidence anyone needs of the progress of our work and the impression we are making upon the people of our land."

He elaborated this statement in an interview with *Prairie Farmer:*

I have letters from bank presidents and captains of industry, many of whom have always been opposed to farmers' organizations, expressing confidence in the purpose and sound business judgment of the American Farm Bureau Federation. We shall do many things they do not agree with, but as long as they believe in our honesty of purpose, we are going to be able to get many things done by diplomacy that we would otherwise have to fight for.

With men from both parties on its governing board, the Farm Bureau quickly established its tradition of nonpartisanship. Silver appeared before the platform committees of the Republican and Democratic national conventions to present a statement of the organization's position. At the Republican convention Silver was embarrassed because Henry C. Wallace, as editor of *Wallaces' Farmer,* had claimed to be agriculture's spokesman when he presented the same planks earlier in the day. The Farm Bureau executive committee followed an open-door policy and the farm press had been present when the board met just prior to the convention. Howard and his colleagues never had any interest in the unsuccessful Farmer-Labor party organized in 1920 by labor leaders and given a name they hoped would bring support from the Non-Partisan League.

One advantage of having headquarters in Chicago was that Coverdale could be one of the godfathers of the 4-H club movement that sprang up about the same time that farm bureaus spread across the country. Although neglected by many organizations, the value of the 4-H work by boys and girls was recognized by both Howard and Coverdale when county farm bureaus were being formed in Iowa. The Department of Agriculture financed the basic 4-H activities but was not authorized to provide prizes for outstanding work. Beginning about 1918, several major corporations picked up part of the expenses of trips to Chicago for club winners at the time of the International Livestock Exposition, but more money was needed. Among the early backers was Thomas E. Wilson, the meat packer, who became interested when he encountered a group of boys at the stock show and took them to dinner. In 1921, Coverdale, Wilson, and three others organized a national committee to support Guy L. Noble, the underpaid one-man staff of the National Club Congress. The AFBF provided office space, clerical help, and financial aid for Noble, who came from Marshall County and whose brother was the Howard family doctor. Noble's committee raised money for 4-H awards and scholarships.

Leading roles were played by Coverdale and Wilson in establishing the National Livestock and Meat Board, which did not involve itself with marketing but promoted the consumption of meat through advertising and the development of better types of animals. The Farm Bureau in 1921 contributed $10,000 and appointed the first directorate of the Meat Board, which was composed of representatives of packing companies, the Farm Bureau, livestock associations, and stockyard exchanges. Two years earlier at a Kansas City conference Henry C. Wallace had blocked the creation of such a board because he feared it would be dominated by packers.

Coverdale served as chairman of the Committee on the Relation of Electricity to Agriculture, which was a forerunner of the rural electrification movement and, at his suggestion, was patterned after the Livestock and Meat Board. The Farm Bureau helped finance the cooperative study in which power companies, equipment manufacturers, agricultural engineers, and the U.S. Department of Agriculture also participated. The committee confined its work to the development of the use of electricity on farms and did not involve itself with legislation and rate regulation. Working from a Farm Bureau office, Earl A. White, an agricultural engineer from the University of Illinois, began research that led to standardization of lines and equipment. In this field, as elsewhere, Howard showed a willingness to either oppose or work with business interests, depending upon their attitude.

17

Gray Silver Goes to Washington

T H E talents of Gray Silver, a West Virginia apple grower who became one of the great figures among Washington's twentieth century lobbyists, might have gone unnoticed without the Farm Bureau movement. For Silver, as for Jim Howard and John Coverdale, the Farm Bureau provided an avenue to national leadership.

Howard discovered Silver on his first train trip to Washington after the founding convention. The president's usually excellent memory had slipped a cog and he could not recall the face of the executive committeeman from Martinsburg, West Virginia, who had participated in the postelection meeting in the hotel room. Howard needed to become acquainted with his board members and he knew that Martinsburg was an express train stop on the Baltimore and Ohio Railroad. Silver accepted a telegraphed invitation to join him on the last two hours of the Pullman ride.

They talked about the federation's future relations with Congress and governmental agencies and about problems that would have to be faced. Before the train pulled into the station Silver accepted an invitation to become the new organization's Washington representative. He held the position for five years and was influential in establishing the American Farm Bureau Federation as the nation's dominant farm organization. Howard, who had a high opinion of the character and intelligence of the original executive committee, regarded Silver as the ablest of the founding group.

Tall, handsome, and genial, Silver combined intelligence, aggressiveness, and persistence with a rare insight into human nature that made him effective in dealing with individuals and groups. He had never gone to college but he instinctively understood economic and governmental problems and knew what policies would benefit farm people. The Farm Bureau's original Washington representative also was a superb manipulator of congressional committees and an effective negotiator with governmental officials. Within a year after he started work with one assistant and several secretaries, he had organized the farm bloc that made the AFBF widely known, and in some places feared, for its unprecedented success in passing major legislation over the objections of the establishment.

The technique of exerting political pressure from the grass roots might have been devised earlier during agitation for prohibition and woman's suffrage, but credit for perfecting it goes to the West Virginian. At his disposal were district-by-district tabulations of responses to public sentiment polls taken by county farm bureaus at the request of the headquarters in Chicago. As a member of the executive committee, Silver had a hand in deciding what questions should be submitted to the membership. If the inquiries had to do with issues with which the people back home were not fully informed, they were submitted in a manner that clearly indicated that the national office regarded the matter as important. Whether or not the inquiries were impartially worded, most of the responses agreed totally with the stands taken by the Farm Bureau. Despite the handicap of a small staff, Silver operated an efficient office. If a congressman seemed to be wavering in advance of an important roll call or if someone had the temerity to challenge the Farm Bureau's position, Silver did not hesitate to show him the poll results. In an emergency, he would telegraph directly to state or county offices and know that a flood of wires would pour into his office as evidence that the grass roots were informed and aroused. The final step in operating as a pressure group was to keep the members informed whether their congressmen had supported the Farm Bureau.

Typical of Silver the politician was an appearance with a delegation of farmers before an unfriendly House committee that was considering an appropriation for extension work. When the chairman announced that the committee would go into executive session, Silver pretended not to understand that his group was to leave the room. He and his friends, identifying themselves as farmers, stayed in their seats. When they were asked to depart, Silver explained that farmers had sent them to Washington to report on the committee's work and that, of course, the committee would not do anything that the congressmen would not want known. He was so friendly and persistent that the chairman changed his mind and approved the appropriation without a reduction.

Silver, the son of a Confederate colonel, was a Democrat who counterbalanced Howard's Republican background in the nonpartisan organization. Descended from Scottish Presbyterians, he was born February 17, 1870, in Frederick County, Virginia, where his maternal grandfather had been prominent and well-to-do before the Civil War. He was fifteen, the oldest in his family, when his father died. In the impoverishment of the Reconstruction era, a college education was unthinkable for this oldest of five children. He became a livestock dealer at the age of eighteen by borrowing one hundred dollars and buying an unattractive band of thirty-two ewes and twenty-six lambs for ninety-six dollars. Within a few days, after the sheep had filled up on grass and the rain had washed their fleeces, he sheared the wool and sold the ewes for one hundred dollars, leaving the wool, the lambs, and four dollars as profit. By the time he was twenty-one he was an established entrepreneur and reputed to be the largest livestock dealer in six counties.

Silver was a cooperative marketing pioneer. In 1896 he organized fruit growers in Berkeley County, West Virginia. At Inwood he helped establish the first state-owned community packing house. In 1900 he became a leading citizen of Martinsburg, where his wife's family had business interests. By the time his Farm Bureau career started, he owned or had an interest in nearly one thousand acres of land within ten miles of Martinsburg. Most of the acreage was devoted to apple orchards, but on his own farm, Silver also raised Shorthorn cattle and Shropshire sheep. His landholdings also included farms in Madison County, Illinois, and in Arkansas. He also was president of a bank and active in management of a wholesale grocery firm established by his father-in-law.

In West Virginia, where he served two terms as state senator beginning in 1907, Silver's political exploits included the legendary breaking of a legislative deadlock in 1911, when he was president pro tempore of the senate and acting lieutenant governor. The house of representatives was solidly Democratic, but the senate could not do business because each party had fifteen members. Although stricken by pneumonia at Martinsburg, Silver insisted on making the 500-mile train trip to and from the capital. He was carried into the senate chamber on a stretcher and spent several days in public maneuvers and private negotiations with Republicans who boycotted the session. His powers of persuasion won a settlement under which a Democrat was elected U.S. senator, a Republican who had been selected by the Democrats took over the senate presidency, and both parties ratified legislation for which Silver's forces had voted during the deadlock.

In the legislature, Silver sponsored West Virginia's original good roads legislation and was appointed by President William Howard Taft to a commission on wool tariffs.

While they were together in Washington, Howard and Silver looked over possible arrangements for an office there and checked on the status of bills, such as those proposing regulation of packers and the return of railroads to private ownership. In the interim, Howard Leonard of the Illinois Agricultural Association was the chief Farm Bureau watchdog and spokesman in the capital.

Silver began the rounds of officialdom as soon as he found a manager for his farm and orchards. As he studied economic problems, the

AFBF's program began to expand and he talked to treasury officials about extending more credit to farmers. Legislation was not his only concern. Where state and local officials had failed, he proved his worth by arranging with railroad officials and the Interstate Commerce Commission to rush 106,000 empty boxcars to the wheat regions and for the U.S. Shipping Board to assign thirty-five vessels, unused since wartime, to service on the Great Lakes.

Soon after he opened the Washington office, Silver became aware that he was being followed about town by a large, dimpled, and smiling man whom it would be difficult to forget. The stranger obviously was a private detective, employed by someone to keep track of where the Farm Bureau's representative went and to whom he talked. On their daily rounds the two men developed a casual acquaintance. In time Silver made a deal that was intended to give him some privacy and the stranger less work. Each day he gave the detective a report on where he had been.

Howard, inclined to be skeptical, was warned that he, too, undoubtedly was being followed by undercover operatives, not only during his frequent trips to Washington but probably when he was in Chicago and other cities as well. Silver's theory was that the emergence of the Farm Bureau as a strong influence in national affairs presented a threat to a considerable number of powerful interests. He had no idea whether the detective was hired by a business organization or by someone in the political establishment, but it was possible that they wanted more than information. Blackmail might be attempted. Both men realized that eventually they would have to react. Meanwhile the sophisticated Silver patiently watched the situation. He knew that the Farm Bureau president, a man of high discretion and morality, was not in the least vulnerable.

Silver later told Howard that matters he had discussed confidentially by telephone seemed to become public knowledge rather quickly. He suspected that the Farm Bureau telephone had been tapped. To check this possibility, Howard went to a nearby hotel, called Silver, and talked at length about a situation that was both sensational and fictitious. The next day they heard about the matter from outside sources. Silver did nothing about it.

The climax came on Howard's next trip to Washington. Two women who said they were from Kentucky had asked to see Howard and Silver to tell about work being done among farm women in their state. Howard asked if they had been checked by the U.S. Department of Agriculture, but Silver didn't think it was necessary. When the women showed up, Howard said his time was entirely at the Washington representative's disposal. The women had much to talk about and Silver invited them to dinner at the Willard Hotel at seven-thirty. When Howard asked about dinner clothes, Silver merely told him to "forget it."

Just before the dinner hour, Silver went to an untapped telephone and told the women that an emergency made it necessary to cancel the dinner. All hands were exceedingly sorry. Soon the same phone rang and Silver learned that the two women and a man had talked for several minutes in the Willard lobby. Thus Howard learned that Silver had his own detective reporting on the women.

When the persistent women called again the next day, Silver told them that he and Howard would be busy until 9:00 P.M. With great appreciation he accepted an invitation for the two men to call at their apartment at ten o'clock. At that hour, again from an outside phone, Silver with regrets cancelled the appointment. Silver's detective then watched from a parked car as the women went across the street and talked to the man who had been in the hotel lobby the night before. That was the last social engagement.

The next day Silver asked the phone company to check his line. The tap led across the street to a private office that Senator Boies Penrose of Pennsylvania used as his political headquarters. Silver went there with the telephone technicians and found Penrose, who was chairman of the Republican National Committee, with Congressman Roy O. Woodruff of Michigan, who had professed to be a close friend of the Farm Bureau. They were apologetic about the telephone. Silver asked them to introduce the third man in the room. He was Gaston B. Means, the private detective who had followed him in the past.

Means, a notorious swindler and detective, later was appointed a special agent for the Federal Bureau of Investigation by Attorney General Harry M. Daugherty. Means was implicated in numerous frauds, one growing out of the Lindbergh kidnapping case, and twice was sentenced to federal prison terms.

Nell V. Price, Silver's secretary, remembered Means's fat, smiling face and head of blond curly hair. He had called, she said, when she was alone in the office, identifying himself as a member of Congressman Woodruff's staff and asking for the Farm Bureau's file on Muscle Shoals legislation. She turned him down. Miss Price also told about but would not name a highly placed Washingtonian having close ties to the Republican National Committee who called to warn Silver about a "dirty piece of business."

In later years Howard wished that he had kept a diary about his Farm Bureau career. His recollections were quite clear, however, about the detective and the tapped telephone line. Experiences such as those do not often happen to an Iowa farmer. If detectives trailed him in other cities, he didn't know about it.

In the early years, before Franklin D. Roosevelt established the Tennessee Valley Authority, the fertilizer industry seemed to be the Farm Bureau's permanent enemy. A large sector of rural opinion wanted chemical fertilizers produced at a nitrate plant that had been built during World War I at Muscle Shoals, Alabama, for the extraction from the air of nitrogen needed for the manufacture of explosives. Chemical companies, which had one of Washington's powerful lobbies and were dismayed at the thought of government competition, opposed passage of a 7.5-million-dollar appropriation for the completion of a Tennessee River dam to be used in generating electricity for the nitrate plant. On their side were Republican majority congressmen who were liquidating wartime facilities as rapidly as possible and seeking opportunities to charge the Wilson administration with waste.

In Iowa, Howard had never seen a sack of commercial fertilizer, but farm bureaus in other parts of the country wanted the dam completed and the executive committee endorsed the project. Silver, who bought fertilizer for his apple orchards, privately believed that the proposed government plant would greatly boost farm prosperity. Howard answered that immense surpluses could result. In public they put up a united front for, in Howard's words, "a good pulling team holds the ends of the doubletrees as evenly as possible."

As the appropriation bill neared a House vote, Silver worked single-handedly against a swarm of fertilizer lobbyists. Harry Hull, an Iowa congressman who was a close friend of the Farm Bureau, said it was the largest lobby he had seen. There were reports that congressmen were being entertained at an unusual number of dinner and theater parties.

In Washington it was an open secret that Silver planned to keep a permanent record of roll call votes on legislation vital to agriculture. In advance of the Muscle Shoals vote he kept a detailed record of promises and reactions. His surveys showed that the appropriation would carry by a safe margin. He had expected the clerk to call the roll of the house membership and record how each congressman voted. The Speaker, however, called for the ayes and nays and announced that the bill was defeated. The Farm Bureau did not have a record vote and Silver's advance work was wasted.

That night, when he showed up on business that had nothing to do with Muscle Shoals, Howard was met by a glum-faced group that included Silver and his assistant, Orville M. Kile. They talked for several hours about what might be done to bring grass roots pressure on Congress. Howard, who never had specialized in the formulation of policies in a hotel room at midnight, went to bed after announcing that he would support whatever the group decided.

"We made up our minds to call their hands," Silver told him at breakfast. A letter had been composed, over Howard's signature, that would be on every congressman's desk that morning. The text of the letter dated January 5, 1921, read:

All competent and impartial inquirers have agreed that the Muscle Shoals project would result in greatly increased nitrate supplies and materially decreased costs. Hence the farmer as well as the consumer is intensely interested.

It is evident to the farmer that the Muscle Shoals appropriation yesterday was defeated through the influence of large corporations who have a selfish interest in maintaining fertilizer costs.

The American Farm Bureau Federation has a paid-up membership exceeding 1,500,000 active farmers. These farmers expect us to keep them informed on legislative matters.

We regret that the vote yesterday was not one of record. In order that we may do justice both to Representatives in Congress and to our membership, will you kindly notify our Washington Representative—Mr. Gray Silver, 1411 Pennsylvania Avenue—whether you voted for or against the proposition.

The letter had seemed reasonable, but by noon a roar of indignation shook the Farm Bureau office. In the 1920s it was unthinkable that Congress should be called to account by anyone, and the upstart farm organization was threatening the prerogatives and political security of congressmen who courted rural votes but played ball with urban campaign contributors. The first instinct of the establishment congressmen was to protest that they were the innocent victims of slander. The second was to teach the Farm Bureau a lesson.

A select committee on war expenditures, which had nothing to do with the appropriation, summoned Howard and Silver to appear on January 10, 1921, to explain why they had charged that the bill had been killed through the influence of large corporations that had a selfish interest in maintaining high fertilizer costs. The chairman was William J. Graham of Aledo, Illinois, a Republican from a major hog raising district who showed no compassion for the Farm Bureau officials. They were told that they could not bring a lawyer, since the session would be secret. Unfamiliar with congressional procedures and trusting that they would be treated fairly, they faced seven obviously angry congressmen. One staff person also was in the room.

The official transcript shows that Howard was not impolitely questioned about the idea that congressmen might be influenced by corporations. Howard could not give names but he insisted that fertilizer lobbyists had been in the city, a statement the committeemen seemed unable to believe. One congressman asserted that he had never seen a fertilizer lobbyist. The witness made it clear that he did not intend to affront any lawmaker. Subject to recall, he was courteously excused in time to catch an afternoon train.

The transcript conflicted with Howard's clear memory of an unpleasant three hours that was more of an inquisition than an investigation. He remembered that Chairman Graham angrily began: "In a letter to every member of Congress you have charged that Congress is corrupt. The charge is criminal unless you can prove it. We demand proof."

Thunderstruck, the Farm Bureau president insisted that the letter be read. He asked whether it was criminal to ask a congressman to explain his vote. The demand for proof was sternly repeated by Graham and by the other committee members. When he wrote about the occasion in later years, Howard said that his answers were not always respectful as the congressmen refused to believe that Washington was overrun by lobbyists.

Later Silver scored points by filing a statement that cited parallels between propaganda issued by American Cyanamid Company and a letter in which a congressman explained to a farmer why he had voted against the Muscle Shoals appropriation.

Howard was at a disadvantage because he had not been in Washington during most of the Muscle Shoals maneuvering, which had been handled by Silver. During the long proceedings, the belligerent questioning focused on identification of the head lobbyist for a major corporation. The Farm Bureau president had heard his name but could not recall it. Just before train time he was told that he would be recalled under subpoena for a major investigation, but that unstated penalties might be avoided if he identified the seducer of congressional morals. At that moment, Howard's memory clicked. He named the head lobbyist and suggested that he be questioned.

Within a minute or two, the lobbyist walked into the room and indignantly demanded to be heard. Howard stopped at the door to say: "It was just a minute ago your name was mentioned and your office is a mile and a half from here. That's good time."

On the train to Chicago, Howard decided that he would have an experienced lawyer at his side at the next hearing. Just then a telegram from Harry Hull told him that all was well, that the Farm Bureau had triumphed at the hearing.

The alert Silver, who had followed Howard on the witness stand, saved the day by asking why the lobbyist had been allowed to listen to the proceedings from an anteroom. Silver had seen the man sneak out, his hat pulled down and his coat collar turned up, just before he strode through the main door. There was no more questioning about lobbyist influence, but Silver also underwent bitter cross-questioning on other matters. At the end of the day the Muscle Shoals letter had not been retracted or amended.

Graham never sought reelection in his rural district. Five months later he resigned from Congress to become a federal judge.

Muscle Shoals remained a lost cause for the early Farm Bureau. A special committee of Chester H. Gray of Missouri, W. G. Jamison of Colorado, and John G. Brown of Indiana recommended that a government corporation produce power and fertilizer at Wilson Dam. For lack of something better, the executive committee approved an offer by Henry Ford to lease and operate the plant, but Congress continued to listen to fertilizer lobbyists.

Coinciding with the Muscle Shoals controversy, a backfire of misinformation was started in the grass roots. Officials of county and state farm bureaus heard that Silver's activities were antagonizing government officials and giving the AFBF a bad reputation. The matter came to the attention of the executive committee when it met in Chicago on February 21. Howard and a few others understood the situation in Washington, but the majority argued that something should be done. The board voted to reorganize the Washington office and make Silver responsible to a committee of five. The West Virginian was demoted and his effectiveness reduced, but not for long.

It was a low point in the Howard administration, but Silver quickly recovered. He had friends in both houses of Congress who respected the Farm Bureau and its leaders and who believed that the old guardsmen had been unfair. They were a minority but they were not impotent.

The turning point came in less than two months. Between April 11 and 23, the Farm Bureau's executive committee held a long conference in Washington with presidents and secretaries of many state federations. The chief purpose was to study national legislative problems and to determine what stand organized agriculture should take. They met with prominent men in and out of govenment, including farm-state senators and representatives who were fully informed about the effectiveness of Silver's work and the cause of his troubles. The Farm Bureau board made an unhurried investigation and restored Silver to his original authority.

A willingness to cooperate with the AFBF prevailed when some one hundred senators and house members attended a meeting in the House caucus room. Speeches by Howard and others laid the groundwork for one of the Farm Bureau's greatest achievements. On May 9, the senate's farm bloc held its first meeting in Silver's office.

One result was that Silver thereafter operated with a larger staff. Two executive committeemen, Gray and Jamison, spent considerable time in the capital on research and liaison work.

During the April conference, the executive committee authorized Howard to sign a friendly agreement with A. C. True, head of the Department of Agriculture's states relations services, that county agents should not participate in the commercial activities of farm bureaus.

Under pressure from other farm organizations and some corporations, True pointed out that the Farm Bureau had become involved in cooperative marketing and was getting into commercial activities. Howard said the county agents would be hurt more than the Farm Bureau movement. The close relationship between the Farm Bureau and the extension services continued to be a touchy matter until 1954, when a complete separation was ordered by Secretary Ezra Taft Benson.

The True-Howard memorandum of agreement, designed to limit county agents to educational activities, was a concession to fertilizer companies. The county agents had been obtaining wholesale prices for Farm Bureau members, which increased the demand for fertilizers, but the industry complained that its distribution system had been dislocated and its retail volume reduced. Small farm organizations meanwhile were unhappy about the spectacular rise of the Farm Bureau to first place in their league. The Farmers Union, some state Granges, and lesser groups protested that the Farm Bureau was receiving favored treatment, including a subsidy, from the government.

As an ex officio member, True had attended meetings of the executive committee, beginning with the ratification convention, at which there was a continuing discussion of the rising volume of complaints and a feeling within the department that a change should be made. By mid-October the federation's governing body cooperated by adopting a resolution that was the basis for further compromises.

County agents were allowed under the lengthy document to aid all farming people regarding "the problems of production, marketing and formation of farm bureaus and other cooperative organizations," but thereafter the business of running the agencies would be up to the farmers, without Extension Service assistance. The agreement declared that county agents could not "engage in commercial activities or take part in other farm bureau activities which are outside their duties as extension agents." Specifically they were barred from soliciting members, handling funds, and editing or managing publications. The document specified that the county agents, who received part of their salaries from public funds, were "part of a public service as defined in the Smith-Lever Act."

True continued to show up at quarterly meetings of the Farm Bureau Board and Secretary Wallace clarified the agreement four months later by adding that it was proper for an organized group of rural people to contribute funds to support county agent work.

Complaints about the close relationship between the farm bureaus and the government had been a side issue during the House agriculture committee's hearings on packer regulation in early 1920. The opposition was led by the Farmers' National Council, a highly vocal organization that was affiliated with some state Granges and Farmers Unions, the Society of Equity, the National Non-Partisan League, the National Order of Gleaners, and other associations of less consequential membership and influence. The council was headed by Benjamin C. Marsh, who claimed to speak for a membership of 750,000. That claim was challenged by Howard Leonard, who had credentials from the Illinois, Iowa, and American federations when he testified in behalf of control of the packing industry. Neither committee members nor departmental officials were impressed with Marsh. Even in its formative stage, as far as they were concerned, the Farm Bureau was the real power in the rural United States. At least it had prospects of achieving more than the older organizations ever had.

Later, one resolution at the ratification convention denounced the Farmers' National Council for seeking to ''ally the agriculturalists of America with the radical element of the industrial world.'' Howard, who was usually charitable in his judgments, described Marsh in his memoirs as a ''man of socialistic bent who claimed to be the representative of every farmer in America.'' Marsh's assistant, George P. Hampton, was the Washington correspondent of the *Iowa Homestead.*

The Department of Agriculture and the agricultural committees of Congress, which were the agencies that counted, recognized from the outset the primacy of the Farm Bureau. Trouble kept popping up, however, and in the summer of 1921 the dissident Pennsylvania Grange prevailed upon the House Banking and Currency Committee to investigate all farm organizations. During a long hearing, some congressmen from urban districts threatened to have Smith-Lever appropriations withdrawn from support of county agent work. Howard, Coverdale, and Silver underwent repetitious questioning. Howard, who in speeches and statements had said that the effectiveness of the national office depended upon strong county units, was heckled about a statement directed to county agents. At the hearing he described county agents as semigovernmental employees and testified that the Farm Bureau encouraged them to do better work:

The county farm bureau is organized to aid to the fullest possible extent the work of the county agent. You have no right persistently to misrepresent the case and put the cart before the horse. The farmers join the Farm Bureau in order to secure maximum efficiency for the extension work of the Department of Agriculture. Do not forget that where there are strong farm bureaus, the farmers raise enough money to employ and retain highly trained and experienced men as county agents and pay them proper salaries. This enables them to carry out the real programs of work adapted to the special needs of the county.

Last week two governors came to me and voluntarily paid high tribute to the work of the Farm Bureau in keeping down dangerous expressions of unrest. They declared the Farm Bureau to be the great sober, thoughtful, careful, practical organized force in the country today. I declare the Farm Bureau to be a movement of the farmers themselves for the good of the whole people. Every cent of revenue received by the American Farm Bureau Federation comes from its members, fifty cents a head. We file here a full membership report. The Farm Bureau is four-square with all the jealous winds that blow.

Many Americans at that time were alarmed at the success of the Russian Revolution. Fear for the nation's traditions had been intensified by labor unrest, in which the Industrial Workers of the World were prominent, and by "red scare" activities of the attorney general's office at the end of the war. When his 1919 convention keynote speech included a statement that he "stood like a rock against radicalism," Howard had been in the mainstream of current opinion. The Farm Bureau president believed it was fortunate that rural people had confidence in the college-trained county agents whose educational work was not limited to vocational agriculture.

Several state legislators turned down Farmers Union petitions seeking a cut-off of state funds.

18

❧❧❧❧❧❧❧❧❧❧❧❧❧❧❧❧❧❧❧❧❧❧❧❧❧❧❧❧❧

Failure in Cooperative Marketing

F OR the early Farm Bureau and its first president, the major objective, the highest hopes, the greatest effort, and the worst failure lay in the field of cooperative marketing. Eight months after the founding convention in Chicago, before the mechanics of organization had been completed, the AFBF was backed by some of its agrarian rivals in an overly amitious attempt to take over the functions of the Chicago Board of Trade. The story involves the controversial Aaron Sapiro, a San Francisco lawyer, whose ego exceeded his accomplishments and who stirred up a row that almost destroyed the national federation.

The time had come for a great marketplace confrontation. For decades rural people had regarded the terminal markets as the common enemy chiefly responsible for the low prices received by the farmer and for the high handling charges he paid. In an effort to correct the situation, rural cooperatives had been successful locally and in some cases had banded together into statewide organizations. Howard and others believed that national or regional cooperatives, provided they had strong memberships and facilities, could make needed corrections in the marketing and distribution system. A demand for action arose from the midwestern grass roots and was agitated by officials of some state federations, especially the Illinois Agricultural Association (IAA). There was no consensus about the details of a solution but the membership wanted the American Farm Bureau Federation to take some action.

Howard did not hesitate to accept the responsibilities of leadership. On other occasions he had warned that the recently formed federation should not move impetuously or engage in too many arenas of action, but he believed that the establishment of grain and livestock marketing cooperatives should be at or near the top of the Farm Bureau's priorities. As one step, he believed that a farmer-owned commission house was needed at the Chicago Stock Yards and that it should have been set up years earlier.

142

"It is not fair or right that farmers should continue to sell their products at prices dictated by those who buy," he told the IAA convention in January 1920. Without reservation, he made it clear that the AFBF should involve itself not only with local and terminal markets but possibly with world markets as well.

Under those circumstances, cooperative marketing became the Farm Bureau's first large project. The twelve executive committeemen who had been strangers in November quickly put aside regional differences and were converted to Howard's concept of a national organization that would work harmoniously for the betterment of agriculture without forgetting the best interests of the nation. By mid-August, when the committee met in Denver, they were marching in step. "This federation has been in existence since March and the preliminary work has been done," the president told them. "We ought to know what we are going to do and what is to be the future policy of the Farm Bureau."

Unanimously they followed his leadership. They agreed that the federation, along with its other activities, should push economic programs. Even the New Englanders gave their approval to efforts already begun by the midwesterners who wanted major changes made in the established system of marketing grains and livestock.

For years economic controversies had involved the grain elevators—some of which were owned by farmers—which were the tallest structures in midwestern and plains towns. As part of a study of the cooperative movement, Howard wrote:

Many of the earlier farmer elevators were of few days and full of trouble. One of the first to survive was located at Rockwell, Iowa (founded in 1868). Its first car of grain was shipped to Chicago, consigned for sale through a commercial company. The company did not accept it because it did not recognize cooperative associations. After some delay the cooperative sent its attorney, E. G. Dunn of Mason City, to Chicago to see what could be done. The commercial firm knew nothing about what had become of it. Mr. Dunn spent some time tramping through the switch yards of various railroads before locating the car. After he located it, he tried to get other firms to sell it on commission. None of them would handle it, all offering the reason that the Chicago Board of Trade did not recognize cooperative marketing associations.

This claim was probably bogus because Mr. Dunn did later arrange with a young dealer on the board who had not yet built up a profitable clientele to sell the grain for him. This man was Lowell Hoit, who for many years has continued most helpful in farmer marketing. It is much more probable that the resistance came from privately-owned elevators that for years had handled grain at local stations. Most of those were what were known as line elevators; this is, one company owning and operating all the elevators along a certain line or division of a railroad, thus constituting a monopoly.

As the elevators increased in number, the line elevators would bid for grain in the territory of a newly established farmers' elevator at a materially higher price than the market would justify and make up their losses by depressing the price at other elevators. The writer has personally known of these old line elevators bidding as much as ten per cent above the market in order to crush the new farmer-owned cooperative.

The line and independent companies formed state associations that put pressure on railroads and banks as well as on the terminal markets. Loaded cars lost in freight yards were only part of the problem. For years commission firms and track buyers boycotted the cooperatives, railroads balked at providing box cars and sites for cooperative elevators, and banks provided uncertain service.

By the time the Farm Bureau organized, some 4,400 farmer-owned elevators, not all of them cooperatives, had survived cutthroat competition. They also organized on a state or regional basis but were not strong enough to make a noticeable impact on the city markets. One of the most successful was a subsidiary of the Farmers Union of Nebraska, a major handler of livestock as well as grain. Members of the National Farmers' Grain Dealers Association, based at Chicago and with years of experience, also owned a sizable number of elevators. In Kansas and Oklahoma the National Wheat Growers Association at Wichita was the dominant marketing agency. The independent Missouri Farmers' Clubs represented a sizable group of cooperative elevators, but their leader, William A. Hirth, would not work with other farm groups. The Equity Cooperative Exchange of Minnesota had headquarters in St. Paul and extended its operations into the Dakotas, where it came into conflict with the Non-Partisan League. In general, the cooperative associations were not interested in cooperating with each other on an interstate basis. Many of their officials were jealous of their prerogatives, ambitious to become more important, and fearful that they might lose status if the grain-handling organizations formed a united front.

Dissatisfaction with livestock marketing was prevalent in the Midwest, where livestock shipping associations were at their peak in 1920. First formed in Nebraska in 1883, they sought to obtain higher prices for uniform carload lots and to eliminate part of the cost of sending cattle and hogs to distant markets by rail. On a regional basis they were represented by the Corn Belt Meat Producers' Association, with which Howard had been familiar in Iowa. State Farm Bureaus worked on the problem and in 1919 the Illinois Agricultural Association had conducted an interstate conference on livestock marketing that the Iowans considered to be of value. Jim Howard considered himself a pioneer in that field, for during his New Providence banking days he had organized a hog shipping pool.

In the pre–Farm Bureau era, the most cooperative progress had been made by the dairymen clustered around major cities. Such organizations as the New York Dairymen's League took the side of the cow owners, who thought milk prices too low, against the distributing companies that wanted a larger profit margin for handling a perishable product. In 1917 they federated into the National Milk Producers' Association, with whose officials Howard established good relations on his first trips to Washington. The organized dairymen, who claimed 400,000 members, won milk marketing battles in Boston and Chicago in 1915–1916 and in New York in 1916–1917. Nevertheless, they still needed protection.

When the American Farm Bureau Federation was organized, dairymen were under indictment at Cleveland, Chicago, and St. Paul, charged with selling their milk cooperatively in violation of the Sherman Anti-Trust Act.

The first pages of the history of American farm cooperatives involved the processing and sale of dairy products early in the nineteenth century. A futile attempt to make and sell butter cooperatively began in 1808 in Connecticut. Before the Civil War, local associations of farmers in New York and Wisconsin operated successful cheese rings, creameries, and cheese factories. By 1872 a fluid milk association had been formed in the Boston area, and cooperative creameries and cheese factories functioned in the Fox River valley of Illinois until a market for fluid milk opened in Chicago. For two generations surplus cream from the Howard farm had been churned into butter at the cooperative creamery at Clemons and then marketed in attractive packages.

Elsewhere, producers of other commodities had joined forces to express their dissatisfaction with the marketing system. In Kentucky, a cooperative tobacco warehouse began operating in 1873. In 1885, a year after Aaron Sapiro was born, California citrus growers began the organized advertising and marketing of their crops at Riverside. Four years later at Fresno, raisin growers began to organize. Walnut growers formed an association at Santa Paula in 1895 and almond growers at Davis in 1897.

Rural cooperation was not confined to the field of marketing. Most rural fire insurance risks were handled by locally organized mutual insurance companies.

They had known it all along, of course, but the AFBF officials found that U.S. agriculture was surprisingly diversified and complex. Grain and livestock marketing could not monopolize their attention, since truck, fruit, cotton, dairy, and tobacco farmers also had marketing problems they wanted someone to solve. In that emergency, Howard and his overworked staff invented commodity marketing conferences.

No one believed more fervently in the future of cooperative marketing and in the evils of terminal market speculation than William G.

Eckhardt, who headed the grain marketing department of the Illinois Agricultural Association. A graduate of the University of Illinois, he had been one of the first county agents in his state and had attended the Ithaca conference.

Eckhardt believed that grain prices could be stabilized if the producers owned terminal facilities large enough to store the crop until it could be shipped directly to the points of consumption. For that type of operation farmers would have to open their own brokerage house, organize farmer-owned elevators where none existed, and set up a midwestern exchange for the buying and selling of elevators. Eckhardt also wanted livestock commission firms established at the Chicago and East St. Louis markets. Inspired by his enthusiasm, the Illinois Agricultural Association adopted an aggressive marketing program and invited managers of farmers' elevators to a series of meetings.

At a regional meeting in Ames in the spring of 1920, Farm Bureau presidents and secretaries from eleven midwestern states agreed on the need for an all-out battle for cooperative marketing. Asking for a united front, they invited the Farm Bureau's rivals and officials of elevator associations to meet with them in Chicago on June 22 and 23. It would be the first commodity marketing conference and the agenda called for the formation of a planning committee.

Dissension was audible as five hundred men gathered at the LaSalle Hotel. Many were jealous of the prerogatives and openly suspicious of if not antagonistic to the effort to harmonize rural interests for the greater good. Howard, who needed his talents for leadership, in an effort to make the goal clear announced:

The American Farm Bureau Federation is not going into the grain marketing business itself. It is going to see that the whole system is changed, however, through existing organizations if possible. We are going to establish a bureau of cooperation with competent men at the head to direct the work. We are here today to discuss the plan that should be followed.

During two difficult days as presiding officer, Howard refused to compromise. The National Board of Farm Organizations, representing most of the state Farmers Unions, boycotted the meeting because Howard would not let them name half the members of the all-important committee. Farmers Union men from some important states were on hand, however, along with officials of the Grange, Equity Societies, and cooperative associations. During the program Agriculture Secretary E. T. Meredith pronounced the government's blessing on the venture and Eckhardt repeated before the larger audience the speech he had been delivering in downstate Illinois.

A new controversial element was added when the magnetic figure of

Aaron Sapiro strode into the opening-day limelight. As chief attorney for fourteen California cooperatives that handled 300 million dollars of crops a year, he held the center of attention as he bubbled with confidence that methods he had used in stabilizing prune prices could be duplicated across the wheat belts. Sapiro was ambitious and brilliant, controversial and self-centered, and at the moment largely unknown east of the Rockies. He already had made converts of Eckhardt, Clifford V. Gregory of *Prairie Farmer,* and some others. Introduced simply as an authority on cooperation in California, Sapiro talked for an hour and thus began one of Howard's longest headaches.

The dark-haired Sapiro had been born thirty-six years earlier in San Francisco, where part of his boyhood was spent in an orphanage and all of it in poverty. People who recognized his potential sent him the University of Cincinnati, where he was graduated as a Phi Beta Kappa. Returning to San Francisco, he headed a young law firm that was highly successful in a practice not confined to cooperative law. His interest in that field had developed early when he did legal work for the California state market bureau.

The Sapiro success story began among Fresno raisin growers in 1911. Almost ruined financially, they had sold at prices below the cost of production. Prices doubled the year after he formed an association whose members signed five-year, ironclad contracts that enabled their cooperative to control 75 percent of the crop with the financial assistance of bankers and merchants. Sapiro repeated his success among specialists who grew prunes, other fruits, and nuts in comparatively small areas.

On the floor and in private conversations, delegates debated the Sapiro thesis that the teminal markets could be eliminated if corn and small grain growers would sign California-style contracts that they would sell their crops only to cooperative pools. Sapiro insisted that the cooperatives be organized on single-commodity lines and that experts be hired to handle sales, traffic, advertising, and warehousing. The enforceable contracts would allow the marketing association to know how much of the crop it would handle. Long-term contracts would assure permanency, with adequate supplies at fair prices year after year. Speculation would end, since the cooperative would set prices on the basis of cost of production plus a fair profit. Farmer-members who failed to deliver their grain to the local cooperative would be penalized by heavy damages for nonperformance of contract. The national or regional associations would enter the terminal markets and take over the work done by the line elevators, commission houses, and other middlemen. Sapiro also contended that if production increased the expert managers could open new markets by advertising techniques.

In the critical situation that faced the quarreling delegates, President C. H. Gustafson of the Nebraska Farmers Union came to the front as a strong man who supported the Farm Bureau president. He spoke for forty thousand Nebraskans who paid annual dues of two dollars, considered educational activities to be secondary, and since 1913 had formed a half dozen successful cooperatives. The Farmers Union Livestock Marketing Association, of which he was also president, was the largest commission house at the Omaha stockyards and had branches at Kansas City, Sioux City, Denver, and St. Joseph. Gustafson, who also headed grain marketing and insurance subsidiaries, took the position that the cause was larger than any organization or individual. Howard needed to demonstrate that not all the leadership came from Farm Bureau ranks, and before overnight adjournment he appointed Gustafson chairman of a five-man committee to recommend a course of action.

The next day Gustafson recommended that a committee of not more than seventeen members be appointed to represent the various organizations present in formulating a plan under which grain producers would market their crops cooperatively through one or more central organizations.

As the meeting closed, Howard received a personal tribute from the Farm Bureau's rivals. For a time arrangements for selecting the committee of seventeen were held up with debate over a formula that would not put the Farmers Union, Grange, and Equity leaders in a secondary position. Eventually they solved the problem by permitting Howard to make the appointments. His competitors had known him for only a few months but they trusted him. They believed that under his leadership they would be treated fairly and would have the best chance of achieving their goal.

Meanwhile the National Farmers' Grain Dealers Association played dog-in-the-manger. Its ambitious officers did not want a secondary role in an all-powerful cooperative movement. They announced formation of a competing committee that would put into operation its own marketing plan. Others could join them, but elevator men insisted on having majority control of their movement, which never materialized.

The Farmers' Grain Marketing Committee of Seventeen was appointed two months later by Howard, who considered 150 names and refused to be hurried in a search for men who were experienced in the grain business and would provide a geographical and organizational balance. Eckhardt was one of three men with Farm Bureau backgrounds and Gustafson one of two from the Farmers Union. Equity Societies, the Grange, and the Missouri Farmers' Clubs were recognized, as were grain dealers' associations. A place was found for Gregory as representative of the American Agricultural Editors' Association. The Midwest was well represented, but no one from the Northwest was appointed. The North Dakotan on the committee was the state's new U.S. senator, E. F. Ladd, president of the state agricultural college. Howard had displayed tact and diplomacy in a difficult situation and in general his selections were well received.

As the group began its work with Gustafson as chairman and Eckhardt as treasurer, Howard issued a denial that either the Farm Bureau or the Committee of Seventeen intended to fix grain prices. The goal, he said, was to evolve a marketing system that would eliminate useless handling costs, unnecessary selling expenses, and ruinous price fluctuations. He wanted the farmer to have a reasonable profit over the cost of production and the consumer to have an adequate and uninterrupted food supply at the least possible mark-up over actual costs.''

Gustafson's committee inspected U.S. and Canadian exchanges, held hearings in rural areas, and sought the opinions of experts. It ignored the advice of Julius Barnes, who had been wartime head of the U.S. Grain Corporation, that farmers should not attempt to set up corporations that would operate in the terminal markets. Barnes held that prices will always fluctuate, that the grain business is unusually complicated, and that farmers should confine themselves to local markets.

Gregory and many others were carried away by Sapiro's vision of California-style cooperatives controlling the wheat belt, and there was no unanimity of opinion during the deliberations of the Committee of Seventeen or in the grass roots. No one objected to Howard's thesis that farmers' cooperatives should retain control of the crop through the marketing process and get the highest price consistent with supply and demand. Many were obsessed with the idea that the grain exchanges should be abolished on the ground that price fluctuations were the result of speculation. Many wanted arbitrary price fixing. Others complained that pooling would promote monopolies and that individual independence would be lost.

In midwinter the committee agreed on an ambitious plan that incorporated many of Sapiro's theories. Individual farmers would pay ten dollars for memberships in a nationwide cooperative association to be known as the U.S. Grain Growers, Inc. (USGG). They would sign contracts with local elevators that for five years would restrict the sale of grain to specified channels. The facilities of existing cooperatives would be utilized and the USGG would have district sales offices, export and finance corporations, and other subsidiaries.

"This morning of April 6, 1921, marks sun-up for American agriculture," Howard announced at the opening of a ratification conference in Chicago. Representatives of nearly all rural organizations from the twenty-three grain states were in the audience as he asserted that farmers had reached their Runnymede in a fight against uneconomic and speculative marketing. If he had private misgivings about the scope of the committee's recommendations, they were concealed; he did his best to form a united front. He continued:

This right to follow our products to the manufacturer, processor, or consumer in no essential differs from the universally accepted right on the part of all classes to consolidate capital and effort. We are seeking no class privileges. We are seeking a stabilization of market wherein the farmer gets the benefit of the economic working, not the effect of the manipulated working, of the law of supply and demand. . . .

Let no man say the farmers of America want to lower their production output. That would be contrary to the natural courses of our calling. The farmer wants to produce. He must produce. He insists that unnatural barriers to production be removed. The time has come in our national life when the consumer interest is only safeguarded by the adequate and economical distribution of things produced, so that the farmer may not only maintain but expand his operations. The most potent cause of our present social unrest and commercial stagnation today lies in the fact that there is no farm market. The farmer's purchasing power is gone. His prices are far below par. His costs of production are deep in red. His markets are gone.

Do you want to know what will start again the hum of the mills and the song of the laborer throughout the land? I'll tell you: A prosperous agriculture. It is the foundation of all permanent prosperity and contentment. It has been so in all nations and ages. Delay in bringing about this speedy readjustment is fraught with untold dangers.

The delegates ratified the recommendations of the Committee of Seventeen, which then appointed a board of twenty-one directors for the U.S. Grain Growers. To head the cooperative, the board elected Gustafson president and Eckhardt treasurer. Reaching into the Northwest, it made George C. Jewett, general manager of a cooperative at Spokane, one of the vice-presidents.

Sapiro, who preferred to prosper from legal fees collected from cooperatives he organized, was not interested when Illinois friends proposed that he be placed on the payroll of the AFBF, which acted as financial angel for the Committee of Seventeen. During the transition period, Gustafson headed the Farm Bureau's division of cooperative marketing and gave some attention to livestock, fruit, tobacco, and sugar beets. He continued in that position for several months after be became president of the Grain Growers. The second-year report of AFBF Secretary John W. Coverdale did not give details of the financial arrangements.

Howard's contribution was "full farmer time." Starting in mid-1921, the federation's president did double duty by assuming personal charge of the cooperative marketing division. Already he had a heavy load of desk work and a travel schedule that now required he make speeches explaining the necessity and objectives of the grain marketing program. Long train trips were welcomed, for in a Pullman car he learned how to ignore distractions and, while his body rested, to plan the next speech and read the documents that had piled up on his desk. The strain of the heavy responsibilities and long hours began to show in his face. He missed occasional meetings because of brief illnesses. He would have been in better health had he stayed on the farm.

A harmonizer who wanted all men to work together, Howard soon learned to keep Sapiro at arm's length. During his three years as Farm Bureau president, he never permitted the lawyer to become an official part of the organization. Eventually, under heavy pressure, the executive committee authorized his retention to do some organizational work in the South. Howard stalled and finally told Sapiro that he wouldn't get the job because it was not important enough for a man of his talents. Never given to unkind judgments, Howard once characterized Sapiro as having "a great appreciation of himself."

Hardheaded John Coverdale didn't care for Sapiro from the beginning, at least after he submitted a bill for $1,600, which included $600 for expenses, for the Chicago speech he had volunteered to make. "I knew right then that he wasn't working for the farmers," Coverdale recalled. "He was working for Sapiro. He would bear watching."

The U.S. Grain Growers never got off the ground, although three years would pass before its death was officially conceded. Its membership campaign encountered stiff opposition from grain dealers, who collected a jackpot, and from officials of commodity exchanges from New York to the Missouri River, who formed a national committee to defend the status quo. For financial backing, the cooperative venture could count only on the midwestern resources of the Farm Bureau. To pay start-up expenses, Gustafson and Eckhardt borrowed $229,188 from state and county farm bureaus, but only 62,878 farmers signed up in thirteen states, far less than the Sapiro disciples had anticipated. Liabilities exceeded assets by $102,524. Meanwhile Coverdale in his third annual report on AFBF activities noted that "dissension among the board of directors on matters of policy finally resulted in bringing the organization to the brink of ruin." He did not elaborate and minutes of USGG board meetings have not been located.

The midwestern farm bureaus did their best to start the cooperative in the business of selling grain. Just before the notes came due, state presidents and secretaries ordered an investigation by a committee headed by E. H. Cunningham of Iowa. On its recommendation, another $10,000 was loaned, but by the summer of 1921 the Grain Growers had given up. Cunningham took over the presidency from Gustafson and other Farm Bureau men replaced the original board of directors. In a period of reconstruction, Coverdale and some others believed that the program could be salvaged on a less ambitious scale by using existing market facilities, and $75,000 was raised, of which $50,000 came from the Iowa Farm Bureau. All possibilities were explored and on December 8, 1921, a letter to Commerce Secretary Herbert Hoover suggesting a temporary loan to the Grain Growers was signed by Howard and four state Farm Bureau presidents—J. G. Brown of Indiana, C. W. Hunt of Iowa, Ralph Snyder of Kansas, and Howard Leonard of Illinois. In a reply to Silver, Hoover recalled that he had previously offered a personal loan of $5,000 if others would contribute $45,000. He said the offer was still good, "conditioned upon neither credit nor publicity. I simply wish to help solve the farmers' problem to the best of my very limited financial ability where help may be needed."

Hoover in June 1921 had invited officials of the Farm Bureau and the Grain Growers to meet in his office with representatives of the grain trade to discuss improvements in warehousing methods that might give producers more control over marketing. The meeting was not held because Howard and his associates believed it would be unwise, at the height of the Grain Growers membership campaign, to meet publicly with the opposition.

Applications of the Grain Growers for seats on the Chicago and Omaha boards of trade were rejected on the grounds that patronage dividends would be an illegal rebate. At the same time, the Chicago Board of Trade challenged the constitutionality of the Capper-Tincher Futures Trading Act that had been passed by Congress at the request of the Farm Bureau. Valuable time was lost; not until late 1923 did the reorganized Grain Growers form a sales agency that began selling grain at Minneapolis, and the cooperative subsidiary never was able to pick up steam.

At a time when cooperative marketing was being opposed from outside and debated within the federation, Howard's views on the right to market were stated in the August 10, 1922, AFBF newsletter:

The AFBF contends that the farmer has a right to follow his produce through his cooperative associations just as far down the marketing and distributing channels as will meet his best interests. We claim we must have the greatest freedom in the exercise of this right and that there must be no organized barrier or unfair practices thrown in the way of its freest functioning. What the farmer demands is service at a fair and equitable cost. If the cooperative selling associations at the livestock markets can render that service adequately and economically, they ought to succeed and have the support not only of the farmers but the general public as well. If they cannot succeed in competition with already established agencies they will fall of their own weight.

Therefore, we can but view any organized opposition or propaganda against cooperative selling as an admission that cooperation is fundamentally sound and promises success.

It has never been the thought of the AFBF that the farmer-controlled agencies would or should ever displace entirely the present existing machinery. Rather, we believe there should be the keenest competition between the two different types of selling agencies, both in grain and livestock, in order that the producer may have the best market facilities. We shall continue to stand on our rights to sell cooperatively, prorating back to the producer the profits of the business, but as an organization we have not nor shall we do other than meet our competitors with that spirit of fairness which we, in turn, expect from them.

Thirty years later, in an interview, Howard commented on the failure of the Grain Growers cooperative:

Yes, it was a big experiment and we just lost by the skin of our teeth. That was due to too much expenditure, too much money. They borrowed too much money from various county Farm Bureaus. . . . Bill Eckhardt was treasurer, an Illinois fellow, and he had big ideas. The committee, on the whole, had rather large ideas. It was a sorry mistake and we corrected it in the livestock committee.

Coverdale, a conservative who believed that action should be preceded by careful study of the basic problems, thought that the federation moved too quickly into the marketing field. In his "Early Days" reflections on the development of the Farm Bureau movement, he pointed out that creation of the Committee of Seventeen was endorsed by the AFBF executive committee as soon as the proposition was advanced. His style would have been to postpone a vote at least until the next meeting. Coverdale also was critical of committeemen, whom he did not name but who were newer members of the Farm Bureau board, who were enthusiastic backers of a proposal they had not studied in depth.

Some postmortems contend that the Howard administration organized the campaigns for cooperative marketing too quickly and depended upon high pressure salesmanship. The first president recognized that situation when he addressed the AFBF convention in Atlanta in late 1921. Repeating previous statements, he said:

The danger of cooperation is in its too rapid development in an overexpectation regarding its benefits. If it succeeds, it must be on the basis of sound and efficient merchandising, coupled with a real spirit of cooperation and mutual helpfulness among producers themselves. Thus assured, cooperation will not only shorten the road to market but will result in material economies.

Such cautionary advice had to be ignored by a leader who believed in the theory and practice of cooperation and, as a practical matter, could not attempt to restrain the enthusiasm of a new organization. Of necessity, the AFBF presidency was a crash course in practical economics, and Howard was not ignorant of the vast expanses of the wheat growing region and the complexities of the marketing system. His public statements include a few oblique references to the parallel situation fifty years earlier when Grange-owned enterprises failed because their farmer officers lacked business training.

Another handicap was the traditional independence of the men of the soil. A sizable proportion would not pay Farm Bureau dues even after they had been told time after time about the educational and economic benefits that would come from membership. Similarly, many valued independence more than loyalty to a cooperative association, be it local, state, or regional. More than a decade earlier Kenyon L. Butterfield, president of Massachusetts Agricultural College had written:

Among no class of people is individualism so rampant as among farmers. For more than a century the American farmer led the freest possible social life. His independence was his glory. But when the day of cooperation dawned he found himself out of tune with the movement, was disinclined to join the ranks of organized effort, and he prefers even yet his personal and local independence to the truer freedom that can be secured only through cooperative endeavor.

In a quieter but more effective manner the Farm Bureau achieved solid progress in the marketing of other commodities, especially livestock. After establishment of the grain Committee of Seventeen, in rapid succession Howard appointed a livestock marketing committee of fifteen, a dairy committee of eleven, a fruit marketing committee of twenty-one, and a wool marketing of twenty-five. In these ventures the Farmers Union and the Grange did not participate actively. Sapiro showed no interest in perishables. The commodity committees called the attention of both producers and consumers to the need for improvements in the distributive system, and with pride the Farm Bureau took credit for originating the system of national commodity marketing conferences.

At a time of general enthusiasm over prospects for farmer domination of grain marketing, livestock men asked the Farm Bureau to sponsor a cooperative system that would improve the distribution system for fattened cattle, hogs, and sheep. With the approval of his executive committee, Howard called a meeting in Chicago on October 8, 1920. Without controversy, he was authorized to appoint a Committee of Fifteen to study the existing machinery and, if possible, to recommend changes. After consultation with Vice-President Oscar E. Bradfute, a prominent cattle breeder and showman, Howard announced the appointments three months later. In the only duplication, Gustafson also headed the Committee of Fifteen. A marketing plan that largely was the work of Dean H. W. Mumford of the University of Illinois was unanimously adopted in November 1921, at a conference to which thirty-one organizations sent delegates.

The executive committee appointed the first board of directors of the National Livestock Producers' Association, to which $7,000 was contributed by the Illinois, Indiana, Iowa, and Ohio federations. John G. Brown, president of the Indiana federation, became its president and Cunningham its secretary. Without delay, they began in 1922 to set up subsidiary commission houses similar to those already operating successfully in Sioux City and South St. Paul. Individual farmers, who paid a ten-dollar membership fee, and local associations consigned shipments to the producers' agencies, which competed with privately owned firms for the best prices available under supply-and-demand situations but did not attempt to influence the general level of prices. Sales were made at regular commission rates and savings set aside for substantial patronage dividends. Stocker and feeder subsidiaries were set up to help midwestern farmers obtain replacement stock.

The ultimate hope was that by controlling shipments to the various stockyards the producers' cooperatives could stabilize prices. That did not happen, but subsidiary commission houses handled from one-third to one-half of the total receipts in some cities.

In contrast to the Grain Growers, the livestock cooperative wasted no time in starting. When the Chicago producers' sales agency opened in June 1922, Howard consigned the first five carloads of steers, which had been fed at Homelands Farm by Roe Hiatt and brought within ten cents of the top price. Subsidiaries at East St. Louis and Indianapolis had opened earlier in the year, and in Peoria, East Buffalo, and Fort Worth subsequently. Operations began the next year at Kansas City, Cleveland, Evansville, Pittsburgh, Sioux Falls, and Oklahoma City, but the latter two soon closed. In following years agencies opened at Sioux City, Cincinnati, and Michigan City. Producer agencies in some cases competed with cooperatives backed by the Farmers Union. Throughout the Iowa Farm Bureau's fifty-year history, in some cases—despite partially interlocking directorates—state associations of shippers did not affiliate with the National Livestock Producers' Association.

Farmers in specialty areas also petitioned for help. The normal procedure was for the executive board to authorize the president to call local organizations of producers into a conference. Upon request, Howard would then appoint a committee that had the backing of the cooperative marketing department as it worked out a plan of action. In some cases, a committee staff member went on the federation's payroll.

The National Milk Producers' Association, whose members operated on a regional basis around large cities, soon asked for the assistance of the younger federation. After appointing a Committee of Eleven, the Farm Bureau oversaw the reorganization of the Chicago Milk Producers' Cooperative Marketing Company and helped with organizational problems elsewhere.

Another Farm Bureau committee, to which Howard appointed one man from each interested state, recommended establishment of a national wool pool. A drastic price drop made that impossible, but some state pools were consolidated and sectional pools encouraged. The Washington office helped by backing legislation for an emergency tariff and for a truth-in-fabrics labeling law. Some 20,000 double bed blankets were manufactured for Iowa farmers whose wool could not be sold at acceptable prices.

A few agencies like the California Fruit Exchange could operate independently, but most fruit and vegetable marketing cooperatives were localized and sold their produce through established commission houses. Requests for Farm Bureau help from organizations of vegetable and canning crop growers resulted in the formation of the Federated Fruit and Vegetable Growers, which at the start of 1923 took over a commercial house with some 140 sales outlets. It was operated as a cooperative with headquarters in New York until it failed in the depression.

A Cotton Belt conference at Memphis called by Howard in 1922 encouraged the rest of the South to support the American Cotton Exchange, which had been set up by Arizona, California, and Texas cooperatives and which in time handled about 20 percent of the crop. Sapiro was active in that field.

Elsewhere a tobacco marketing conference endorsed cooperative session, sugar beet producers met and recommended a uniform national contract, and a cooperative coal buying service was set up for five state federations.

The AFBF newsletter listed those and additional accomplishments at the end of 1921, adding "All for 50 cents from each Farm Bureau member."

19

Depression, Gift Corn,
and Herbert Hoover

HISTORY repeated itself for the man who was born at the start of the panic of 1873 and who entered the job market in the severe economic depression twenty years later. In 1920, his first year in the AFBF presidency, prices for farm commodities dropped drastically and steadily. For the owner of Homelands Farm and for other Farm Bureau members, the raising of crops and the feeding of livestock ceased to be profitable, but from past experience they were confident that a cyclical upturn would reverse the trend and they hoped it would be soon.

For the rural depression, which continued during the 1920s, Howard and his associates blamed the nation's banking system rather than the fact that grain, livestock, and cotton surpluses had clogged the overseas markets when wartime credits were terminated. Bankrupt European nations as a result could not buy the U.S. food they needed. During wartime prosperity, farmers had been encouraged to increase production, if necessary by going into debt to buy more land. Lulled into a sense of financial security, they had expected a continuation of the period of high prices that had been uninterrupted since 1900. Here is Howard's account, given during his first year in office, of the events that started the price tailspin:

On May 18, 1920, the Federal Reserve Bank called on its correspondent banks to take up their collateral. They had authority to fix rediscount rates. They raised them to a point where banks could only rediscount at an operating loss. Correspondent banks must therefore demand payments from the country banks, whose only recourse was the maker of the note. The only way the farmer could pay was to sell something, and in May there was little to sell. The previous year's hog crop had been sold and it was farrowing time for the current crop. The cattle in feed lots intended for the fall markets were not half fat. The 1919 cotton, wheat and corn had been marketed and maturity for the new crop was weeks ahead. It

157

meant flooding the market with unwanted and immature products, which in turn meant sacrifices. In my own state of Iowa the immediate call exceeded 85 million dollars.

The Federal Reserve Board, created in 1913 at the start of the Wilson administration, in its newness was an obvious target for blame as an increasing number of families lost their farms. Writing in 1928 to a friend, Howard said:

It seems to have been an inevitable result of the war. In many instances, but not all, the banks took a very arbitrary course. First they forced prosperity in order to induce people to buy Liberty bonds and finance the war and after the war was over they forced deflation which lowered prices and caused the trouble.

During the decade overproduction continued with the encouragement of the extension services. Tractors replaced horses, commercial fertilizer came into increased use, and crops were grown on marginal land. The depression of the 1920s was limited to rural areas and was made worse because the price of things farmers bought kept rising. Except for brief recessions in 1924 and 1927, the businessmen in the cities were prosperous until the stock market debacle of 1929 brought on the general economic collapse of the 1930s.

Occasional downturns of fairly brief duration had been common in the past, and the severity of the depression was not recognized at the time of the 1920 political campaign, during which the platforms of both parties contained their customary agricultural planks and at the end of which farmers contributed to the Harding landslide. By fall, however, Howard had discarded his fears about the ability of American farmers to feed the nation. His presidential speech at the Indianapolis convention, where he was reelected by acclamation, outlined three remedies for the price slump. He wanted longer term credits through a period of orderly marketing, tariffs that would protect against competition from imports, and a constructive policy of cooperative marketing. The president said that grain price declines already had cost $7 billion, and he argued that "there is entirely too much spread between the farmer and the consumer" and that it might be necessary for farmers to organize their own agricultural banking institutions. Federal Reserve Governor William P. Gould Harding, to whom Silver already had appealed for help, told the convention there had been "no policy looking toward a broad curtailment of credit, but efforts have been made to correct abuses and bring about moderation and better judgment in the use of credits which a year ago were being diverted to all kinds of speculative channels." The delegates nevertheless asked Congress to act immediately to extend and renew the discounted farm obligations. Also on the program, to discuss the financing of crops and meat, was Willis K. Booth of the Guarantee Trust Company of New York.

Howard, who had never studied economics in college, was getting a practical education. The Farm Bureau's executive committee, impressed with the importance and complexity of subjects it had discussed with governmental officials and financiers, recognized the need for continuing forecasts, price analyses, statistics on agricultural conditions around the world, and information on weather, credit, foreign competition, shipping, tariffs, and internal revenue. The committee set up an economics department under the temporary guidance of six agricultural economists. A program worked out by G. F. Warren of Cornell University and Henry A. Wallace of Des Moines called for special marketing courses at leading agricultural colleges, the establishment of one or two graduate schools in economics and statistics, the collection of cost-of-production data and other statistics, legislation for short-term credits, and a study of corn imports from Argentina.

Supervision of the AFBF bureau of farm economics, which was headed first by S. W. Tabor and then by H. W. Morehouse, was the responsibility of a four-man committee of which Howard was a member. In 1921 several columns of statistics and production data were a regular feature of a Farm Bureau newsletter edited by Samuel Guard, who left *Breeders Gazette* to head the publicity department.

As a result of the rural depression, Jim Howard met Herbert Hoover for the first time. Thereafter he never wavered in his admiration for the mining engineer, another native Iowan of Quaker ancestry, whose career as a humanitarian had begun in Belgium during the First World War.

Hoover in late 1920 took charge of a campaign, financed in part by public contributions, to alleviate famine conditions in parts of Europe and Asia. Because of low prices, farmers did not have money to contribute to Hoover's cause. They began to write to the Farm Bureau that they would like to donate the corn they could not sell at a profit. Howard sounded out sentiment when he addressed the Illinois Agricultural Association's convention on January 14, 1921, saying:

Things are out of balance. We have an abundance of food and food products, more than the markets can absorb. But over in Europe millions of children and babies are underfed and undernourished. The mortality rate is frightful. And in China there is a region containing five times as many people as there are in this city. All must starve before another crop unless there is relief.

And here we are in the land of plenty. Are we our brother's keeper? Are we doing to others as we would have them do to us? What can we do to help this acute world situation? My own county in Iowa suggested the other day that we, as farmers, offer of the abundance of this corn for the feeding of those starving children.

His suggestion that farmers donate surplus corn and that city people pay for its transportation brought an emotional response, and in a few minutes the Illinois delegates pledged forty-seven carloads.

By resolution the convention asked Howard to confer with Hoover about collecting and shipping the grain. He sent a telegram, went to New York, telephoned the European Relief Council, and was given a five-thirty appointment. He sensed a common interest with a man who worked as long as farmers, and their first meeting made a lasting impression on the Farm Bureau leader:

Before three minutes passed I knew that here was a man of thorough information, broad sympathy and definitive action. He was better informed than I was about Corn Belt crops and conditions. He knew the details of freight rates and shipping routes. At the end of his tongue were more facts about nutrition and calories in corn in relation to prices and in comparison with other foods than most domestic scientists know.

Hoover knew all about the plight of farmers and he sincerely appreciated their offer of corn for relief. There was no better food than corn, but in only a few places in Europe did the people eat dishes cooked from cornmeal. The women would not know how to cook mush or make corn bread. The corn would have to be converted into grits or hominy, corn oil, or corn flakes. He had used all these for Belgian relief with excellent results. So acceptable were these forms of corn that he had built corn processing mills in Belgium. They were operating at capacity, but mills at Louisville, Argo, Milwaukee, and Cedar Rapids were running only part-time.

According to Howard's memoirs, when Howard estimated that a million bushels of corn could be collected, Hoover said a special organization to handle it would be justified. The U.S. mills should be willing to process the corn as their contribution, the railroads should furnish the cars, and the railroad workers should man the trains, he said. Howard was asked to return at nine in the morning.

"I have been able to get only three of the corn mill superintendents on the phone since you left last night," Hoover told him then. "We won't wait for the other, for he will have to come along. The railroads and the brotherhoods are with us. We can sell the gluten feed and other by-products to the farmers in the Eastern states for dairy feed—"

"Hold on," Howard interrupted. "The farmers will demand that the by-products go too. Any kind of livestock feed left over will depress the market for every other kind.''

"That's so," Hoover replied. "We will take the tail with the hide.''

A genius for organization, Hoover requested that a general administrator, a transportation expert, and a bookkeeper be added to the Farm Bureau staff. He required a full accounting of all grain and money received in the charitable project.

"When you return to Chicago, I wish you would go to see Archbishop Mundelein about that dairy feed,'' he said. "He is interested in the babies in a part of what was Austria where crops have failed and fresh milk is greatly needed. He is doing a most important job and I am sure he will want the feed. How soon do you think you can get the corn moving?''

Wondering how a surplus of food and fiber could exist in the face of starving and shivering humanity, Howard hardly slept on the Pullman ride to Chicago. His decision was that only after every need was satisfied could a surplus exist.

The archbishop the next morning pointed out on a map of Europe the areas of need and the transportation difficulties. He hoped that the first corn could be shipped from Norfolk the next week. Howard accepted his offer of help from a rural organization headed by Father Edwin V. O'Hara, who later became bishop of Kansas City.

The Farm Bureau drafted Carl Vrooman of Bloomington, Illinois, who had been assistant secretary of agriculture in the Wilson administration, to take charge of the emergency program. Deere and Company sent a traffic expert and A. R. Simpson, the AFBF office manager, kept a detailed account of every carload from farm to shipside.

In bushels and wagons the corn went to local elevators, to mills, and then to the docks. Donations from ten states were 413 cars of corn and $59,883 in cash. Part went to relief in Palestine and the Near East.

Later Hoover told Howard that the gift corn was so acceptable that he bought an additional $40 million of corn for European relief and that 8 million children and adults were fed. Removal of the surplus gave new strength to the corn market in 1921.

On the invitation of Hoover, who was secretary of commerce in the Harding administration, Howard in the summer of 1921 joined a group that as guests of the Canadian government inspected the site of the proposed Great Lakes–St. Lawrence Waterway between Niagara Falls and Quebec. He immediately and permanently became a strong supporter of the project that was designed to permit ocean-going vessels to load cargoes at Duluth and other lake ports and thus reduce the cost of shipping grain to foreign markets. Howard called it the "greatest resource development project before the American people'' and added that the possibility for generation of hydroelectric power was impressive. On his recommendation, the Farm Bureau repeatedly endorsed the project.

Howard's days were filled with surprises, spur-of-the-moment dealings with strangers, questionable proposals advanced as guarantees of farm prosperity, decisions that could not be delayed, and travel schedules suddenly revised. In late 1920, while reading a newspaper at St. Paul, he first encountered the name of W. W. Brauer of New York, an agent for the German government who wanted Congress to authorize a billion dollar loan to purchase foodstuffs for European countries. The brief item was intriguing; increased exports of farm products were one of the federation's goals.

A more interesting dispatch from Washington the next day stated that the American Farm Bureau Federation had endorsed the loan. Since no such endorsement had been made, Howard sent a telegram to Silver asking for details. Silver replied that Howard was needed in Washington at once to help put across the largest proposal ever to come before Congress in behalf of U.S. agriculture.

In his executive capacity Howard delegated authority but watched his subordinates closely. Silver, he knew, was farsighted and loyal and was making a great record as the AFBF's Washington representative. A man of action, he would push any cause if he personally thought it was right. In a second telegram, Howard instructed him not to make further commitments until he reached Washington.

Brauer, it turned out, was a U.S. citizen who before the days of transoceanic refrigeration had prospered in the business of shipping live cattle to Europe. A pending bill would give Germany a credit, equal to the funds—nearly $1 billion—held in the United States as proceeds of wartime sales by the alien property custodian. Eventually the money was to be returned to Germany, which in 1920 was in dire need of food and which had authorized Brauer to negotiate with Congress. Congressional leaders later told Howard they were ready to pass the bill, provided it had Farm Bureau backing.

Wanting more information, Howard met Brauer at his hotel. In a strong German accent, Brauer explained that he had maintained his German contacts and now had an opportunity to help both nations. He had a contract and he offered to read it. Howard remembered enough German from his academy days to read it himself. The contract was intriguing. In the event that the existing German government should fall, there was no commitment binding its successor. Neither was there any protection against depreciated currency. Brauer's commission would be 5 percent, or $50 million on a $1 billion transaction.

There were other questions. Since most of the crop surplus was in the hands of speculators, producers would profit little from the proposed transaction. At the prevailing prices, nearly 20 percent of the 1920 food production would be committed to Germany; the result could be that some Americans would go hungry. And it was strange, with diplomatic channels open, that Germany would pay such an enormous commission to one man.

Brauer insisted that Howard was wrong in his analysis and single-handedly was preventing approval by Congress. If Howard would consent, the legislation would be passed in three days and Howard would be well paid for his services. The amount mentioned was $1 million. The farm leader stated that neither he nor Silver was authorized to act, but he promised to withhold a final decision until the next morning.

At breakfast, he instructed Silver to tell Brauer that the loan would be endorsed on three conditions: that the original contract be produced so that the Farm Bureau could have its own translation made, that Brauer produce a memorandum from the State Department approving the trans-action, and that he pay the expenses of a special meeting of the executive committee to consider the matter.

Then Howard, some of whose land was under mortgage, made it clear that he could not be bribed. He dictated a letter to Brauer, dated January 7, 1921, stating that the Farm Bureau's sole concern was "to serve the interests of the country through the maintenance and improve-ment of the interests of agriculture." He continued:

Our decision in refusing to go further with you in this matter is due to your offer of remuneration for our services. As I told you plainly at the hotel, you could not give us one cent for any service which we could render, but the fact that you made the proposal to me which you did, making us believe that there may have been other similar proposals made by you to other representatives and possibly public officials [*sic*]. Such practices we view as absolutely corrupt.

You will not understand this letter to mean that we will not support any measure coming from proper sources. We still believe it essential to the farmers that all markets be open as freely as possible.

Brauer replied with an intemperate five-page letter of denial. Still hoping for approval of the billion dollar transaction, he sent copies of the correspondence to the White House. It can be found in the Woodrow Wilson Papers in the Library of Congress.

That was the last the Farm Bureau heard from Brauer. Never positive of the wisdom of his decisions, Howard wrote an account of the incident because it was typical of many nostrums that had to receive his full and prompt consideration. A penciled memorandum among his papers said that Howard had called in the Washington staff one by one, beginning with Silver. To each he said, "Look me in the eye and tell me if you accepted any money from Brauer."

A postscript written in a shaky hand, probably when he was reading some of his papers for the last time, added that he had fired one man whose offense was that, having been told that commissions would be paid, wrote a news release to the effect that the federation favored the legislation.

At the outset the Farm Bureau was internationalist in its outlook. The newsletter in early 1921 mentioned that Howard, who frequently went to Washington, had conferred with Secretary of State Charles Evans Hughes about international agriculture. Earlier the government sent Harvey J. Sconce of the Illinois Agricultural Association and W. S. Hill, president of the South Dakota federation, as official delegates to the International Institute of Agriculture held in Rome.

Reflecting his Quaker upbringing, Howard advocated worldwide disarmament in advance of a conference called by President Harding in November 1921. In the AFBF newsletter he wrote:

Our failure to ratify the Versailles treaty in some manner in 1919 is largely responsible for the slough of despond through which we are struggling today. The blame for agricultural stagnation must be placed squarely at the door of those who blocked peace ratification two years ago. If America had in some way or another ended the state of war in 1919, we farmers would be fifty percent better off than we are today.

Some 300,000 Farm Bureau members, about one-third of the claimed membership, signed petitions approving the Conference on Limitation of Armaments.

20

The Triumph of the Farm Bloc

THE president of the United States held up his hands in a gesture of surrender when the president and the Washington representative of the American Farm Bureau Federation were ushered into the Oval Office. "Well, boys, you have us," said Warren G. Harding. "What do you want us to do?" Nothing like it had happened before. President Harding and the old guard Republicans, established in power by the landslide election of 1920, could not adjourn the United States Senate without the consent of J. R. Howard and Gray Silver.

The Farm Bureau leaders wanted—demanded would be more accurate—Congress to stay in session until it passed and the president signed a series of bills backed by a bipartisan farm bloc that Silver had organized and masterminded. From past experience, the bloc knew that legislation important to agriculture would have been killed had Harding been able to force adjournment.

Having no alternative, the president agreed that Congress would promptly pass and that he would sign a half dozen farm bloc bills. Two of them for the first time put grain exchanges and the packing industry under federal regulation. Others provided emergency credit for agricultural marketing and made more money available for farm mortgage loans.

As responsible men, Howard and Silver did not insist upon immediate action on all of the farm bloc agenda. That came later in the Sixty-seventh Congress, to the chagrin of the Republican leadership and the alarm of the East Coast power structure, when additional farm bills of major importance were enacted.

When the Sixty-seventh Congress adjourned in early 1923, Silver passed this judgment: "It is not too much to say that the twenty-six laws passed . . . are of far more importance to American agriculture than all the legislation relating to agriculture passed since the adoption of the Constitution."

The legislative triumph cancelled the Farm Bureau's concurrent failure to establish the U.S. Grain Growers as a cooperative powerful enough to force marketing reforms. Long-standing complaints about grain exchanges, packers, and stockyards died away when the federal government began regulation of those industries.

"You haven't heard a peep from farmers about the inequities of grain marketing from that day to this," Howard said thirty years later when he reviewed his career. "And you haven't heard any serious complaints about the Packer and Stockyards Act. The most important thing the Farm Bureau did in those early years was that conference with Harding in which we demanded legislative relief."

Pressure blocs were by no means new around the halls of Congress. This one attracted attention because it was rural and because it had superior leadership. For its achievements primary credit goes to the Farm Bureau's man in Washington. Silver conceived the idea of organizing a bipartisan group of senators who would insist upon passage of farm legislation. To be its chairman he picked Senator William S. Kenyon of Iowa, who had been elected as a progressive Republican ten years earlier. Kenyon, who previously had been an assistant attorney general in charge of antitrust enforcement, recruited a group of twelve southerners and westerners, equally divided between the two parties and including a majority of the Committee on Agriculture. Its members were respected, influential, and not subject to disciplinary pressures. E. D. (Cotton Ed) Smith of South Carolina and Arthur Capper of Kansas were recognized as leading farm spokesmen. Robert M. LaFollette of Wisconsin and George W. Norris of Nebraska were others with national reputations and upper house seniority. Among the Republicans, only LaFollette came from east of the Mississippi River. The group met Silver's specifications. It was large enough to be effective but not so large that it would be involved in leadership responsibilities. For one session of Congress it held the balance of legislative power.

In advance, an extensive legislative agenda had been prepared by men who were concerned that farm commodity prices had not begun to recover from the 1920 downturn. Covering in some detail such subjects as finance; taxation; rail, ocean, and highway transportation; tariffs; and the federal trade commission, it had been drafted by the Farm Bureau's executive committee during a conference with representatives of state federations that lasted from April 11 to 23. Before resolving what position would be taken on legislative issues, the group sought information from governmental officials and other experts, including Henry C. Wallace and Herbert Hoover, members of the new cabinet; W. P. G. Harding, governor of the Federal Reserve Board; Edgar E. Clark, chairman of the Interstate Commerce Commission; and A. F. Lever of the Federal Farm Loan Board.

As far as the Farm Bureau men were concerned, they were only seeking the same consideration that businessmen previously had received from government. "Are we going to ask special privileges for agriculture?" Howard asked the group. The answer was a unanimous no.

It was at this time that Silver, who had been demoted several weeks earlier by the executive committee, was restored to his original position as the AFBF's Washington representative. Again he and Coverdale were Howard's top assistants.

Silver acted quickly and on May 9, 1921, the farm bloc held its first meeting in his office. Several departmental specialists were on hand to provide technical help as Kenyon's group set up its own committee system to study transportation, the Federal Reserve Act, commodity financing, and miscellaneous legislation. Advice on previously introduced bills was sought from government officials, leaders of other farm organizations, and men of national reputation, such as Gifford Pinchot, Bernard M. Baruch, Eugene Meyer, and Thomas A. Edison.

When the bloc held its second meeting in June, the agenda included requests for legislation providing better financing of farm marketing, personal credits for farmers, the privilege of cooperative marketing, readjustment of freight rates, packer control, and regulation of grain futures trading. By that time the senators were demonstrating that legislative progress is possible if expert testimony is given in support of bills previously introduced and if someone of Silver's capacity oversees the marshaling of public sentiment.

The crisis came quickly and demonstrated that Republican leadership was weak in Congress and the White House. Higher tariff rates were the administration's top priority, and the president asked that the Senate adjourn until a bill could be drafted and passed by the House of Representatives. Remembering what had happened at previous sessions, farm bloc members feared that their bills would be tabled when work began on the tariff bill. In the emergency, Silver alerted state and county farm bureaus, whose members responded with a flood of protesting telegrams. On July 5, Henry Cabot Lodge of Massachusetts, symbol of old guard power, moved for adjournment and was beaten on a twenty-four to twenty-seven roll call. The ailing Boies Penrose of Pennsylvania, summoned to bring in absentees and enforce discipline, was told by the party whip, Charles Curtis of Kansas, that the necessary votes could not be obtained. Harding then gave up and asked for peace terms. Kenyon told the president that he would have to deal with the Farm Bureau. At Silver's request, Howard made another hurried trip to Washington. The two men went to the White House, by then familiar territory, to tell Harding which bills must be passed promptly. The Senate stayed in session through most of August and fulfilled its part of the bargain made in the Oval Office.

Howard played a main role in making possible passage of the Packer and Stockyards Act, which had been defeated by previous Congresses and which he regarded as the Farm Bureau's major legislative achievement of 1921. Signed August 15, it cleared both houses by margins of better than three to one. With enforcement in the hands of the secretary of agriculture, the law prohibited packing companies from engaging in such unfair practices as division of territory and establishment of monopolies. As public service corporations, stockyards were subjected to regulation of their rates and practices.

The Capper-Tincher Futures Trading Act, designed to do for grain growers what packer regulation was designed to accomplish for livestock men, had to be reenacted in 1922. In answer to complaints of farmers who believed that speculation on boards of trade had caused a collapse in grain prices, it levied a tax of twenty cents a bushel on all grain sales for future delivery and for certain questionable practices such as "puts and calls." That provision soon was invalidated by the Supreme Court as an improper use of the taxing power. As a compromise, in September 1922 Congress passed the Grain Futures Act, which limited the amount prices could fluctuate in a given trading period.

One of the first bills passed helped the cooperative movement by rejuvenating the War Finance Corporation with authority to loan $1 billion to finance the marketing, storage, and exportation of surplus farm products. The Emergency Agricultural Credits Act also permitted the government corporation through bank loans to finance the raising, fattening, and marketing of cattle. The bill, which had high priority in the farm bloc program, was a precedent for the creation eight years later of the Reconstruction Finance Corporation. The Farm Bureau regarded the law, a compromise, as a "stabilizer of business and enormous help to agriculture." Commerce Secretary Herbert Hoover had objected to the original farm bloc proposal to set up a government corporation that would buy for cash and sell on credit for a five-year period.

After passage of the credits act, Howard and Silver conferred frequently with Eugene Meyer, who headed the War Finance Corporation and at first did not favor loans to cooperatives. Later he became a strong supporter of the legislation.

Also passed were two bills amending the Federal Farm Loan Act in an effort to make more money available for farm mortgages. One encouraged investment in federal loan bonds by raising the interest rate for investors from 5 to 5½ percent without increasing the rate to the borrower. The other increased by $25 million the working capital of the federal farm loan system.

The Farm Bureau also took credit for an emergency quota law limiting annual immigration to 2 percent of foreign-born residents as recorded in the 1920 census. A permanent, more stringent act was passed three years later.

Toward the end of 1921 the early successes were repeated and to the congressional leadership it became embarrassingly evident that the only major bills being passed had farm bloc sponsorship. In this unique situation, Silver's bloc itself was unique. Other Congresses and state legislatures have had loose coalitions, called blocs, made up of men with similar backgrounds who would support economic or social causes, if no one interfered, but the farm bloc of 1921–1922 was different. Primarily and wholeheartedly it was interested in the enactment of farm legislation and its members were willing to put aside other matters, at least for the time being. They had a cause, a leader in Kenyon, and a strategist in Silver who was backed by an activist organization with a widespread membership. Furthermore, the political situation was favorable, since the established powers were vulnerable to a bipartisan assault. It was a now-or-never situation that had not existed before and would not be duplicated.

In time, Kenyon's group was enlarged to twenty-two senators without disturbing its bipartisan character. In the House of Representatives, Lester J. Dickinson of Iowa mobilized some one hundred congressmen into a farm bloc of less clearly defined membership. Throughout the session, the hardest fighting was in the Senate, since the House could pass the farm bills with larger proportionate majorities. During the session of Congress the key men were Kenyon and Silver. To the bloc meetings, Silver would frequently invite officials of the National Grange and occasionally Charles W. Holman of the National Dairy Council, but the farm bloc was a Farm Bureau operation.

The bipartisan group of southerners and westerners, not yet identified by the metropolitan press as a disciplined bloc, demonstrated that it could prevent passage of legislation it did not like. Howard, Silver, and their tax expert, H. C. McKenzie, went to the White House in mid-September to tell President Harding that the administration's new tax bill was unfair to those least able to pay. Soon the Senate Finance Committee agreed with the bloc that the bill's disputed features should be amended to increase the maximum surtax, reduce the lower rates, and retain the capital stock tax. When finally passed, the revenue law was more progressive than the administration had intended.

The bloc scored again at the start of 1922 with enactment of a bill giving agriculture representation on the Federal Reserve Board. A top priority item, it reflected a conviction that the Federal Reserve system, then less than ten years old, had manipulated rediscount rates to the detriment of producers. Furthermore, an original reason for federating local farm bureaus was to give ''dirt farmers'' a seat on governmental and quasi-governmental boards at state and national levels. The bill was vigorously opposed by financial and other interests. Several influential eastern newspapers criticized President Harding, implying he had demonstrated weakness in signing the compromise measure, which also gave seats on the Federal Reserve Board to representatives of industry, commerce, and finance.

The Farm Bureau spokesmen asserted they were only interested in a fair deal for the long-neglected farmers, and Howard repeatedly stated that his organization was primarily concerned with the nation's welfare. The Harding administration, big business, and the Republican party felt threatened, however, especially when it seemed that only bloc legislation was being passed and when major bills, including those dealing with taxes and tariffs, were repeatedly stalled in committee because the rural interests wanted to change them. Eastern opinion makers were predictably alarmed at the unexpected domination of Congress by hitherto voiceless farmers. Failing to realize that the Farm Bureau had acted responsibly since its organization, they remembered the western agitation for free silver in the previous century, the Non-Partisan League's more recent socialistic laws in North Dakota, and a 1920 effort to form a Farmer-Labor Party. They feared that the government would be taken over by radical elements.

"The leaders of the Senate no longer lead," the *New York Times* gloomily observed on October 3, 1921. "They follow." Complaints were repeatedly voiced that Congress was passing laws for the benefit of one class. *Wallaces' Farmer* thought it humorous that eastern publications were alarmed at the display of agrarian power: "They denounce what they call class legislation. They decry legislation in the interest of a group. They seem to think that this is a criminal novelty in legislative chambers."

Howard, who went to Washington frequently but of necessity left most of the legislative situation in Silver's capable hands, made major speeches explaining the farm bloc's genesis and objectives. Especially he denied that the Farm Bureau was creating a class consciousness in America. That was a predominant theme when he addressed the Minnesota federation's convention at St. Paul on January 3, 1922:

Repeatedly have we said that there is but one interest in this country and that is the interest of the whole American people. Time and again we have asserted our interest in and dependence upon transportation lines and facilities, manufacturing establishments, distributive institutions as well as the American laborers and the consumer in general. We have called the attention of all classes of our citizenry to the fact that no one of us can prosper without all others also prospering. We have endeavored constantly to look across our own fence lines and to study the other man's problems and I want to assert plainly that the American

Farm Bureau Federation has not knowingly or wittingly and never shall advocate any policy which is not for the well-being of all our various interests.

The farmer's income creates the bank balances of the nation. If his prosperity were doubled or tripled, the prosperity of industry and commerce and transportation would be likewise enhanced. That fact is self-evident. Every thinking man admits it. How then, under Heaven, can that which would help bring prosperity to the whole people of the nation, through the building up of the prosperity of our basic producers, be termed class legislation? Is the farmer to continue to develop improved standards of living? Is he to educate his children and continue to send part of the brightest into the cities to become leaders of commerce and finance? Is his purchasing market to be of continuing importance in the trade channels of the world? Or is he to be reduced to serfdom and peasantry?

Denying that the farm bloc was playing politics, he said that its members were trying to correct economic maladjustments:

The bloc has to its credit practically all of the constructive legislation which has been passed during the last six months and none of it would have been enacted if party leaders had had their way. It is just as true that the questions interesting the bloc to date are vital to the nation as a whole.

In mid-February, Howard went to New York and told a luncheon meeting of the American Association of Advertising Agencies that for years preelection promises to farmers had been forgotten almost before the votes were counted. In the first six months of the bloc's existence, he said, more constructive agricultural legislation had been passed than in the ten preceding years.

The bloc might be bipartisan, but its activities became a political issue. Tom Heflin of Alabama in a Senate speech said Harding had lost no opportunity to denounce the bloc. William Jennings Bryan, the old Populist, took a predictable stand for the bloc. So did Norman Thomas, the durable Socialist. Otto H. Kahn, the New York financier who was Howard's friend, refused to be antagonistic to farmers and urged all Americans to work together. A succession of easterners made speeches and gave interviews pleading for solidarity. Business houses also expressed alarm that the nation might come under the economic domination of farmers to the detriment of business and financial interests. President Harding, whose leadership increasingly came under criticism, on several occasions asked that majority lines remain firm. During a plea for party solidarity at a Lincoln day dinner he inserted a rebuke to the farm bloc.

In another major achievement, in early 1922 the bloc pushed to enact the Capper-Volstead Act that legalized cooperative marketing by exempting farmer-owned cooperatives from antitrust prosecution. Under the Clayton Act of 1914, cooperatives formed on a stock basis were subject to challenge and many milk associations had been harassed by legal action. The broader definition in the new law held that the existence of a large-scale farm cooperative, with or without capital stock, was not a crime. Monopolistic situations were legalized providing there was no agreement to restrain trade or to increase prices unduly.

Howard's memoirs say the Capper-Volstead Act was passed by the Farm Bureau as a favor to Charles W. Holman and the National Dairy Council, which as a member of the National Board of Farm Organizations had worked for years to free its members from the threat of antitrust prosecution. The bill had been passed by both houses in the 1920–1921 lame duck session but was allowed to die because of nullifying amendments. It was making progress in the new session until Clifford Thorne, the Farm Bureau's transportation expert, interfered.

"Thorne was a whiz on freight rates but a little out of his level on other legislation," Howard recalled.

He was a lawyer and he picked several flaws in the bill just when Holman and his friends almost had it out of committee. They were very incensed because it looked like a delay in the passage of a bill that they thought was very important in their milk marketing work.

I think that was the only time I ever really interfered with a subordinate. I had to call Thorne off and let the bill go through exactly as the other fellows had drawn it and wanted it. We included it in our list of bills, but it wasn't our work or our bill. That will illustrate a little bit about our committee work. We did cooperate with the other fellows and it was Holman who called our attention to Thorne's testimony. We did claim credit because we made it possible for it to pass.

Early in 1922 the bloc had a new chairman. Kenyon, whose lifetime ambition had been the federal judiciary, resisted temptation in October when Harding offered him a judgeship in the northern Iowa district. Determined to break the power of the bloc, the president upped the ante and Kenyon on January 31, 1922, accepted appointment to the Circuit Court of Appeals, one notch below the United States Supreme Court. Disruption of the bloc was widely predicted.

In the immediate speculation about a successor, Howard's name was prominently mentioned at Des Moines for appointment to the Senate. In farm circles it seemed logical that the Farm Bureau president should step into Kenyon's role as bloc leader, even though he would be at the bottom of the seniority list and knew nothing about Senate rules and procedures. Reached at Columbus, Ohio, Howard said only that if the appointment were tendered he would submit the matter to his executive committee and abide by its decision. The next day an announcement from AFBF headquarters said he was not a candidate. Two weeks later C. A. Rawson of Des Moines was appointed senator by Governor Nate Kendall.

A Senate appointment would have been attractive to Howard, at least at first glance, but it would have stirred up complications. To rural people the Farm Bureau presidency was second only to the office held by President Harding. If Howard resigned, the AFBF would be subjected to turmoil during a change of command. Furthermore, an appointive Senate term would have lasted only a year. Smith W. Brookhart, a demagogic Republican who for several years played a controversial role in Iowa politics, already was attacking railroads and befriending voters as a prelude to his own election in a period of declining prices and, in a primary contest with Brookhart, Howard would have been a sure loser. Stump speeches were not his speciality and his intellectual integrity would not have permitted changes in position. The Farm Bureau did have a Senate candidate in the Iowa primary. Clifford Thorne resigned as general counsel to make the race and was beaten by Brookhart.

As bloc chairman, Senator Arthur Capper of Kansas succeeded Kenyon. Contemporaries said his leadership was weaker, but nevertheless the Senate continued to pass most of the bills that Silver considered important.

Silver's views prevailed again when Congress appropriated funds for a system of federally supported highways that at least would connect county seats and would be a precedent for farm-to-market road financing. The alternative would have been emphasis on expressways connecting large cities. It was one of several instances in which the Farm Bureau won approval of legislation for which the Grange had worked several years without success.

Because not all of its members could agree, the Kenyon-Capper farm bloc did not involve itself with the tariff issue, but with considerable overlapping of membership a farm tariff bloc of twenty-four Republicans was organized by Senator F. R. Gooding of Idaho. The issue was partisan, for on March 3, 1921, the last day of the previous Congress, President Wilson had vetoed an emergency bill that would have abolished the low rates of the Underwood tariff that had been in effect since 1913. Gooding's bloc, with the support of President Harding and a Joint Commission on Agricultural Inquiry, which studied farm relief under the chairmanship of Congressman Sydney Anderson of Minnesota, took an active role in having sharp increases in duties on wheat, corn, meat, wool, and sugar written into an emergency tariff law enacted June 7, 1921. Controversies over farm bloc bills and taxation delayed until September 1922 enactment of the permanent Fordney-McCumber tariff that the Harding administration pushed. The Senate Finance Committee repeatedly heeded the voice of the farmer more than that of the eastern establishment.

Tariffs had not been mentioned in the resolution Howard drafted at the 1919 convention, but the next year he asked state federations to study the problem. A policy of nondiscrimination, holding that farmers must be protected against foreign competition to the same extent as manufacturers, was agreed upon by national and state Farm Bureau officials during the conference in Washington in April 1921. At the same time, the AFBF recognized the difficulty of writing a tariff law that would be effective for surplus agricultural commodities.

As explained in the AFBF newsletter, surplus commodities such as cotton, wheat, corn, and vegetable oils must be sold abroad on the world markets. In those cases, a tariff would be helpful only in preventing temporary price fluctuations. The domestic market for corn, the newsletter pointed out, was not infrequently depressed by the arrival in some port of a cargo from Argentina. But the Farm Bureau did not want copra to be on the free list in competition with vegetable oils. The final conclusion was that farmers might lose as much from high tariffs as they did from low schedules.

"Any tariff so high as to prevent free exchange of commodities will defeat its own ends," Howard told the National Association of Manufacturers May 9, 1922, at a New York meeting. He described himself as a protectionist but he insisted that a tariff law must be flexible so that rates can be changed in emergency situations without prolonged hearings. "The agricultural interests of this country are not best served by tariff walls so high as to become artificial barriers," he said a week later in a speech before the United States Chamber of Commerce. "It is only as Europe can sell to us that she will be able to absorb our agricultural surpluses."

The farm bloc's batting average was sensational but not perfect. The Muscle Shoals appropriation was not passed and the guarantee clause of the Esch-Cummins bill was not repealed. Congress did not act on the question of reducing freight rates on agricultural products and the truth-in-fabrics legislation was still dormant, as were several other bills of lesser significance.

After two years, the farm bloc went out of existence. Most of the major legislation had been enacted, the political situation had changed, and Silver did not attempt to set up another bipartisan combination when the Sixty-eighth Congress convened in 1923. He concentrated his attention more and more on specific bills and had the support of bipartisan veterans of the Farm Bureau's first great demonstration of top-level influence.

The agreement that made possible enactment of the Packer and Stockyards Act was reached in Howard's private office in Chicago. There an old and troublesome problem that had been before Congress for years was solved in one afternoon by the presidents of the American Farm Bureau Federation and two of the nation's largest meat processing companies.

For years farm organizations agreed that the government should control the packing industry. Two congressional committees had conducted expensive hearings without conclusive results. The Federal Trade Commission had issued a voluminous report cited by economists and farm spokesmen when they demanded relief from unfair practices and monopolies, real or imaginary. Suggested remedies included government regulation and government control. The packers meanwhile were united and adamant in refusing to tolerate anything that would lead to government interference with their industry.

Howard's guidelines were resolutions adopted at two AFBF conventions. At the founding convention, the resolutions committee he chaired wrote a plank recommending regulations of all purveyors of foodstuffs, including packers, wholesale grocers, commission men, and all similar industries, in "such manner as will be just and fair to producers and consumers as well as to the industries." A typical statement of Howard's philosophy, it asked that action be taken in behalf of his membership—the consuming public would also benefit—while also pledging justice and fairness to the industries involved. The Farm Bureau wanted to be reasonable, and it did not indulge in bombast and demagoguery. The second resolution, adopted at the 1920 convention in Indianapolis, asked Congress for prompt enactment of legislation "necessary to bring under federal inspection, supervision and control all interstate agencies which prepare for consumption meat and vegetables."

the American Association of Meat Packers and then had several informal talks with its president, Thomas E. Wilson. Founder and head of a major packing company, he was one of the top breeders of Shorthorn cattle and had done as much as any man to advance 4-H club work.

At one session, Howard told Wilson that the AFBF was committed to federal regulation in a way that would be fair and just to producers, consumers, and packers alike. Afraid of governmental interference, Wilson said that the packing industry would close its plants if unfavorable legislation were to be enacted. Then or later, Howard did not doubt his sincerity.

For fourteen years, Wilson said, the industry had spent more than a million dollars a year in opposing antipacker legislation. That cost, both men agreed, did not come out of earnings but was an expense item that had the effect of reducing prices paid for live animals. The cost of lobbying was a needless waste. Wilson's main concern was that the industry in some cases needed both reorganization and refinancing but its executives could not make decisions so long as there was uncertainty about what Congress might do.

Howard sensed that a settlement might be possible. Chiefly, he wanted farmers to have a constant market for their livestock on a fair and open competitive basis. He frankly stated that the Farm Bureau stood for regulations that would prevent discrimination, assure open markets, and assure publicity regarding all transactions. He would be glad to talk to the packers at any time on that basis. Wilson took it under consideration.

A week later Wilson and J. Ogden Armour, another giant in the industry, came to the Farm Bureau headquarters. Howard called Coverdale into the meeting that lasted several hours. The two Farm Bureau resolutions were read at the start of a thorough discussion that ended with agreement on the outlines of what became the Packer and Stockyards Act. Wilson and Armour accepted legislation to assure open markets, prevention of discrimination, and open accounts both in the purchase of livestock and sale of by-products. It was agreed that in fairness the law must apply to stockyards and commission firms. Howard pledged that the Farm Bureau would not make additional demands and would resist any effort to have the government take over the industry.

In strict conformity with the agreement, details of a bill were worked out in the Washington office in conferences with several congressmen. When the bill came up for action, packer opposition was withdrawn. The Packer and Stockyards Act became law. The conference had solved in a half-day a problem that had baffled Congress for years. Although the law drew some criticism, no serious effort has been made to amend its fundamental principles.

Armour was dead by that time, but Wilson on December 16, 1927, said Howard's account of their conferences was "pretty much in keeping with the facts."

21

Personal Diplomacy

AS a specialist in private conferences with important men from other industries, Howard in late 1921 convinced officials of the Association of Railway Executives that, for the nation's good, they should not make it necessary for the American Farm Bureau Federation to begin another long and expensive freight rate hearing before the Interstate Commerce Commission. It took several weeks of his time, but the result was a voluntary 10 percent reduction in freight rates paid by farmers, effective at the start of 1922. In a decade of falling prices, the Farm Bureau estimated that the action, which was without precedent and for which Howard was primarily responsible, saved U.S. farmers $127 million per year.

After he retired, Howard believed that the freight rate reduction was his major personal accomplishment as Farm Bureau president. His second most important achievement, he believed, was the private agreement with Thomas E. Wilson and J. Ogden Armour that led to enactment of the Packer and Stockyards Act. The third, another case of a farmer meeting with millionaires on equal terms, was the dinner given by Otto H. Kahn at which a roomful of important New York executives listened to a recital of the troubles and hopes of Liberty Township farmers.

In the summer of 1921, the Farm Bureau was not satisfied with the reduction in livestock, hay, and grain rates granted by the commerce commission on evidence submitted by Clifford Thorne. Howard had decided there was little prospect for repeal of the Esch-Cummins Act's controversial guarantee clause, which was intended to compensate the carriers for higher wages ordered by the Railway Labor Board. Furthermore, he did not believe that its repeal would necessarily bring lower freight charges. While Thorne's transportation department began assembling evidence for new rate reduction petitions, Howard tried a new strategy. "I called personally on a number of railroad executives, urging upon them the seriousness of the farmers' condition and the part transportation had in the whole economic situation," he told the 1922 Iowa Farm Bureau convention. "I urged a general freight rate reduction as the quickest and most potent remedy." He did not leave a record of the men with whom he conferred. One apparently was President Charles H. Markham of the Illinois Central Railroad.

In testimony before the Interstate Commerce Commission, in speeches, and in private conferences, Howard's basic argument was that freight rates were higher than farmers could afford to pay, especially after commodity prices dropped drastically in 1920. Freight bills were an unavoidable expense, added to the cost of manufactured goods and deducted from payments for livestock and grain. When transportation rates were increased, the load was heaviest on producers of bulk commodities, such as grain, that had to be shipped long distances. When farm prices declined, the burden became unbearable. In some cases, the freight bills exceeded prices paid at terminal markets. He knew that a reduction in freight rates would not restore farm prosperity, but it would materially reduce a major expense.

His main supporters were Floyd R. Todd, vice-president of Deere and Company, and Sherman J. Lowell, master of the National Grange. In March Todd had attended a shippers' conference called in Chicago by the Farm Bureau and attended by men from twenty states whose markets had been curtailed by the economic situation. Later he arranged for the National Association of Manufacturers to call a meeting of officials of railroads, the Farm Bureau, and the Grange in New York on September 25. Lowell presided. Also present were representatives of manufacturing, mining, and shipping industries.

Howard and Todd argued that the farmers' plight was serious and "that only by remedying it could the entire national industrial situation, already getting worse, be alleviated." Railroad executives who feared bankruptcy were told that "we sympathized with them, but not more than we sympathized with the wives and children of thousands of farmers left destitute because of bad economc conditions for which high freight rates were in part responsible."

Negotiations were turned over to Howard, Todd, Lowell, and three men from the Association of Railway Executives: Howard Elliott, board chairman of the Hill lines; W. W. Atterbury, who became president of the Pennsylvania road; and W. B. Storey, president of the Santa Fe. The AFBF newsletter kept the membership informed:

In this small committee Mr. Howard took the position that the railroads should not continue any longer to enjoy special favors but that they must stand up on their own resources and responsibility, exactly as the manufacturer and farmer is compelled to do; that the present high prices are stifling all business; that recent reports indicate the railroads to be more prosperous than any other class of business in the nation; that railroad labor has recently taken a 12 percent reduction, and that the costs of steel and coal will in the future probably be decreased.

Therefore, he asked that the railroads immediately announce freight rate reductions for basic commodities, including agricultural products, building materials, coal, and iron ores, and that any further economies in the form of wage cuts be reflected in decreased rates until the general rate increase of 1920 was wiped out. Howard made it clear that the Farm Bureau did not like the Esch-Cummins guarantee clause and that it wanted authority in intrastate matters to be restored to state railroad commissions.

The executive committee of the Association of Railway Executives agreed to adopt Howard's wage-cut formula, but approval was withheld when presidents of all lines held a special meeting in Chicago. Immediately, Thorne filed with the Interstate Commerce Commission a petition asking that it order the rate reductions that Howard had asked them to make voluntarily. On the defensive, the railroads offered a compromise that Howard refused. He consulted with Thorne and advised the carriers that they should gracefully agree to a 10 percent reduction on all agricultural commodities not already reduced by that amount or more.

A month after the New York conference, the rail officials agreed that freight rates on agricultural products should be reduced 10 percent on January 1, 1922. The commerce commission promptly signed the order that put into effect the only general freight rate reduction of the 1920s. To make certain that individual farmers were benefiting from his diplomacy, Howard wrote to more than two hundred local elevators and shipping associations. In all cases the full reduction was reflected in price increases within three days. He was grateful, but the Farm Bureau president contended that the rate reductions were not sufficient. The railroads promised further conferences after they had replenished rolling stock and rebuilt roadbeds that had deteriorated during the war.

Previous reductions had cut $93 million from freight rates paid by farmers, so the Farm Bureau computed that total savings were $220 million during the Howard administration. They were obtained with the cooperation of the Grange, but no other farm organization tried to negotiate freight rate reductions. The results of the conferences could not have been obtained by congressional enactment or formal hearings. The magnitude of the achievement was acknowledged by *Traffic World*, which was quoted by Howard as saying:

It seems to have been a game of heads the farmers win and tails the railroads lose. The agricultural bloc seems to have the carriers just where it wants them—afraid to call ther souls their own. Let us hope that the American Farm Bureau Federation and Mr. Howard, its president, will not be too unreasonable or grasping and that in their newly acquired role as administrators of the tariff policies of the railroads they will not disregard utterly the rights of others.

In one quarter, Howard was wrongly accused of selling out the interests of farmers. At the end of 1921, the railroads asked for a second conference with Howard's group. At an informal meeting at the Racquet Club in Washington a number of observers were in the room. One was a Washington representative of the National Association of Manufacturers, who kept a record of the discussion under the heading of "minutes." A copy was obtained by Senator Robert M. LaFollette of Wisconsin, who charged in a Senate speech that changes in the Esch-Cummins Act had been discussed by the Farm Bureau at a secret meeting with officials of the Association of Railway Executives and the National Association of Manufacturers. At that meeting, the farmers had insisted upon repeal of the guarantee clause and asked that Congress restore former powers to state railroad regulatory commissions. Despite explanations by all parties, LaFollette never retracted his charges.

The Howard policies were deflationary, intended to cut the costs of all articles into which transportation figured. Payrolls, of course, were one of the costs and the farmer never has been sympathetic with the city man who joins unions, calls strikes, and obtains higher wages that are reflected in costs paid by rural people and other consumers. During the New York conference, Lowell had rejected a proposal that the farmers join an effort to convince the brotherhoods, which were threatening a strike, that railroad wages should be reduced. He saw no reason for taking sides in a labor dispute involving city men. Later, while putting pressure on the railroads, Howard played an antilabor role. To make possible the rate reduction the Farm Bureau president asked for, the Railway Labor Board gave permission for a 12½ percent wage reduction. When the brotherhoods announced they would strike, Howard kept in touch with Todd and Atterbury while they met with the contending parties. Simultaneously he issued a statement criticizing the brotherhoods. The unions, which generally were on the losing side of wage disputes in the 1920s, stayed on the job.

As indicated by the resolutions adopted at the 1919 convention, the Farm Bureau from its inception regarded the city laborer as a valued customer but wanted him to earn a full day's pay and not interfere with the marketing process. In July 1920, in a tense situation just before the Railway Labor Board granted a $500 million a year wage increase, Howard in a statement issued from the Washington office said that farmers would lose hundreds of thousands of dollars a day in a train tie-up.

In a 1922 strike of 400,000 shopmen, which protested cuts of the previous year, he announced that only immediate settlement would prevent heavy rural losses. At the same time he pointed out that the AFBF was opposed to government ownership. That strike was settled largely in favor of the carriers.

No one kept records, but Howard believed that in some seasons he slept in Pullman berths half his nights. His office was deluged with invitations to speak to audiences of city men who wanted to know more about the new agrarian movement with a strange name that had made a stir in governmental, business, and banking circles. Many had to be declined, but Howard believed that it was his duty to meet face to face with individuals and groups of many types. For a time he was a member of the Chicago No. 1 Rotary Club, but he could not regularly attend the weekly businessmen's luncheons. Quickly it became obvious that the Farm Bureau had no sympathy for the 1920 third party movement that was launched unsuccessfully by organized labor and given the name of Farmer-Labor party in hope of support from the Non-Partisan League in North Dakota. Frequently Howard went to Washington, sometimes on short notice, to hold strategy sessions, testify before congressional committees, and confer with cabinet officers. Contact with the rural membership was one of his duties and he could have occupied most of his time by going to state and county meetings, especially in states where new federations were being established or strengthened. In his first year he spoke at the South Dakota State Fair, participated in a New England conference, and aided membership drives in Pennsylvania and Nebraska. During the next two years his speaking tours took him into most of the states and before meetings of many national and regional organizations. Once on a vacation trip he got as far as the Wisconsin north woods before he was called back to the city. He did not play golf, but when he spoke at a conference of bankers at White Sulphur Springs he enjoyed some fresh air by acting as caddy for financiers with whom he was discussing intermediate credit problems.

Howard was above average as a public speaker but not a spell-binding orator. His standard speeches, both expository and explanatory, were carefully thought out and tailored to the audience. Without a prepared text, he could follow an outline with sentences that were logical, grammatical, well rounded, and varied in structure. When he was on familiar ground, explaining the Farm Bureau's antecedents and objectives, his speeches were examples of good language, perhaps unexciting and seldom humorous, but capable of holding an audience's attention. At least twice in extemporaneous addresses before annual Farm Bureau conventions he was inspired to a rapid-fire delivery that bordered on sermonizing. Sentence structure could be halting, however, when as a digression he injected new material into a speech on short notice. When the AFBF hired a publicity man or when a specialist wrote an important address, it was obvious that a ghostwritten speech was not vintage Howard.

As far as Howard was concerned, his best speech, entitled ''The Cadence of the Corn,'' was delivered at a Chicago Association of Commerce dinner on October 27, 1921. Also on the program were Chairman Eugene Meyer of the War Finance Corporation and former Agriculture Secretary E. T. Meredith. Both were able speakers, and for days the Farm Bureau president had pondered about what he should say. It was a time of depression, the gloom affecting both business and agriculture. The night before the dinner he was on a train. About 2:00 A.M. he looked out the Pullman window and noticed that the sky was fairly bright. When he again pulled up the shade it was quite dark. He recalled many seasons of corn picking and the outline of a speech came to him. At the banquet, Howard was an optimist when he was called to the rostrum:

Through my long years of experience on the farm, I have come to consider this season the most charming of the year. It's the time of the shortening day and the lengthening night. I know full well what it is to be awakened by the flapping of the blind, the crow of the rooster, or the sighing of the wind in the trees outside the window and to note that it is darker than it was an hour or two before or when I went to bed. I cannot see my hand before me. It is the darkest hour of the night. Instantly I know that that darkest hour is the time when I should arise and go to work.

It is the night's darkest hour when the farmer gets up. He takes his lantern and goes to the barn. He feeds his stock. He milks his cows. He curries and harnesses his team. He goes to the house and eats breakfast, all before there is yet the first rosy hint of dawn in the East.

Breakfast over, the farmer hitches his team to the wagon and rattles off down the hill, across the bridge, and up the road to the cornfield. He pauses for it to get a little lighter; he cannot yet see the row. And while he is putting his sideboard over and getting off his coat he listens. From every direction there comes the sound of other corn wagons going to other corn fields. Soon there reaches his ears the rhythmic beat of the ears against the sideboards—the cadence of the corn, the corn which is converted into the gold and silver of commerce and manufacturing and industry. Where in all the world is there another song to equal it? Before noon the farmer brings in his load, and another at night.

We want to get these chores done and our breakfast over, for morning is close at hand. Let's put on an extra sideboard and grease up the wagon, for we have the biggest job we ever had ahead of us in America. It is going to take the energy and faith of the American businessman to put it over. But we have one common interest—service to the whole people.

As a farmer of this country, I ask you businessmen to join us in the procession toward national prosperity.

On no other occasion was the applause he received so loud and long. Andrew Stevenson, Jr., who was a high school boy when he heard the speech, remembered sixty years later that the speaker's delivery reproduced the rhythm of ears of corn bouncing off the sideboards of a wagon.

Witticisms and humorous rejoinders were not the Howard style. He never tried to remember stories, in dialect or otherwise, and he never used them in speeches. Occasional one-liners or understatements were appreciated by audiences. Now and then in a debate situation he bested an opponent with a spontaneous response that surprised the speaker as much as anyone in the room.

At one period many of his speeches argued that the Federal Reserve Board had caused rural distress in 1920 by suddenly increasing rediscount rates. He was on the popular side with at least half of the audience when he used that theme extemporaneously before an audience of business men and farmers in Spokane. When he finished, the program was interrupted for a rebuttal by a stranger who had a resonant voice, a commanding stage presence, and a rapid-fire repertoire of facts and figures. Howard was thoroughly deflated before the stranger closed his speech with this statement: "I understand Mr. Howard is a fair-minded man and I am going to ask him if, in the light of what I have said, he will not come again to the platform and say that the Federal Reserve has been as fair to the farmer as to any other industry?" Howard's memoirs contain this account of his dilemma:

I was completely licked and I knew it. The spotlight was on me, and I had no time to prepare an answer to his sophistries. At best a slow thinker, I am my worst before an audience. When a fellow is licked, about all he can do is own up. So I thanked him for his illuminating address which had showed me the error of my ways and acknowledged that, from what he had said, it did appear that the Federal Reserve had been eminently fair and helpful to the farmer.

I thought I was finished when something within me clicked. I felt it from foot to head. What it was I never knew, but I went on scarcely knowing what I was doing. I said:

"It reminds me of the farmer in Nebraska who made rabbit sausage. His friends asked him if it was pure rabbit meat. "No," he said. "It is part horse. Fifty-fifty. One rabbit, one horse."

The audience broke up and the stranger disappeared. Howard could not recall that he had ever heard the story and never understood by what mental process he had told it in a moment of crisis. Also, he thought it was an illogical joke that proved nothing. The stranger, he was told, was an official of the San Francisco Federal Reserve Bank. When Howard came back to Spokane a year or so later, a man in the hotel lobby inquired about the farmer who made rabbit sausage.

On a few occasions, Howard was under pressure when he testified before unfriendly congressional committees, but transcripts show he was tenacious in adhering to the Farm Bureau position. His testimony was in clear and grammatical sentences that were never obtuse and seldom lengthy. If he gave ground, it was a slow retreat that kept out of corners and allowed maneuvering room. If circumstances required an answer that had strategic weaknesses, he made it calmly and briefly, without advertising the fact that he might be in potential trouble. He did not filibuster; he made the interrogator carry the burden of the attack and he kept his temper.

22

Voluntary Retirement

HOWARD retired voluntarily as president of the American Farm Bureau Federation. After his surprise election at the 1919 founding convention in Chicago, he had been returned to office by acclamation in Indianapolis at the end of 1920 and in Atlanta in 1921. He had wanted to retire at Atlanta, where he told the delegates it would be his last election. That determination was repeated within a few weeks before two state conventions and at the end of October in a letter to executive committeemen, thus giving advance warning that a change of command would take place at the four-day convention scheduled to open December 11, 1922, in the Sherman Hotel in Chicago.

Howard wanted to limit his tenure to three years for two reasons: "First, I stayed a year longer than I said I would when I went into the work and I felt someone else could probably carry it on better than I. The second reason, and the principal one, was that I was very rapidly becoming physically unfit."

The strain of long hours, heavy responsibilities, and almost continual travel had taken a physical toll. Several times fatigue and minor illnesses had forced him to cancel speeches and miss conferences. During the second quarter of 1922, for example, he addressed eighteen meetings but cancelled three others because of illness.

As a result of his personal contribution, he was confident that the national federation had been established on solid foundations and that rural areas at last had a coast-to-coast organization that would be permanent. To him the cause was more important than the man and he had no intention of imitating the self-perpetuating dynasties that witnessed the reelection year after year of the top officials of some of the Farm Bureau's competitors. Having risen suddenly from Liberty Township obscurity, he believed that a vast pool of leadership talent existed among county farm bureau members. Howard did not believe that he was ordained to grow old in the national presidency.

185

His last year began with a salary cut. Membership campaigns had been thwarted by the rural depression and economizing again was in order after the Atlanta convention. As part of a general retrenchment, Howard volunteered for a 16.6 percent reduction to $12,500 a year. On the new scale, Coverdale and Silver were paid $10,000 each. For 1922 the executive committee budgeted $224,000, plus another $72,000 that could be spent if the money came in. Nine state federations had been added during the year, and Coverdale's report said forty-six states had Farm Bureau federations "with a total membership, with the water squeezed out, of 772,634." For the 1922 fiscal year the AFBF's total income was $248,140. The annual audit showed a bank balance of $979.25 on October 31, 1922.

The shortage of money made it impossible to organize a women's department of the national federation. At the Indianapolis convention in 1920, two women were among the speakers for the first time—Mrs. John W. Ketcham of Michigan and Mrs. Charles W. Sewell of Indiana. The next year Howard appointed a women's committee headed by Vera B. Schuttler of Missouri to widen the scope of Farm Bureau work. Other members were listed as Mrs. Ketcham, Mrs. W. G. Jamison of Colorado, Mrs. Izetta J. Brown of West Virginia, and Mrs. A. E. Brigden of New York. Not until 1927 did the AFBF establish a home and community department.

On June 30, 1922, the Farm Bureau movement celebrated its tenth anniversary in DeKalb County, Illinois, in the midwestern center of its greatest strength, rather than in Broome County, New York, where it was founded. A presidential speech and a pageant emphasized the importance of the rural home and family as the foundation for the unparalleled growth, strength, and promise of the young organization. Howard emphasized that the basic unit is the county Farm Bureau and said that the federation's programs are educational and social as well as economic. During his final year in office he made that point repeatedly.

The regional differences over the relative importance of economic and educational programs continued to cause trouble. The AFBF's cooperative marketing department was still under the president's personal supervision and he and Coverdale worked with midwestern state presidents in an effort to provide members and business for the U.S. Grain Growers. Howard and Coverdale, however, did not want the Farm Bureau to become directly involved in cooperative marketing to the extent that it would become the federation's major activity. They wanted a balance between economic and educational programs and they had private questions about a trend in some state federations toward commercial activities. Under their leadership, Yankees, southerners, and westerners had backed midwesterners in the drive to reform the established methods of marketing grain and livestock. Now Howard did not want the pendulum to swing too far, and the Iowan found himself in the position of being the champion of men from outside the Corn Belt.

"The American Farm Bureau Federation is not and never will be a marketing organization," Howard told the Iowa federation's convention in Des Moines on January 10, 1922. "Its business or mission is largely promotional and educational. We have always taken the position and still hold that our mission toward cooperative associations . . . is one of helpfulness and not domination."

In the Des Moines speech, he reviewed the farm bloc's achievements in pushing legislation through Congress and told of freight rate reductions that were the result of his conferences with railroad presidents. He also responded—with a complete denial—to charges then being made by Senator LaFollette of Wisconsin that he had betrayed the interests of agriculture by attending a meeting at which the guarantee clause of the Esch-Cummins Act was a secondary issue. He noted that he had been warned against meeting with railroad officials, packers, bankers, and other representatives of big business. He said:

My reply has always been that I am the representative of the biggest interest in America—American agriculture—and that it is the duty of those who represent, through their various organizations, the farmers of America to sit across the table with any and every other interest where questions of large moment are discussed.

He reviewed the work of the marketing committees established by the Farm Bureau and continued:

Opposition is being strenuously made from two sources—one from already firmly entrenched and established distributive agencies with whose profits cooperation will interfere. More money has been raised to defeat this work than the American Farm Bureau Federation has yet spent in all its activities. The second line of objection is internal. It comes in the main not from the farmers but from the leaders of farmers' movements who too often are more interested in their jobs than in the welfare of the farmers themselves.

That my own skirts may be clear and that the American Farm Bureau Federation may never be accused of building up a self-perpetuating or a political machine, I am resolved to return at the earliest moment to the ranks and carry out the aspirations of my life up in Marshall County.

After his retirement, Howard called "absolutely untrue" statements that he had supported passage of the Esch-Cummins law's guarantee clause, unpopular with farmers, providing that the freight rate structure should keep postwar railroads from operating in the red. He contended:

The American Farm Bureau Federation was not in existence until after the Esch-Cummins Act had been written. The act was passed within two months of our organization meeting. Hence to have taken any action with no organization built up and with no previous study of the bill would have been an impossibility. Neither did I approve or disapprove, personally or otherwise, the act before its passage except to say that it was my opinion that the farmers would not stand for the so-called guarantee clause. Any statement to the contrary is absolutely untrue. Following the passage of the act I had repeatedly condemned the guarantee clause and publicly and privately said that the whole act ought to be repealed and rewritten. I have made these recommendations at two annual meetings of the American Farm Bureau Federation.

Howard added that he had not stood for repeal of section 15(A) of the Esch-Cummins Act, in its entirety, because seventeen of its eighteen clauses were commendable and desirable. He added:

I stand exactly where I have always stood. All guarantee clauses should be removed from the Transportation Act of 1920 and never allowed in another transportation act or any other act of Congress. In order to do this it is better to repeal and rewrite the whole measure than to repeal 15(A), thus nullifying a number of beneficial provisions.

Thirteen years after he resigned as cashier of the Providence State Bank, Howard was invited to address a convention of the American Bankers Association at White Sulphur Springs, West Virginia, on May 10, 1922. In an hour-long speech and in three days of private talks, he lined up support for intermediate credit legislation that Gray Silver and the farm bloc were pushing toward enactment at Washington.

He urged that Congress establish a group of specialized banks so that farmers could borrow money at reasonable interest rates for periods from six months to three years. The Federal Land Banks created in 1916 had made excellent progress in the long-term financing of farm mortgages, and local country banks provided adequate ninety-day loans, but Howard complained that another source of credits was needed. From his own experience he told about borrowing money to buy feeder cattle that would not be ready for market until long after his note had matured at the bank, which had to keep its assets liquid. Other examples were the financing of crops kept in storage because of unfavorable market conditions and credit for the construction of buildings and other facilities necessary for more efficient production. By 1922 Howard was an experienced lobbyist. To gain support of the bankers, who were alarmed at the growing multiplicity of government agencies and institutions, he agreed that the Federal Intermediate Credit banks should be under the jurisdiction of the Federal Farm Loan Board:

I spent three days visiting with these men around the hotel lobbies and even went out on the golf course and caddied for some of them. The result was that some of them gave open support to the Intermediate Credit Act which became a law the next year. Without this support it would have failed. The growth of the intermediate credit banks was, as anticipated, slow at first, yet within three years their assets had passed above the 100 million dollar mark and have rapidly increased since then. To facilitate their handling of business there have been added such affiliated organizations as the Production Credit banks and Banks for Cooperatives.

I have always considered those three days at White Sulphur Springs well spent.

Howard participated in numerous meetings with Federal Land Bank officials and whenever possible was joined by Coverdale. Their basic stand was that the farmer needed increased credit, but always of sufficient duration to enable the note to be paid off at maturity.

The future of the American merchant marine became a controversial issue among midwestern farmers in the spring of 1922. During the war the government had spent $3.2 billion to build 1,700 steel cargo ships with a 12-million-ton capacity. So that the United States Shipping Board could keep some of the vessels in operation, President Harding proposed a subsidy and sought the support of the Farm Bureau. Howard replied that he had no opinion on the question but would have it investigated by the federation's staff. The most respected available economists were consulted and conferences held with the Chicago Association of Commerce and the National Association of Implement and Vehicle Manufacturers. Howard notified the president:

While the American Farm Bureau Federation is opposed to any subsidy on principle, we realize the necessity of developing an American merchant marine as a naval auxiliary and as an agent in the development of foreign trade. We approve aid temporarily until our flag can be established on the high seas, but no longer. Subsidies like tariffs should be flexible and not continuous. If a subsidy be supported on naval grounds it is essential that merchant ships be available and used for training of naval reserves.

Testifying before a joint hearing of the Senate Commerce and House Merchant Marine and Fisheries committees, Howard refused to discuss specific bills but said that a merchant marine was needed, that farmers were vitally interested in foreign trade, and that farm products were the largest item in balancing exports against imports. He noted:

The United States is no longer a debtor but a creditor nation and must seek the business. Other nations will be competing in Europe where we market our goods and we must be prepared to put our products into the European market promptly and cheaply; transportation, the servant of business, must be available when needed, for it will be available only if we control the ships; the service afforded by foreign-owned vessels is second rate, hampers our exports, and makes impossible proper increase of our overseas business.

The AFBF newsletter listed twelve reasons for supporting the subsidy. The first was that the United States as an agricultural nation must have access to world markets and that the farmer pays the freight, whether by rail or water. Another was that, by enabling independent operation of ships, the subsidy would protect against Wall Street domination. "The ship subsidy is like a tariff," Howard said at the next meeting of the executive committee. "It is just as reasonable to protect the carrier of the goods as it is the manufacturer."

The committee took no action. Critics of the Howard administration, led by Dante Pierce of the *Iowa Homestead*, complained that the AFBF was more interested in doing favors for shipowners than it was in helping Corn Belt farmers. Smith W. Brookhart, the new senator from Iowa, was instrumental in blocking action in Washington. Farm Bureau referenda in the Midwest showed heavy majorities against the subsidy.

Howard stood by his convictions. In the next year or so in a personal letter he wrote:

I merely stood by the American Farm Bureau Federation organization and gladly bore the brunt of the criticism. The lies that were told and misrepresentations made would fill many volumes. I am still for the American merchant marine. I still think that the passage of the ship subsidy bill would have saved the taxpayers of this country many million dollars. I have been in New York a number of times since and it is very interesting indeed to note that the international bankers and traders of Wall Street are tickled to death over the defeat of the ship subsidy. It is the first time I have ever known the farmer and the most vicious of the Wall Street crowd to work in complete harmony, which they certainly did do.

George N. Peek, president of the Moline Plow Company, and Hugh S. Johnson, his counsel and assistant general manager, sought Farm Bureau support as soon as they began promoting a two-price formula for restoration of rural prosperity. Howard and Coverdale sympathized with their objectives but were not impressed with the practicality of the Peek-Johnson "equality for agriculture" theories that evolved into the McNary-Haugen equalization fee proposal for exportation of crop surpluses while maintaining high domestic prices. In May, a few days after Peek and Johnson came to the Farm Bureau office, Howard went with them to Washington for a conference with Henry C. Wallace and Henry C. Taylor, head of the Department of Agriculture's division of economics. With White House permission, Wallace later explored the plan at a small meeting attended by Charles G. Dawes, Chicago bank president; Otto H. Kahn, New York financier; Julius H. Barnes of Baltimore and Frederick Wells of Minneapolis, both grain men; and Judson C. Welliver of the White House staff. Howard and Silver, the only farm organization men present, did not commit themselves when Peek and Johnson argued for their two-price plan.

Three years later, the American Farm Bureau Federation's top priority was a series of McNary-Haugen bills that embodied the Peek-Johnson exporting theory. Howard and Coverdale, who never endorsed it, in 1922 were still hopeful that cooperative marketing could improve grain and livestock prices. They doubted that the equalization fee would work with cotton, a large part of which was exported, and they did not see how it would solve problems of dairying and specialized crops.

While economists and public officials debated what could be done to improve farm prices and markets, Howard's attention was diverted to economic history. In the spring of 1922 he asked the Department of Agriculture for extra copies of a mimeographed circular that was later published as "Food Control during Forty-six Centuries—A Contribution to the History of Price Fixing." Mary G. Lacy, librarian of the Bureau of Agricultural Economics, had presented it as an address on March 16 before the Agricultural History Society of Washington. Her study of governmental efforts to control food supplies began with Egypt in 2830 B.C. and in succession dealt with China, Athens, Rome, Great Britain, Belgium, India, colonial America, and France. She found that the results were astonishingly uniform and concluded that in the attempts of government to ease the burdens of the public by setting artificial limits on high prices, "the people are not relieved but only exchange one set of ills for another which is greater."

The Lacy speech, which Howard had read before he went to Washington with Peek and Johnson, had a profound effect on his thinking. Since it dealt with governmental efforts to help consumers when food was scarce and prices high, it was not directly applicable to the depressed situation of the early 1920s. It did raise questions, however, since a corollary would be that governmental efforts to raise prices also would be suspect. In the weekly newsletter, the federation's economists were contributing columns of statistics and miscellaneous information, and the Farm Bureau president was getting an education in a field he had not studied at college. One lesson was that the economic forces that affect the United States are worldwide and complex. Nevertheless there were fundamentals, and Howard remembered what he had been taught in the 1890s by his nonpopulist father, who had faith in the United States but not in nostrums advanced in political campaigns. There had been a partial turnover in membership of the executive committee, but the holdovers from the original group had never been inclined to be stampeded out of conservative positions and John Coverdale, for one, doubted that Congress could legislate rural prosperity. Howard made a point of reading the heavy incoming mail that kept him informed about membership sentiment and included theories about how the price situation could be corrected. He did not close his mind to new ideas, and he felt duty bound to investigate any proposal that might have merit. Therefore he arranged for the proponents of "equality for agriculture" to obtain a hearing at the Department of Agriculture, but he withheld a personal endorsement.

Inside the Farm Bureau and at the top levels of federal government, the downturn in commodity prices was still regarded as part of an old-style business cycle that in time would be reversed, rather than a major economic dislocation that grew out of the war and had some of its roots in Europe. The situation was thoroughly studied by a congressional Joint Commission on Agricultural Inquiry, which in early 1922 issued a series of recommendations that were primarily refinements and extensions of Farm Bureau and farm bloc proposals.

While Senator Kenyon was farm bloc chairman, the Harding administration on January 23, 1922, convened a five-day National Agricultural Conference that gave attention to rural complaints. Sixty men from Farm Bureau ranks were among the 300 delegates. Recommendations made by President Harding in the opening speech included part of the Farm Bureau program and several noncontroversial subjects. He also made an extemporaneous and unfavorable reference to bloc interference with national concerns. The conference's final report praised the farm bloc's stand and declared that emergency economic measures were needed. Howard served as chairman of the conference's waterways committee. For diplomatic reasons, since White House goodwill was important to the legislative program, after the conference he commended Harding for his interest in rural affairs.

As the rural depression dragged on, Howard was under constant pressure to have the Farm Bureau do something about the economic situation. At the same time his heavy administrative work load, coupled with his inability to find a sensible solution, added further stress to his already complicated physical condition. Something had to be done and the former schoolteacher invited fifty business leaders, mostly Chicagoans, to a luncheon in October. His gloomy report on the financial plight of their rural customers was seconded by Alexander Legge, president of International Harvester Company, who said that the situation could be improved by organization of cooperative marketing reforms. Officials of the American Bankers' Association and the United States Chamber of Commerce also offered support and sympathy. Thomas E. Wilson, the meat packer, held hope for a remedy through economic rather than legislative channels. On his motion, a committee of five was appointed to see that city men understood the situation.

When he presided over the executive committee for the last time, Howard told the members that the Farm Bureau was trying to do too many things. He didn't mention cooperative marketing and other economic involvements, but he wanted the committee and the forthcoming convention to limit rather than expand its work in the next year. He made it clear that the organization must not deviate from its original community and county activities. He held to the Yankee concept that educational work had a major place in Farm Bureau programs and indicated disapproval of the efforts of some Corn Belt delegates to involve the federation directly in marketing.

Clifford V. Gregory in the columns of *Prairie Farmer* gave the fullest and apparently fairest account of backstage activities at the 1922 convention. His analysis of Farm Bureau politics, contained in a "John Turnipseed" column, accepted Howard's intention to retire and said that Bradfute was "a bit too conservative to suit the farmers who elected Brookhart, Shipstead and Frazier" to the United States Senate. Gray Silver, popular as a result of farm bloc successes, would not take the presidency but might accept the job of vice-president. Iowa had "started a nice little boom" for E. H. Cunningham. Illinois, which "gave much credit to Howard's leadership," supported its president, Howard Leonard. Other possible candidates were W. S. Hill of South Dakota, John Orr of Texas, and C. W. Hunt of Iowa. W. H. Walker of California, a three-year veteran of the AFBF executive committee, was listed as a dark horse, but *Prairie Farmer* said the darkest horse was former Governor Frank O. Lowden of Illinois.

Under the Turnipseed by-line Gregory said in the issue of December 9, 1922, that Howard probably "is slated for the dirt farmer appointment to the Federal Reserve Board, a position he would find very attractive." Gregory continued:

Jim has made a pretty good president, everything considered. Leading the embattled farmers to victory is a big job and the victory has to be won a trench at a time. Jim has succeeded in convincing the business interests that farmers don't wear horns and that they are not organizing to put a depth bomb under the Statue of Liberty. Opinions may differ as to the value of a friendly attitude on the part of businessmen toward agriculture, but for my part I'd a good deal rather have them for me than against me.

The column then discussed the difficulty, if not impossibility, of satisfying Farm Bureau members in the period of economic deflation:

They don't know what the federation could have done to prevent the calamity, but they think it should have done something. They don't know what it can do now, but believe if it is any good at all it ought to be able to do something. They want aggressive action. They think there has been too much watchful waiting. They would rather have the federation do the wrong thing than not do anything at all. . . . Very likely they are expecting too much from a new organization. But the important thing is that they expect it. . . . Plans for more educational and community development on the part of the federation leave them cold.

Howard had been ill for two weeks before the convention and his annual address was extemporaneous. It also was confident and wide-ranging. Because of shortages of funds, staff, and time, the federation hadn't achieved all of its 1922 goals. Howard warned against expansion into new fields, which by inference meant that the AFBF should not become directly involved in the management of marketing cooperatives. Specifically, he said that Farm Bureau membership could be increased by concentrating on home and community programs. He said that the transportation system was a national economic problem that would take years to work out. The future work of the farm bloc, he advised, should be not so much in the passage of legislation as in the defeat of measures that are not economically sound. He called Silver one of the great men of America. Expounding free enterprise views, he was confident of the future and incidentally certain that the nation would never have a Farmer-Labor party. Personally, he was for prohibition, which he credited with increasing farm markets, and he deplored the lack of law observance that came with it. Before he closed, he came back to the subject of the federation's priorities. He said he was confident the Farm Bureau would be permanent, "anchored to the farm home and to our best American institutions. I have the utmost faith in it because it is more than an economic movement.

He was supported by Coverdale, whose 100-page annual report pointedly noted that "organizations directed toward economic wrongs fade as soon as the wrongs disappear." The secretary advocated that the federation's chief activities should be research and education, accompanied by some attention to legislation, transportation, and marketing.

There was nothing provincial about the opening day's program. Georges Clemenceau, the "tiger of France" and one of the great figures in postwar Europe, made a plea for an international outlook and said that farmers suffer most from a policy of isolation. Clemenceau, who had pleaded the cause of his country before eastern audiences, had delayed his return voyage until he could address the Farm Bureau convention.

Another speaker was Bernard M. Baruch, the New York financier and economist who was a friend of Howard's and who had been instrumental in arranging for Clemenceau's appearance. He received close attention when he proposed that the volume of rural credits be increased by establishing a warehouse certificate system tied to a new finance corporation.

During and since the war Baruch had been an advisor to governmental officials and had been one of the guests at the dinner given for Howard in Otto II. Kahn's Fifth Avenue mansion. Baruch made an intensive study of farm financing and was consulted by the Farm Bureau on several topics, including the organizational difficulties of the U.S. Grain Growers. In a letter to Howard in early January 1923, he said: "My connections with agricultural matters have been a continual source of pleasure and interest. And my work was made easier and my interest increased by my contact with you. The movement was fortunate in having a man of your character and ability as its leader, particularly in the trying times of its beginning." A week later, in a letter discussing the Clemenceau speech, Baruch told the retired Farm Bureau president: "There is no man with whom I have come in contact who has grown so much in my respect and estimation as you have. You are sincere in your purpose and courageous in expressing it."

Howard's refusal to run for a fourth term was well advertised. At the Atlanta convention in 1921, when against his personal wishes he stood for reelection, he told David M. Odaffer of Ohio that in a year he hoped to be succeeded by Bradfute. Here is Howard's analysis of the situation at the convention:

A great many people came to me asking me to withdraw the statement and stand for re-election. I persistently refused, stating that I had my full share of honor, that my health would not permit the strenuous work and that the only reason for changing my view would be the necessity or extremity on the part of the AFBF.

In spite of all this, the agitation for me continued. There were a number of aspirants for the office. Mr. Odaffer told me early in the convention that if I desired another year I would have Ohio's support in spite of my previous year's statement favoring Mr. Bradfute. Thirty minutes before the election session convened word came to me that a majority of all delegates were assembled in one room of the hotel, had pledged me their vote and requested that I stand for reelection. I positively declined, knowing at the time that Mr. Bradfute would be elected if I did not get into the race myself. It is interesting to note that the Ohio delegation and two other middle west states which were my hearty supporters were not included in the majority pledged to me. Intimations were given me that if I had accepted no other candidate would be named. I think such would have been the case because Mr. Bradfute's strength was my strength and none was named against him.

For four days, while state workers told about their community and membership campaigns, there was grumbling on the sidelines that not enough time had been allocated for debating resolutions and discussing new directions. At a poorly attended session at a late hour, the resolutions committee adopted a ship subsidy plank that repudiated Howard's position. *Prairie Farmer* reported that midwestern advocates of economic programs had lined up enough votes to elect E. H. Cunningham of Iowa as the new AFBF president.

On the final afternoon, Howard's farewell speech chided delegates who, beginning at the Indianapolis convention two years earlier, had engaged in wire-pulling and held late night caucuses.

"The American Farm Bureau is big enough for the office to seek the man, and no self-seeker ought ever be elected," he said. "He ought to be disqualified."

The short speech, increasingly interrupted by applause, closed with appreciation for the honors he had received and with a declaration that he did not know what he would do in the future. He had received many offers of employment and in advance he had rejected those that he considered antagonistic to agriculture.

"No man is ever going to accuse me [applause] of going back on the man whose hands are on the same plow handle with mine," he concluded. "I only hope to be in that place of service where I can accomplish the most in a broad way for my fellow man, and I ask your heartfelt continuing prayers." The official transcript then showed "prolonged applause and three cheers and a tiger given for President Howard."

He had the convention under control and, as the cheering began to subside, he pointed his gavel at one of the old guardsmen, E. B. Cornwall of Vermont, whom he had known since Ithaca. "Is it time to elect a president?" Cornwall asked. "Ebby" Cornwall wasn't a typical Yankee farmer. The son of a Princeton chemistry professor, he had gone to a New England preparatory school, had been graduated from Princeton and a law school, and had clerked briefly for a New York City law firm before he took up a new occupation as a farmhand in Vermont. He owned 170 acres near Middlebury, sold eggs, lambs, and hay for a cash income, practiced some law on the side, and still served as the president of the state Farm Bureau he had helped organize. In later years he would be a part-time college professor, a tennis coach, and a member of state commissions as well as the operator of his farm, with the help of a hired man. At the moment he was thinking of what had been achieved since Ithaca and of the many families who hoped that the work would go forward on a broad scale. "I won't take but a minute," he began. "Farm Bureau members, I wish I had the privilege of renominating Jim Howard, the First Farmer of the land."

Applause again swept the hall. Against his own wishes, because Jim Howard has asked him to and because he did not want the Farm Bureau to deemphasize its educational work, Cornwall quickly put Bradfute's name in nomination as the logical successor. Attention switched to the South and two Texans seconded the nomination. The western states were on the bandwagon, knowing that W. H. Walker of California, a member of the original executive committee, would become vice-president. Cunningham gracefully moved that the nominations be closed, and by acclamation the convention passed the presidency from Howard to Bradfute.

There would be difficult times ahead, but the American Farm Bureau Federation would continue to be a national organization having a broad base and a wide program of activity.

For the rest of his life Jim Howard would have the satisfaction of knowing that the job he had not wanted had been well done. As he phrased it, "I always felt that I did the job better than any reasonable person had a right to expect."

23

The Exit of Aaron Sapiro

D U R I N G the first year of Oscar E. Bradfute's presidency, the American Farm Bureau Federation survived a crisis generated by the ambitious Aaron Sapiro, to whom only cooperative marketing was important. Sapiro's protagonist was John W. Coverdale, who lost his position as secretary for five days but became the hero of the 1923 annual convention.

Bradfute, an able administrator for whom Howard was a chief adviser, was handicapped by a constitutional flaw that called for the annual election of the officers and the executive committee. In the interest of stability and continuity, it was corrected by an amendment for two-year overlapping terms, but beginning at Indianapolis in 1920, the early conventions saw the gradual replacement of most of the veterans who had participated in the debates and decisions that had achieved unity behind broad-based programs that could be supported by men from all regions. By 1923 two-thirds of the committee were new members whose backgrounds were limited and whose support was cultivated by Sapiro in his effort to dominate the American Farm Bureau.

The San Francisco attorney's personal bandwagon became crowded. His home base was on the Pacific coast and in the Midwest he had the strong backing not only of the Illinois Agricultural Association but also of the Indiana Farm Bureau, where William H. Settle had replaced the conservative John G. Brown as state president. As a result of preliminary success in setting up cotton and tobacco cooperatives, Sapiro had partisans among southern committeemen. He helped organize the National Council of Farmers' Marketing Associations, a potential competitor of the Farm Bureau. He was personally acquainted with eastern financiers and government officials. Influential friends included Robert W. Bingham, publisher of the *Louisville Courier-Journal*, who applauded Sapiro for a twin success—which turned out to be temporary—in setting up cooperatives among burley and dark leaf tobacco growers. Another admirer was Frank O. Lowden, who three years earlier had been governor of Illinois and a candidate for the Republican presidential nomination. A successful Chicago attorney, Lowden believed in cooperation and devoted much of his time to the study and advocacy of steps to restore rural prosperity. He owned a large farm in northern Illinois and a cotton plantation in Arkansas. Among other rural credentials, he was president of the Holstein-Friesian Association of America.

By autumn Sapiro had the AFBF executive committee under control. His backers forced the appointment of Walton Peteet, secretary of the Texas Farm Bureau, as director of the cooperative marketing department. Sapiro quickly moved in as Peteet's legal adviser. He finally had become an official part of the Farm Bureau organization, but he was not loyal to the federation's policy that wheat should be marketed through the U.S. Grain Growers. Soon he was ambidexterously helping the National Wheat Growers Advisory Committee, a new organization of which Lowden was chairman, in an effort to encourage Sapiro-type marketing pools in each of the grain belt states. The advisory committee, organized by Bingham and other city men, hoped that its membership campaigns would be more successful than the Farm Bureau's had been with the Grain Growers. Active in the movement were Peteet, Sapiro, and Settle. Conspicuously absent were Bradfute and Coverdale.

Coverdale, who did not like Sapiro, believed that the Farm Bureau was spending too much time and money on cooperatives and that it should concentrate on "a well-balanced program that renders service not only to marketing but to legislation, organization, transportation, research and community development." He was the chief obstacle in the path of the Sapiro faction on the executive committee. As a result, he lost his job. At the old committee's last meeting before the 1923 convention, eight of the twelve members of the committee voted to discharge him, an action they soon regretted.

As delegates arrived, Chiciago newspapers printed Coverdale's claim that his dismissal was part of an effort by Sapiro and Lowden to elect the former governor to the presidency of the American Farm Bureau Federation. "I opposed their desire to make the organization a strictly marketing enterprise, whereas I stood for a balanced program," Coverdale said. "It was evidently their purpose either to absorb the federation in the Lowden committee or to get rid of it altogether." A Sapiro supporter retorted that Coverdale wanted farm bureaus to be "glorified agricultural extension organizations." By telegraph, Lowden denied that he had had any part in the discharge of Coverdale and said he would decline the AFBF presidency if it were offered to him. That ended talk of replacing Bradfute with Lowden, who a year earlier when Howard retired had been mentioned vaguely as a possible dark horse. The Farm Bureau had adopted its nonpartisan stance, and Lowden, who had sought the Republican presidential nomination in 1920, would be active in national politics again in 1924 and 1928. William T. Hutchinson's scholarly biography, *Lowden of Illinois* (1957), presents details concerning Sapiro's association with the wheat committee but has no evidence that Lowden had considered the AFBF presidency. By the time the convention opened, the men who might have wanted to elect the former governor were discovering that their own posts as executive committeemen were in jeopardy.

Coverdale, who had acquired the credentials of an Iowa delegate and who had been scheduled to address the convention on organizational problems, placed before the meeting a large black and red chart on membership trends that divided the state federations into three groups according to their emphasis on marketing, education, and other programs. Beyond question, those with well-balanced programs had made the best showing. Some of the men who wanted the AFBF to go all-out for cooperative marketing had balanced programs in their own states. The chart told the story and Coverdale left the room without making a speech.

The annual election, engineered by his friend President Charles W. Hunt of the Iowa federation, was a triumph for Coverdale. The turnover on the executive committee surprised Sapiro supporters—seven of the eight men who had voted to discharge the secretary were denied reelection. Hunt had followed through on a caucus announcement that only Edward A. O'Neal of Alabama, a future AFBF president, would be returned to the executive board. The Illinois Agricultural Association replaced Howard Leonard with Sam H. Thompson, another future president. One of the casualties was Settle. Bradfute won a second term and the vice-presidency went to J. F. Reed of Minnesota, who had been Coverdale's only midwestern supporter on the committee.

Five days after Coverdale's discharge, the new executive committee reelected him secretary and gave him added duties as treasurer and director of organization. The committee endorsed the U.S. Grain Growers and ignored the wheat advisory committee. Repudiated, both Sapiro and Peteet resigned their AFBF positions and for a few months were allied with Lowden's committee and the National Council of Farmers' Marketing Associations. Settle protested by withholding Indiana's dues to the AFBF for one year.

The impossibility of convincing farmers, or leaders of farm organizations for that matter, to unite in a cooperative marketing venture was demonstrated a third time while Bradfute was president. Since both the Grain Growers and the Lowden committee were slowly declining, the AFBF made a final effort to establish a national grain marketing cooperative that would be controlled by farmers. Four grain elevator companies at Chicago and Kansas City with a total storage capacity of 40,000 million bushels were willing to sell their facilities. Bernard M. Baruch, the New York financier, recommended their purchase. Howard advised Bradfute that the proposal was sensible and practical. The executive committee approved.

Gray Silver resigned as Washington representative and Coverdale as secretary to become president and secretary, respectively, of the Grain Marketing Company, which had options to buy the Chicago and Kansas City elevators. Silver said that savings to producers in marketing costs would be at least five cents a bushel, but this membership campaign also failed. Coverdale was unpopular, especially in Indiana and Illinois, with state leaders who had been supporters of Sapiro. The Illinois Commerce Commission refused to permit the Grain Marketing Company, capitalized at $26 million, to operate as a cooperative. For eight months it handled grain at a profit before Coverdale liquidated the company and paid off investors in full.

When Coverdale resigned, H. Styles Bridges, the young secretary of the New Hampshire Farm Bureau, wanted to succeed him but lost by one vote to W. S. Winder of Utah. Disappointed, Bridges then went into politics and served one term as governor and four as U.S. senator.

Sapiro's last hurrah was in the wheat fields of western Canada, where farmers were in a ferment over a proposal that they sign contracts to market their grain through a wheat pool in Winnipeg. Unintentionally, Howard became involved in the agitation when he visited Canada in February 1924 as a representative of the American Farm Bureau. In a report to Coverdale he said:

The province of Saskatchewan was in a feverish heat over a wheat pooling campaign based on the Sapiro plan. The sentiment was more than feverish. It was hectic. I found that the farmers of Saskatchewan, recent pioneers and possessing more or less of the restlessness and impulsiveness which always goes with new settlers of a country, had met the same difficulties following the war which our farmers had met. Their condition was only better than ours through the fact that their land investments were relatively much lower. They blame the Winnipeg Board of Trade for most of their trouble. They had, as a result, rushed toward the Sapiro plan in a sort of desperation and were inclined to adopt it, expecting it to solve all their difficulties. As nearly as I could learn they were not only completely sold on it but oversold in that they were being led, not by Mr. Sapiro but by his lieutenants, to expect more than it was humanly possible for any marketing plan to realize.

On successive nights Sapiro and Howard addressed the annual convention of the Saskatchewan School Trustees Association at Saskatoon. Howard, who had scheduled his speech before he knew of the pooling agitation, said that Sapiro received a great ovation when he "held out an alluring promise of a world wheat pool at Liverpool which would dominate the world trade in wheat and, without necessarily promising, he nevertheless left the impression that the price would be such as to make it profitable to grow wheat in Saskatchewan."

The next night Howard pessimistically told the Canadians that state pools had not been successful in the wheat belt of the United States. Three years earlier in the Pacific Northwest states he had found great enthusiasm for pooling. The situation had changed, however, and he reported that the Idaho state pool was in receivership and that strong sentiment existed for disbanding the Washington pool. The difficulty was that overhead costs were too high for the pools that also were operating in Illinois, Indiana, Kansas, Minnesota, Nebraska, North Dakota, and Oklahoma-Texas. As a result, he held that cooperative marketing could succeed only if it was more economical than the old-line system.

When a Canadian farmer asked him whether world wheat prices could be increased or controlled through a pool or arbitrary measures of any kind, Howard's answer was unequivocally negative. To his stock recital of price-control failures in many nations in past centuries, he added that the British government had recently been unable to regulate the output of rubber. Howard wrote:

I personally believe in cooperative marketing. I believe that in some commodities pooling may be used advantageously. Those commodities are limited to those produced within a limited area and that have outlets through the same gateways so that transportation and other adjustments may be equitably made. Wheat does not come under this category. It will grow in practically every nation in the world and there is not a month but that wheat is being harvested somewhere. Therefore wheat is the most difficult of all crops to pool.

The man who had worked hard to make the U.S. Grain Growers successful pointed out that if pooling should materially increase Canadian wheat prices, more wheat would be grown in the United States, South America, South Africa, Australia, and Asia.

Sapiro, who had moved his residence from San Francisco to Chicago in 1923, soon faded from the picture and four years later went to New York. By that time most of the cooperatives he had organized had gone out of business. At his peak he was credited with organizing or representing at least fifty-five cooperative associations with a half million members in ten states. Still functioning, especially in his native California, are the highly centralized marketing organizations that were his specialty. Sapiro's foray into the Midwest brought two permanent accomplishments: state legislatures adopted strong laws for farmer cooperatives, and the doctrine that they need expert management became widely accepted.

Howard's final judgment of Sapiro was given a quarter of a century later in a letter to C. H. Gustafson:

I have copies of two of Sapiro's addresses and have read them both recently. They are so thin that the wonder grows that how the devil he warped the judgment of seemingly sensible men as he did. So far as Sap [*sic*] goes, it is more than ever clear that he was nothing but a four-flusher. Last time I heard of him he was running some racket. I believe it was a laundry one in New York. What do you know about him? It is my honest belief that if Cliff G. had not brought him into the picture the Grain Growers would have succeeded.

Cliff G. was Clifford V. Gregory, editor of *Prairie Farmer*. In another document Howard said that Gregory shared blame with William G. Eckhardt of the Illinois Agricultural Association and a few others whom he did not name. All were partisans of Sapiro.

Howard wrote this account of his last meeting with Sapiro, sometime around 1930:

We had dinner together: Nothing was said about old times until after the meal. Then he said, "Jim, you owe the farmers of America six billion dollars."

"How so?"

"If you had gone along with me we would have put across the Grain Growers and it would have made the farmers of America a billion dollars a year."

"Well, Aaron," I said. "If I owe it, I want to pay it. I do not have that much money with me, but I will give you my check."

24

Elder Statesman

H OWARD'S career peaked before his fiftieth birthday. He lived thirty more years, most of the time on his Liberty Township farm, but never again was he as influential as when he headed the Iowa and American Farm Bureau federations. Part of the time he was in eclipse, for his conservative economics and intellectual integrity would not accept McNary-Haugenism and the farm relief programs of the depression era. Unchanging through the lean years, he remained a friend and admirer of the unpopular Herbert Hoover. Vindication came two decades later when the Farm Bureau, still firm on the foundations established by its first president, returned to the thinking of its founders and repudiated the doctrine of agriculture's dependence upon government.

As state and national president, he had succeeded beyond his expectations and he hoped to remain in some major but less strenuous capacity in which his time would be divided between Homelands Farm and a city office that would allow meaningful contact with leading men in and out of government. It was not to be. His timing had been providential in 1919 at Ithaca and Chicago when he was chosen for leadership. Four years later, his mission had been accomplished. Out of office, his place was back on his farm as an elder statesman. Somewhat reluctantly, there he returned.

When he gave up the Farm Bureau presidency there was widespread speculation that he wanted and probably would receive a $10,000-a-year appointment to the Federal Reserve Board. In the American Farm Bureau Federation's second year, with a delegation of state presidents, he had called upon President Harding to ask, in recognition of agriculture's importance, that farmers be placed on major boards and commissions. The seat on the Federal Reserve Board had been created by one of the more controversial of Gray Silver's farm bloc bills. At the end of 1922 Howard wrote to Silver that in all probability he would accept it, if offered, but that he would rather have "the position held by the man with whom we held the conference regarding amendments to the Federal Land Bank Act."

The Howard family did not move to Washington. By early summer the Federal Reserve appointment went to E. H. Cunningham, the Iowa Farm Bureau secretary who was able and who deserved the office for his efforts in behalf of the U.S. Grain Growers. Harding gave the Farm Bureau further recognition by appointing Charles W. Hunt, who had followed Howard as president of the Iowa federation, to the Federal Trade Commission, and W. S. Hill, president of the South Dakota Federation, to the U.S. Shipping Board. Sherman J. Lowell, who as master of the National Grange had helped Howard negotiate lower freight rates, became a member of the Federal Tariff Commission.

Howard's failure to receive a presidential appointment can be logically explained. In the Corn Belt, which should have been his power base, he had become somewhat controversial because, with John Coverdale, he steadfastly supported the Yankee philosophy that educational and community activities should not be subordinated to economics. By the end of the Howard administration the emerging strong men in the Midwest wanted the federation's direct involvement in grain marketing to be the all-important activity. Soon they would take up a new crusade and demand that rural prosperity be provided by governmental action. Howard and Coverdale, who were nationalists in their thinking and slow to change basic positions, for two decades would be out of step with their neighbors. They did not believe that the basic concepts of the federation should be altered because of economic problems that, however severe, presumably would not be permanent and, as much as they sympathized with the objectives of farm relief legislation, they doubted its propriety and effectiveness. The first president, who under the Quaker ethic did not ask for personal credit for his accomplishments, also was not especially concerned if the midwestern rank-and-file disagreed with him. He had been and he was going to be his own man.

In his conservative leadership, Howard kept the AFBF from splintering during the early years. At the start of his presidency, he had persuaded men from the East, South, and West to form a solid front and support the Midwest in its crusade for cooperative marketing. Soon he and Coverdale were cautioning that the Midwest would go too far if it insisted that marketing be made all-important. Nationalistic in their outlook, they kept the boat from rocking by preaching that only through cooperation of the state units could the national federation operate at full strength. Had the two Iowans been politicians who adjusted their thinking to changes in rural sentiment in their home state, the Farm Bureau might have fragmented and evolved into several regional federations, which Henry C. Wallace and some other midwesterners had wanted in 1919.

Meanwhile, as far as the Harding administration was concerned, Howard had a special problem in his home state. In the *Iowa Homestead,* Dante Pierce persisted in his long vendetta and did his best to discredit Howard by misrepresenting his stands on the ship subsidy and Esch-Cummins guarantee clause. The *Homestead* had become a spokesman for the Iowa Farm Bureau, which as part of the bargain accepted the publication's animosities. Men with such handicaps as Howard had are easily overlooked when White House favors are passed out.

Howard commented on the Iowa situation in an undated letter written from Chicago in 1923 or 1924:

An interesting bit of information came to me from the Washington office during January. Mr. Silver told me that the president of the Iowa Farm Bureau Federation told him in just so many words that the Iowa Farm Bureau had "traded" Wallace for Pierce. This has since been confirmed by Mr. Pierce to an associate of mine in a conference pertaining to some matters before the Iowa legislature. Hence the whole matter is a political one. Sooner or later the farmers will get awake to conditions there.

The letter was addressed to a Chicago businessman, a personal friend, whose family Howard had known before his involvement in the Farm Bureau movement. The draft copy was not dated. In 1923, Charles Hearst succeeded C. W. Hunt as Iowa Farm Bureau president. In the same letter, Howard gave a lengthy but private analysis of the manner in which his positions on the ship subsidy and guarantee clause had been misrepresented during the closing months of his AFBF presidency.

To be part of the national power structure did not require that Howard hold an office under federal patronage. He had a sense of his own worth and saw the possibility of making a personal contribution in privately financed employment that need not be directly connected with agriculture but could not be antagonistic to it. Without being specific, he wrote to friends that positions he considered honorable were being offered but that he was still considering a return to the farm. His final decision was to involve himself with a project that was national in scope, complex in its ramifications, and worthy of the attention of a man who had successfully organized a farm movement.

Within a few months he had a Chicago office at 30 North LaSalle Street and the title of president of the National Transportation Institute (NTI), which was being organized by a group of Washington men. President Harding, influential congressmen, and the Farm Bureau's executive committee had endorsed the concept that an impartial and reliable agency was needed to collect, analyze, and disseminate information to be used in the formulation of national policies governing rail, water, and highway transportation. A staff member of the congressional Joint Committee on

Agricultural Inquiry in mid-1922 told the AFBF executive committee that steam roads, electric lines, and trucks were operating in an uncoordinated manner and that a new educational institution should be established under the direction of a board on which agriculture and industry, as well as transportation, would be represented.

Bird M. Robinson, president of the American Short Line Railroad Association, seems to have been the chief promoter. Various businessmen were invited to dinners at Chicago and New York, after which Howard was made chairman of a planning committee. By the end of March, incorporation under the laws of Illinois was authorized. The first board of directors included Bradfute, one New Yorker, Robinson from Washington, nine men from Chicago, and seven others from the Midwest. The promotion envisioned an annual budget of $1 million to be raised through $100 membership fees. When he addressed the AFBF's convention in December 1923, Howard said that Edgar E. Clark, former chairman of the Interstate Commerce Commission, would head the institute's research council and that David Friday, former president of Michigan Agricultural College, would be director of research.

Involvement with the National Transportation Institute was a mistake. It soon passed out of existence, under circumstances the Howard papers do not explain. The record shows that Howard spoke, chiefly on railroad matters, before several midwestern audiences without breaking new ground. It is possible that Robinson and his associates erred by assuming that the Iowa farmer would be a skillful membership solicitor. C. H. Gustafson, the Nebraskan who was the first president of the U.S. Grain Growers, was a member of the institute's staff, but correspondence files and payroll records have not been located. That page of the Howard career is largely a blank.

Howard as NTI president and Cunningham as Federal Reserve Board member both spoke at the 1923 AFBF convention. Howard was slow to revise his opinions. When Cunningham reported that he had found no evidence that the board had deliberately taken action detrimental to farmer credit, Howard was not convinced. He insisted that the record might have been altered before Cunningham read it.

After his career in transportation evaporated, Howard was involved briefly in several activities that were transitory or lacked a financial future. As a result of on-the-job training, he qualified as an agricultural economist and on August 25, 1924, he wrote to Commerce Secretary Hoover on the letterhead of the American Economic Institute, 140 South Dearborn Street, of which he was chairman. Most of the other officers and directors were railroad executives and manufacturers.

With H. W. Morehouse, director of the AFBF research department, he formed the Howard-Morehouse Agricultural Business Service. By the end of 1924 it consolidated with the Brookmire Economic Service, which from New York City issued bulletins on receipts and price trends of agricultural commodities as well as on the security exchanges. For many years Howard was listed as a member of the board of consultants for the Brookmire firm. In a letter of recommendation, Hoover wrote: "I have known Mr. Howard for a number of years and regard him as one of the soundest and most constructive leaders in the agricultural field. His practical experience as a farmer, banker and leader gives him unusual equipment for dealing with the economic problems of agriculture." Howard, who for years had studied the trends and factors that cause commodity price changes, contended that agricultural economics was an art, not a science.

From Chicago offices, he was not idle while he recuperated from the stress and overwork of the Farm Bureau presidency. At the beginning of the Bradfute administration he made several speeches and on a trip into Manitoba and Saskatchewan surveyed the wheat marketing situation in Canada. In the 1924 Coolidge campaign, with an office in western Republican headquarters in the Wrigley Building, he was an adviser on farm policy. As the chief speaker at the annual dinner of the Irish Fellowship Club of Chicago, his topic was "The Irish Farmer and His American Neighbor."

In the city, nothing of a permanent nature seemed to work out. On Homelands Farm, Roe Hiatt, who had been the livestock-share renter since Howard's move to Chicago, was ready to retire. At the beginning of the 1925 crop year, Jim Howard, an agricultural elder statesman, again took up on-the-scenes operation of the farm once owned by his grandfather.

About the time that Calvin Coolidge became president, the American Farm Bureau Federation changed directions, abandoned its efforts to unite grain farmers behind a cooperative marketing program, and turned its energies toward elimination of price depressing surpluses. During the Howard and Bradfute administrations nothing had been accomplished about restoring the export markets that were lost when the war was won. As a result of the prolonged rural depression, farmers were in desperate financial condition and the membership began to urge that the government do something. Responding to grass roots pressure, the Farm Bureau became the chief sponsor in Congress of a series of McNary-Haugen bills that were based on the theory that higher domestic prices could be paid if crop and meat surpluses could be sold abroad at the lower prices prevailing throughout the world. Although the five McNary-Haugen bills differed in detail, all proposed that the difference between domestic and world prices be covered by an equalization fee assessed against the producers covered by the proposed law. Before the Great Depression, no one suggested that farmers should be subsidized by the federal treasury. McNary-Haugen supporters were not concerned about either the balance of trade or the international repercussions that would follow the dumping of surpluses.

McNary-Haugenism developed from the George N. Peek–Hugh S. Johnson "equality for agriculture" proposals, which in turn had grown out of a two-tier pricing formula advanced by Henry A. Wallace. Mc-Nary-Haugenism was endorsed by the Iowa and Illinois farm bureaus during the winter of 1923–1924. An active proponent was Sam H. Thompson, president of the Illinois Agricultural Association, who at the 1924 convention defeated Oscar E. Bradfute for the AFBF presidency. In what was primarily a midwestern movement, the Indiana Farm Bureau and the independent Missouri Farmers Clubs also were at the head of the parade. County Farm Bureaus helped win the endorsements of most congressmen from rural districts. The National Grange favored an export debenture plan but also endorsed the equalization fee. The conviction that enactment of the current McNary-Haugen bill would increase rural income duplicated the fervor of the William Jennings Bryan "free silver" campaign of 1896.

In the emotional situation, Howard was almost a Corn Belt minority of one. He wanted farmers to be prosperous, but he did not think the equalization fee would work and he became unpopular by saying so. He sided with President Coolidge, who in 1927 and 1928 vetoed McNary-Haugen bills on consitutional and policy grounds. The president held that the equalization fee was a tax—a point that its proponents conceded. He argued, however, that it could be levied only by Congress and not by an administrative board. Coolidge had additional objections—that the result would be price fixing, which was repugnant to the free enterprise system; that even greater surpluses would be produced; and that the only beneficiaries would be the farmers, chiefly midwesterners, who produced the crops and livestock specifically covered by the legislation.

Howard and Congressman L. J. Dickinson debated the topic in the columns of the July 1927 issue of *Country Gentleman*. The congressman's main points were that farmers needed help, which such a tariff could provide, and that the McNary-Haugen plan would make the tariff effective. From his knowledge of the complexity of the marketing system, Howard raised pertinent questions about when and how, before completion of the harvest, a federal agency could decide how large an equalization fee should be collected across the vast U.S. wheat belt. He said that the 1927 bill passed Congress only in a trade for votes to extend indefinitely the charter of the Federal Reserve Bank. He charged that "all mention of the tariff's relation to farm relief was dropped when the international bankers, seeking payment of Europe's war debt, urged the abolition of all tariff barriers." As a student of economic history, the only precedent he could find for the equalization fee was a 1906 price fixing plan for Brazilian coffee that had not worked.

The former Farm Bureau president still traveled to eastern cities and had influential friends. On one trip to New York he called at the office of Wheeler McMillen, editor of *Farm and Fireside*. Producing a typewritten document of thirty-one pages bound in a blue cover, Howard suggested that it be used for an editorial or article. "I have been requested not to tell you the source of this material, but I can assure you that it is absolutely authentic," he said. It contained figures on foreign trade for which McMillen, who also opposed the McNary-Haugen proposal, had been searching. Years later McMillen learned that the document came from Hoover. The Department of Commerce staff had worked for weeks to collect and verify the statistics but never knew what use Hoover had made of them.

Howard's papers make little mention of his contacts with Coolidge. In writing about his experiences in the White House, the Iowa farmer said that he had been the guest of the president and Mrs. Coolidge at a luncheon also attended by a couple named Sterns from Boston. In early 1924 Howard was appointed a member of the St. Lawrence Commission of which Hoover was chairman. Coolidge hoped that the Great Lakes could be opened for navigation by oceangoing vessels and that the river's hydroelectric power capability could be developed. In company with Canadian officials, the commission toured the waterway from Niagara Falls to Quebec.

A college-aged grandson once was once told by Howard that he had been sent by Coolidge on a diplomatic mission to Canada, where the mayor of a major city was incensed because Chicago officials wanted to increase diversion of Great Lakes waters into the Mississippi River drainage system. Howard succeeded in convincing the mayor, whose identity has been forgotten, that the federal government was protecting Canadian interests. The Coolidge Papers in the Library of Congress do not mention the incident, which is one of many Howard seldom discussed. The grandson, who had returned from a summer job on a water project in Colorado, was impressed by Howard's thorough knowledge of water problems in that area.

For some time Howard was listed on letterheads of the Great Lakes–St. Lawrence Tidewater Association as assistant to Executive Director Charles P. Craig. His mailing address was the Morrison Hotel, Chicago. Had a treaty with Canada been ratified, Howard's ambition was to serve on the international board that would construct and operate the waterway. He was confident that he could have the appointment under a Republican administration.

In 1934 Craig asked for Howard's help in keeping L. J. Dickinson, then a U.S. senator, in line. Dickinson supported the treaty but feared he would lose votes in Iowa cities along the Mississippi. "I wrote Dickinson a very pointed letter yesterday," Howard commented. "For every vote he gains he will lose ten. But that's that."

Discussions of agricultural problems with Hoover and others, including Premier Mackenzie King of Canada, were mentioned by Howard in a 1924 letter to Frank O. Lowden:

During the past six months I have had some correspondence with President Coolidge regarding a plan which has been given careful consideration by a number of people. It has not been pushed because it originated with some of the people in the Department of Commerce rather than in the Department of Agriculture. To my mind it has much merit and I am asking Secretary Hoover to request the President to send you a copy of the plan.

It was common knowledge in Iowa that Hoover disagreed with the current policies of the Farm Bureau and that Howard was his friend. After the secretary of commerce delivered the 1925 commencement address at Penn College, his next stop was at the home of relatives in LeGrand, fifty miles away. The dirt roads were slick with mud as the result of a three-hour downpour, but Hoover did not want to ride in a day coach. At his request, he saw the countryside from the front seat of Howard's Buick, a veteran of slippery roads. En route the former mining engineer helped change a flat tire by using a bridge plank as an auxiliary jack.

The Farm Bureau's first president did not agree with all the policies of the new men in the foundation's hierarchy, but he held his tongue. He had retired voluntarily, and he believed that he should not interfere with those who, under the terms of the constitutions of the state and national federations, had been chosen to take his place. He did not expect that everything they did would have his approval, even though he hadn't anticipated disagreements over questions he considered fundamental. All-important to Howard was the Farm Bureau's future, and he knew that public confidence in its long-range survival could be jeopardized by questioning its day-to-day operations. So he adopted a policy, from which there were few deviations, of ignoring attacks on his own record. He reserved the right to express his own opinions, but he was careful about public statements that might reflect on his successors.

No longer part of the inner circle that guided the federations he had founded, he did not complain that he was not consulted about policies and programs. Until the early 1940s he had no rapport with the officers of the Iowa Farm Bureau. Through the changing administrations he received expense-paid invitations to attend the annual AFBF conventions. He went to some of them, depending on his health, other activities, and depression-era finances.

If the latter years of his career had not turned out the way he had desired, he was nonetheless neither uninformed nor inactive. He had grown intellectually during his Farm Bureau years, and he was still a man of consequence.

By the time he resumed the wearing of overalls, Howard's strong constitution apparently had recovered from the overwork of the Farm Bureau years. Within a few months, however, he developed bronchial symptoms that were diagnosed as tuberculosis by Dr. E. H. Noble, the respected general practitioner in Clemons, and a specialist in Des Moines. A rest cure in the Colorado mountains was financially impossible, but Jim was told that recovery in a year was possible if he confined himself to supervising the farm and a little light work, as long as his temperature did not rise.

Much of his time was spent in a combination office-bedroom that contained an heirloom walnut desk and a four-drawer filing cabinet filled with papers he had brought from Chicago. Also within reach were the *Encyclopaedia Britannica* and the *World Almanac*. In those circumstances he had ample opportunity to read, write, and think. Much of his thinking was about a new career as a writer. After several months of mental activity, he decided to vary his recuperation with travel.

In early March 1928, he started for Philadelphia to talk to friends at the Curtis Publishing Company about marketing his memoirs. Seven months later he gave this account of the journey:

I really was not able to travel straight through but made the trip by stopping off and resting. I stopped at Washington where I knew a very good doctor who wanted to take me under his treatment for several months.

Then I went over to see Herbert Hoover, whom I have known intimately for a number of years, and he asked me if I would not do some writing for him during his campaign for the nomination. So it happened that I stayed in Washington until the middle of May. The doctor took out my tonsils and did more or less other things.

The trouble, however, was a toxic poisoning from bad dental work done years ago and I finally had some of the jaw bone cut away and it has taken a good while for the poison to work out of my system. It is, however, leaving now and I am able to do as much work as I ever did.

Some thirty years earlier a village dentist had used arsenic in treating a tooth.

Even though Howard hadn't followed orders to the letter, the doctors in early June found that the tuberculosis symptoms had disappeared. He had gained twenty pounds and his condition had improved greatly. The doctors repeated the customary warnings about overexertion and fatigue, but Howard paid little heed.

When the Republican national convention met at Kansas City, he spent three weeks in the Hoover-for-President headquarters there. During part of that time, some of his AFBF friends were among McNary-Haugen supporters who demonstrated for Frank O. Lowden. In July, Jim and Anna made an automobile trip to Colorado, but before they returned he received telegrams asking him to come to Chicago and help with the Hoover campaign. It seems to have been good therapy, for by October he had regained his former weight and could easily walk five or six miles, whereas two months earlier he would have been worn out after a mile. He was ready for the rigors of the depression years.

A milestone document, marking the beginning of Howard's literary career, was a twenty-six-page pamphlet entitled "Herbert Hoover's Record as a Friend of the American Farmer." Widely circulated in the 1928 presidential campaign, it was signed by J. R. Howard as former president of the American Farm Bureau Federation. The first draft, which has not been preserved, was written the previous winter when, during convalescence, he had read "a vast amount of original material" in his private papers. He sent it to Washington and in February received telegrams and mail from George Akerson, Hoover's secretary, asking that it be revised for campaign use. Howard replied that revision would be difficult since there was no stenographic help on the farm. It is probable that he worked on the revision in Washington that spring. During that time reports on the Iowa political situation were sent to him at the Willard Hotel. Rewritten to the extent that it lost some of Howard's style, the pamphlet emphasized wartime steps taken by Hoover to protect the interests of American agriculture.

During 1928 Howard had frequent correspondence with W. G. Jamison of Colorado, who had joined Hoover's staff after serving as a member of the AFBF's first executive committee. In one letter Howard expressed scorn that at a meeting in Des Moines Lowden and Senator Albert J. Cummins had lined up for an export bill sponsored by Congressman Lester J. Dickinson.

Another close friend and Hoover supporter was John G. Brown, the founding president of the Indiana Farm Bureau Federation. Howard in a letter said he had made unpopular statements during the preconvention campaign:

The thing that grated most, I understand, is a statement I released showing the loss of membership in the Farm Bureaus of Indiana, Illinois and Iowa during the past five years as a result of the change from conservative to radical leadership. You know that it is true and I share your suggestion that we who were in charge when the movement was conservative need make no apologies.

Stationed in Chicago during the fall campaign, Howard acted as a rural campaign adviser, made some out-of-town speeches, and wrote additional pamphlets, some of which appeared under his own name and some of which were accredited to others. At least twice he was quoted in news releases. He proudly noted that no one had challenged statements in his friend-of-the-farmer pamphlet. A month before the election he wrote to A. F. Styles, his friend from the New Providence days, that "I was for Hoover when scarcely any other farmer in the whole country dared to come out for him and naturally I'm very pleased with the trend."

With some success, for two decades a new career as a writer occupied part of the spare time of the former professor of rhetoric and graduate student in English literature. An unsuspected talent was that, when he became Farm Bureau president, he could dictate to a secretary the advance text of an acceptable speech. Back on the farm, with no stenographers within twenty miles, he was on his own and had to learn hunt-and-peck typewriting. He was a first-class writer on economic and agricultural topics, his field of special expertise, and the articles he typed for himself generally were as good as if he had dictated them. The *Country Gentleman* article opposing the McNary-Haugen farm relief proposal, for which he was paid $500, was both logical and lucid, and it revealed that the author understood the various versions of the complicated legislation. With economy of wordage he anticipated and answered arguments, many of them emotional, that could be raised for the equalization fee proposal. On other subjects, too, he could write as well as speak with logic and force.

He had trouble with "Making an Iowa Farmer," an autobiographical account of his career prior to his involvement with the Farm Bureau. The first longhand draft was written in hotel rooms while he was a field man for the Federal Farm Board during the Hoover administration. It contained valuable material about his early years and was especially good when he took the time to go into the details of an incident or subject. The manuscript was poorly organized, however, with too frequent changes of subject matter, as the author interjected comments about rural life and digressed into historical and social observations. Howard was neither an editor nor a copyreader and he never learned how to revise paragraphs and polish sentences. Pride of authorship prevented his asking for assistance with what could have been the first section of his life story. It and some other manuscripts were difficult to read and "Making an Iowa Farmer" was turned down by several publishers.

The untold stories of the Farm Bureau presidency provided obvious topics for magazine articles, and several were written for *Country Gentleman*. The account of the dinner with millionaires in the New York mansion of Otto Herman Kahn was used by O. M. Kile in *The Farm Bureau through Three Decades.* With a self-imposed censorship, Howard turned down opportunities to write anything that would be even indirectly critical of his Farm Bureau successors. He missed a fine opportunity to tell how the House Committee on War Expenditures badgered him as a result of the letter asking congressmen to reveal how they had voted on the Muscle Shoals appropriation. He hesitated to criticize the legislative branch of government and, even after several years had passed, he seemed afraid that either he or the Farm Bureau might lose the goodwill of congressional leaders.

A serious difficulty was that part of Howard's private papers were lost during shipment from Chicago to Clemons. Although his filing case and desk drawers were rescued when the ancestral home burned in 1929, some documents undoubtedly were destroyed then. As a result, his own records were incomplete and Howard to a considerable extent had to depend upon his memory, which generally was excellent. When uncertain, he omitted time references.

Howard's essays on midwestern farming written during the 1930s for the year-end editions of the *Annalist* demonstrate that agriculture was his specialty and that it was his best subject as a writer. His main focus was on his own farm as he told how work and plans are affected by markets and government regulations.

His unfilled ambition was to write an autobiography, of which "Making an Iowa Farmer" was to have been the introduction. He revised it several times, without great success, and meanwhile wrote separate essays about the death of his sister Mamie and about his teenage train trip to New York. He was persistent and the Howard papers contain three drafts about the return trip with a sack of red bananas.

To his credit was one piece of fiction. *Farm and Fireside* in its November 1928 issue printed "Carolina Love," a short story about a lovesick farmhand from North Carolina who marries the sister of the girl who jilted him. For it Wheeler McMillen paid $300. A second attempt at fiction brought a rejection. "Writing is pretty hard work, as is everything else, I presume, that is worthwhile," Howard said in a letter that has been preserved.

Especially in the 1930s, he corresponded frequently with friends who were editors of magazines in New York and Philadelphia. Despite the financial difficulties of the depression years, they could have used more articles by him. Regrettably it was in one of the fields in which he had highest hopes that he had only average success.

Herbert Hoover was president six months before Howard's loyalty was rewarded with an appointment to a high non–civil service position. Before inauguration, his name was on a list of possibilities for secretary of agriculture, but so was the name of his enemy, Dante Pierce. As a result, they canceled each other. Later Howard was passed over for membership on an eight-man Federal Farm Board created by a special session of Congress. During the summer he supervised construction of a replacement for the family home that dated back to 1861 and that had burned down during the winter. In September he went on the government payroll for the only time in his life when Alexander Legge, the Farm Board chairman, hired him as a specialist in organization. Howard described himself as being "a general utility fielder for the Federal Farm Board team." Substituting for board members when emergencies arose, he spent much of his time in states west of the Mississippi. Hoover did not believe in direct aid to farmers and much of Howard's work involved the administration's efforts to encourage the growth of cooperatives and to improve grain and livestock marketing. In part his speeches were echoes of his 1920–1922 insistence that farmers have a right to market cooperatively and receive a share of the profits of distribution. Livestock marketing was one of his chief interests and in the Northwest he took the initiative in arranging for regional financing. In that field he worked with officials of intermediate credit banks that had been created by a farm bloc law for which he had been largely responsible.

As the financial depression became nationwide and business stagnated, the extension services had more success in increasing production of major commodities than the Hoover administration had in marketing them. Although skeptical, the Farm Bureau avoided an obstructionist role and, when Hoover requested it, Sam H. Thompson resigned as AFBF president to accept an appointment on the Farm Board. By 1930, stabilization corporations established for grain and cotton soon were swamped with unmarketable surpluses.

By the campaign year of 1932, the Farm Board abandoned much of the organization work Howard had been doing and for a time the administration allowed him to work on programs concerned with inland waterways. Always loyal to the president, he hoped to be able to use his specialized knowledge in Republican headquarters, as he had done in 1924 and 1928. Sensing what was politically inevitable, the Hoover campaign did not make the added effort to keep the farm vote lined up.

In the stringencies of the worsening depression, salary checks from the Federal Farm Board helped meet mortgage and tax payments on Homelands Farm, over which Howard's oldest son had immediate jurisdiction. Like all rural people, the family was hard pressed for cash. Jim had optimistically expanded his acreage and increased his debts in 1926 when he bought the adjacent 120-acre Dunn farm, which was not as productive as the older parts of Homelands. His judgment was faulty, for land prices kept dropping.

Inevitably the liquid $4,000 he had at the end of the Farm Bureau career would have been invested in farmland as a down payment. He had written an uncle that he had been offered two other Liberty Township farms, but that one was too large and the other priced too high. As an alternative, he was thinking about acquiring farmland in the Red River Valley. Fortunately, in view of the foreclosure situation of the coming years, the Dunn farm was his last land purchase. That he did not buy more was no doubt due to the fiscal caution of his wife. Anna Howard believed that money should be used to pay debts and retire mortgages. She gave solvency a higher priority than expansion. As the depression wore on, everyone agreed that she was right.

The inauguration of Franklin D. Roosevelt provided a glorious opportunity for men who had been disappointed when Calvin Coolidge vetoed McNary-Haugen bills and who believed that Herbert Hoover should have provided farm prosperity by direct governmental action. Edward A. O'Neal, the Alabaman who had been president of the American Farm Bureau Federation for two years, led an imposing array of proponents when an emergency program to raise rural income by reducing acreage, among other steps, was introduced in early 1933. The Farmers Union, the Grange, and cooperative organizations presented a solid front for the agricultural adjustment plan.

Jim Howard again broke ranks and opposed a program that was immensely popular in Iowa. He wrote to Senator Dickinson that the bill would be detrimental to hog farmers because "you cannot boost the price of pork and lard unless you take similar steps regarding competing food products." He warned Congressman Gilbert N. Haugen that "certain political angles and inequalities" could cause trouble. In replying, neither man disputed his statements.

Identifying himself only as an Iowa farmer and saying nothing about his Farm Bureau background, Howard on the eighth day of a Senate committee hearing testified that the domestic allotment plan was unworkable and would not benefit farmers. He had ridden to Chicago in a stock train caboose and found that thirty-nine of forty-one other men aboard were opposed to the bill. One of the objections he raised was that the legislation would be "the opening wedge of government interference, an essence of socialism." It was on that ground that two decades later the Farm Bureau called for the abandonment of farm relief programs. Howard testified:

This bill is a price-fixing bill. You have aimed at approximately the pre-war averages as a minimum. You are doubtless aware that in every price-fixing experiment since Adam the minimum price has been the maximum price. I want to tell you from my own statements received from four defunct bank receivers that pre-war prices won't save American agriculture. The aid this bill offers would be at best a pittance. It won't bring the equality for agriculture which the farmer demands.

But will it increase prices to any degree? I doubt it. The proponents of the act have overlooked one other essential thing. Just as production is liquid, so is the consumption of food products. There is easy and constant substitution of one food for another. No one article of diet, not even wheat, is any longer essential. The tendency of thrifty people is always to buy on the bargain counter. It is now more so than ever before.

Howard's testimony was ignored in Washington but it was picked up by several publications and received a full column in the business section of the *Chicago Tribune* on February 15, 1933. After he returned home he wrote that he was kept busy reading and answering commendatory mail. Several speaking engagements followed and in June he told the convention of the National Metal Trades Association in Chicago that historically price fixing had never been successful and that its proponents, unversed in geography, "have not learned what a great big place this world is." He went on:

Not a single adventure on the part of any government at any time in the special subsidizing of the interest of farm people has ever succeeded.

. . . It seems to me that all through history in every time of stress the farmer has appealed to government for legislative aid. Just why he does this or tries to do it is not easily explained. Perhaps it is because the farmer's product is and always has been more or less perishable. Maybe it is because he has never been able to control his own marketing. Possibly it is because the demand for the farmer's product is restricted to the human stomach, and therefore is not capable of as easy an expansion as the industrial producer enjoys. It would not be surprising if the desire of the politician to curry favor in order to get votes enters more largely into it than anything else.

A penciled notation that "price fixing is an attempt by a Congress or other human agency to fix valuations based on economic laws over which the human agency has no control" was found in the Howard papers. Whether it was his own definition was not indicated, but in his late years Howard presumably had planned to use it in an essay.

He carefully avoided even indirect criticism of Farm Bureau leaders who supported New Deal farm relief programs and of neighbors who stayed solvent by applying for and cashing the checks mailed from Washington. Like many farmers, he was short of money but his daughter, Janet Paterson, who was familiar with the financing of Homelands Farm operations, says he never qualified for subsidy benefits. But he insisted that a support price guaranteed by law as a market floor of a commodity would quickly become the top or ceiling price. He contended that the farmer's instinctive desire for high yields on the fields he planted inevitably would mean a surplus and that legislation designed to provide individual profits would result in collective losses.

In his late years, his brain was never quiet. He continued to read in search of enlightenment about national problems, particularly those of agriculture. He studied available information about what had happened in past centuries and in far places, and he found much that was pertinent to his time and locale. While tolerant of the opinions of others, he made up his own mind and refused to abandon the conclusions reached by his own intellectual processes. That the majority might not agree never bothered him.

Together, Jim Howard and Homelands Farm survived the depression and two years of drought and made the transition from horse to tractor farming. His papers include a copy of an essay apparently intended to explain to easterners how rural people were existing and why in the "farmers' holiday" movement some Iowans took the law into their own hands. He did not approve of lawlessness but he would not condemn the methods used:

We are reverting to the pioneer mode of life. We're going back to our grandparents' days not because we want to but because we have to. And there are both desirable and undesirable features in this.

Neighborliness, the spirit of helpfulness and cooperation, was one of the commendable characteristics of pioneer life. We have it in Iowa today perhaps as never before. If a neighbor of mine runs out of coffee or sugar I gladly loan him what he needs, without thought of repayment. He will do as much for me. Likewise if a neighbor, after sincere and industrious efforts to meet his payments, is about to lose his farm or equipment through foreclosure, the rest of us take steps to save his home for him.

The procedure is well-known. The sheriff's sale of the property is attended by a number of neighbors. Perhaps a horse is up for sale. One man bids 25 cents for it; another bids 50 cents. Under Iowa law a second bid is all that is required to make a sale effective. There are no more than two bids. Once in a while a third bid is attempted by the agent of the mortgage holder. It is silenced before it is heard and the would-be bidder is escorted to the edge of the crowd and courteously but very firmly told to go home. Livestock and equipment are knocked down for a few cents each, and the successful bidder asks the former owner to just keep the stuff for him for a while. He later buys it back at the bid prices if he so desires.

That's one way in which our debts are being revised downward. Arrangements by which the debtor pays off at so much on the dollar under agreement with the creditor are another method.

The first method, of course, is unfair to the creditor. Yet men become desperate when they see the fruits of their toil in jeopardy and their families threatened with loss of the roof over their heads and their future means of subsistence. We are desperate in Iowa today. We have literally become a law unto ourselves.

We have gone back to the pioneer mode of life in another way. We are depending more and more on our own farms to supply our wants. We must do this because with incomes reduced or nonexistent we spend money only for things which can't possibly be produced or contrived on the farm. We raise more vegetables and foods for our tables. In summer we stock our larders with home-canned foods. We mend our own shoes, and I've even heard reports that ancient spinning wheels are coming out of attics to produce clothing from our own wool clips.

Draft horses are working in the fields while tractors stand idle in the sheds. It takes money to buy gasoline; you can raise horse feed yourself. There is less driving of pleasure cars; that money also is being saved. Farmers drive their draft horses on short trips, and the car stays in the garage. There's a shortage of draft horses on many farms, and since it takes four or five years to raise a good draft animal we may soon be hitching our milk cows to our plows. As one of my neighbors more than half-seriously remarked, "Our county agents have a job at last—they can teach us how to yoke up these cows."

A lot of us are keeping warm this winter at fires fed from our own woodlots. Some of us are burning corn. This, of course, is hard on the coal miners and dealers and is inconvenient to us, but it's another of the many steps we have to take in our efforts to live without spending any money.

What are we thinking about farm relief? Many of us are now convinced that price-fixing plans in all their numerous guises are futile. Some of us see some hope in a plan now being broached under which the government would take 50 or 60 million acres of marginal or submarginal land out of production by outright purchase or leasing. Individual states are involuntarily doing that to some extent right now by taking over tax-delinquent lands for which there are no buyers.

After seeing one after another farm relief plan fail a good many of us are beginning to think that the sooner the government abandons all farm relief plans and concentrates on lowering taxes, with some incidental adjustment of mortgage interest rates, the sooner we'll see happy days on the farm again.

Frugality and hardheaded business sense, supplemented by occasional checks for speeches and writings, enabled Howard to pay taxes and meet mortgage installments. In 1936 he arranged for debt refinancing through a local Federal Land Bank agency and thereby became a beneficiary of one of Gray Silver's farm bloc bills. He wrote to former associates that he would like to have a literary agent and someone to arrange lectures, but no one knew of any and then, too, the times weren't right.

Contacts with businessmen did not bring financial rewards. He told a promoter friend that it would be logical to merge two midwestern railroads—the Chicago Great Western, which had terminal facilities at Chicago, Minneapolis, and Kansas City but leased much of its trackage, and the Minneapolis and St. Louis, which served important rural areas but lacked gateways into cities. His contribution was the idea. He did not invest any money and therefore lost nothing when the promotion failed. Later he acted as consultant for men who tried to establish a flax industry in the Cedar Rapids area. He accepted stock as his compensation but stipulated that his name could not be used unless the project got out of the promotion stage.

"New Uses for New Products" was the topic of a late 1939 speech before the National Congress of Industry and Raw Materials in Sioux City, Iowa. Apparently it was Howard's last appearance before a convention audience.

In politics he was always a Republican, mistakenly confident that Franklin D. Roosevelt would not run well in rural areas. In the 1936 campaign, the Republican National Committee issued a statement quoting the former Farm Bureau president as a critic of Rooseveltian farm policies. Except for his obituary, it was Howard's last entry in the *New York Times Index*. In 1944 he made the introductory speech when Thomas E. Dewey campaigned at Marshalltown. His last vote in 1952 was for a winner. The former 1912 progressive supported Eisenhower for the presidential nomination when his conservative friends were for Taft.

When the AFBF celebrated its twentieth anniversary at a Chicago convention in 1939, Howard was host at a breakfast reunion attended by twelve of the fifteen original officers and committeemen. Memorial tributes were paid to Oscar Bradfute, who had died in 1929, Gray Silver, who had died in 1935, and Silas Strivings. At the start of the Roosevelt administration, Howard had offered to recommend Silver for appointment as secretary of agriculture.

Among those at the reunion was Coverdale, who had returned to Iowa as a businessman after the Grain Marketing Company had folded. Before the depression he had been in the grain, feed, and fertilizer business at Cedar Rapids. Later he joined the Rath Packing Company at Waterloo as manager of its feed and fertilizer department. Upon retirement he was director of the Rath agricultural bureau. He managed a 340-acre farm and as a hobby experimented with orchids and other flowers in his own greenhouse.

Howard returned to the mainstream of Iowa Farm Bureau activities in 1942. At the suggestion of Secretary V. B. Hamilton and with the approval of President Francis Johnson, he was appointed an advisory member of the state resolutions committee. During its session he became a friend of the chairman, Allan B. Kline, and thereafter was in frequent contact with the officers and staff at Des Moines. At the Iowa federation's quarter-century observance, he spoke in response to a welcome from Johnson. The example of the state federation was followed when Howard was made an honorary member of the Mashall County resolutions committee.

The elder statesman had the great satisfaction of attending the 1947 convention at which Kline became the second Iowan to be elected president of the American Farm Bureau Federation. Kline lived only two counties from Homelands Farm and was even closer to Howard in his attitude toward agriculture and its relation to government. When Kline criticized farm relief legislation in testimony before a congressional committee, Howard sent him a commendatory letter. With profuse thanks, Kline replied that the approval of the first president was "one of the greatest things that has happened to me for a long time."

American farmers had decided that they did not want to be dominated by government. The subsidy policies that Henry A. Wallace and the Farm Bureau had jointly sponsored in 1933 had not been effective in controlling production. Government payments had continued even after parity levels had been reached in wartime. Surpluses were expensive and steadily increasing. Price fixing was a panacea that hadn't worked. Howard, the self-taught economist, had known in advance that it wasn't going to work. He had said so on February 2, 1933, when he testified before a Senate committee at a moment when no one was listening.

In his final years he slowed down physically but not mentally. The house on the Dunn farm that Jim and Anna had bought in 1925 was modernized as their final home and later was enlarged when their son-in-law Andrew Paterson retired as manager of the American Royal Livestock Show at Kansas City. The owner of 600 acres, Howard worked only in the garden where for a few years he raised bumper crops of vegetables and flowers and experimented with cotton, tobacco, and peanuts. Twice Jim and Anna went to Sarasota, Florida, for the cold months. In 1950 they held a golden wedding reception in the parlor of the church at Clemons.

Like many country people, Jim frequently went to town on Saturday afternoons. At Marshalltown he could be found in the center of a knot of men at the Marshall Implement store or on a corner of the courthouse square. He could call by name men and women from all over Marshall and surrounding counties, but strangers also would stop to talk to the friendly and obviously intelligent old man. Seldom was the conversation about Jim and his past, for he never got over his interest in people, their problems and their interests. Along with being friendly, he was satisfying his curiosity about public sentiment. A grandson once remarked that if he was the driver on a trip to Marshalltown he could expect to shake hands with half of the people in the county before starting home.

Howard still wished to write a history of the Farm Bureau movement that would go beyond Ithaca at least as far as Broome County and would be full of reminiscences about his career. Kline offered to take care of the publishing details. Help in obtaining information about the old-timers was volunteered by the national and state federations and by the Iowa State Extension Service. The mail carrier brought some but not enough of the information and the dream turned into a disappointment. Incomplete drafts of chapters ended where his memory failed. He had forgotten some of the information he needed was packed into his four-drawer filing cabinet. Had he been experienced in historical research he would have known that much of the rest was as close as the large library on the campus at Ames.

Published only in typescript was a manuscript assembled by Coverdale and entitled, "The Early Days of the Farm Bureau in Iowa and the American Farm Bureau Federation." It bore the joint by-line of Coverdale and Howard and included the former secretary's account of the organization of the Iowa federation and a number of Howard's essays on freight rates, Muscle Shoals, the farm bloc, packer regulation, rural credit, and Gaston Means. The copy on which Howard made marginal notations is in the library of the University of Iowa.

Although he was seventy-eight years old, Howard's memory was sharp on April 6, 1951, when Kenneth Langer of the Iowa Farm Bureau staff and Joe M. Bohlen of the Iowa State College faculty brought a tape recorder to the farm for an interview. The transcript shows that during several hours of questioning Jim answered questions fully and volunteered new information about the organization and growth of the state and national federations. Once or twice he could not immediately recall a name but no discrepancies were revealed when his information was compared with other records.

"I had too much to do with the early days of the Farm Bureau not to have much interest in it and I am proud of its development," the first president wrote when he regretfully missed the 1952 AFBF convention.

Physical problems slowly accumulated. He was exasperated by the static and occasional screeching of a primitive hearing aid powered by a bulky battery strapped to his belt. After an attack of shingles and a series of "cerebral accidents" or minor strokes he gave up driving and typing. Trips to the Marshalltown hospital were few and brief, for the patriarch and his wife both wanted him to spend his last years and days on his farm nursed by his daughter. The doctor permitted it. After the Langer-Bohlen interview he suffered another accident but in a few months he put in the mail a longhand account of additional Farm Bureau anecdotes.

Time never ran out on his desire to leave a written record of his life. When it was too late to sit down before a typewriter, he wrote fragmentary memoranda and short essays in a compact longhand. In a confessional manner, he filled in gaps. On January 30, 1947, he told of being born in a two-room shanty, a term he hadn't used before. The two pages also contain his only admission that it had been a blunder to leave tenant farming in 1904 for banking. On his last Christmas Eve he discovered a long lost essay entitled "A Farmer Goes Afield" that contained important information about his pre–Farm Bureau career. To it he pinned a brief note telling of the circumstances of its finding. When he came across one of his essays about the Farm Bureau presidency, in a postscript he told how and why he had discharged on employee, but with characteristic kindness he omitted the man's name.

Two days after Christmas 1953 he suffered a minor heart attack. He wanted to live until October and observe the centennial of his grandfather's purchase of the quarter section that was the nucleus of Homelands Farm. He was at peace with the world. Except for his mother and possibly two cousins, he had lived longer than anyone in the Howard and Adams families. Frequently his mind went back to the Ithaca conference and the beginning of the American Farm Bureau Federation. Of the men who had been there, he had survived all but Chester Gray and two New Yorkers. Still alive were Herbert Hoover, whom he had followed loyally, and John Coverdale, who had been his strong right arm.

To Anna Howard and her children it was clear that the end was not far away. Peacefully and without struggle, it came at daybreak on January 27, 1954, fifty-six days before his eighty-first birthday. In services at the Clemons church, the pastor included in his brief eulogy a statement that the deceased had a talent for stating complex problems in simple terms. Protestants and Catholics shared the pallbearer duties. He was buried in Bangor cemetery alongside his parents and his sister Mamie. Not far away were the graves of the first J. R. Howard and Talitha Ann, and of Joel Adams, the other grandfather.

One of Howard's epitaphs was written by R. K. Bliss, who had known Howard since the 1908 short course at New Providence and who as state extension director had been close to the Farm Bureau movement since the early days. In 1956 he was a guest when John and Elsie Coverdale celebrated their fiftieth wedding anniversary at Waterloo. In retirement Bliss was writing a scholarly history of extension in Iowa that, when published four years later, concentrated on official programs and philosophies but named few individuals. His personal judgment of the Farm Bureau's founding leadership was given in a signed article published by the *Waterloo Sunday Courier* on February 5, 1956. In detail it recounted Coverdale's four years as Howard's chief assistant. This was his summarization:

Under the leadership of Howard and Coverdale, and with the support of their board of directors, the American Farm Bureau became:

1. National in character, including all states.
2. Nonpartisan in politics.
3. Closely associated with the land-grant college system in a comprehensive educational system.

Influential people presented strong arguments in the early days that the agricultural interests of the various sections of the country would not cooperate in a national program and that it would be better to have a strong Corn Belt (regional) organization than a national one.

Howard and Coverdale stuck tight for a national organization. The soundness of this early position is now universally recognized.

In Bliss's judgment, the nation "can be thankful for the wise policies . . . in which Iowa's President J. R. Howard and Secretary John W. Coverdale had a leading part."

BIBLIOGRAPHIC ESSAY

A MONG J. R. Howard's papers that deal with his Farm Bureau career are typed rough drafts of some of his writings that became part of "The Early Days of the Farm Bureau in Iowa and the American Farm Bureau Federation," by John W. Coverdale and James R. Howard (Iowa Farm Bureau Federation, 127 pages, in Iowa State University Library; hereinafter cited as "Early Days.") The copy annotated by Howard is with the Coverdale Papers in the University of Iowa Library. Howard wrote eight of the fifteen chapters of "Early Days": Chapter 7, "Freight Rate Reductions"; Chapter 8, "Muscle Shoals," which includes the controversial letter written after the House of Representatives defeated an appropriation and which discusses the committee hearing that followed; Chapter 9, "The Farm Bloc"; Chapter 10, "The Packer and Stockyards Act"; Chapter 11, "Farm Credit"; Chapter 12, "Wiretapping and Attempted Blackmail at Washington"; Chapter 13, "Gift of Corn to Herbert Hoover for European Relief"; and Chapter 14, "Cooperative Marketing."

Howard's papers include drafts of essays of varying length and some duplication on the formation of the Marshall County Farm Bureau and the Iowa Farm Bureau Federation, the Ithaca conference, early trips to Washington, the founding convention, the beginnings of the AFBF, visits to the White House, Gaston Means and Boies Penrose, relations with Congress, and the Otto H. Kahn dinner. The last appeared in O. M. Kile's *Farm Bureau through Three Decades* (Baltimore, Md.: Waverly Press, 1948).

An interview with Howard was taped on April 6, 1951, by Kenneth Langer of the Iowa Farm Bureau and Joe M. Bohlen of the Iowa State College faculty. With the forty-one page transcript in the Howard papers is an unmailed letter containing supplementary information written to Langer on November 19, 1951.

Howard wrote numerous unpublished essays and memoranda about his pre–Farm Bureau career. The longest was entitled "Making an Iowa Farmer."

Coverdale's private papers in the University of Iowa Library include an unpublished autobiography entitled "The History of John Walter Coverdale." The Cornell University Department of Manuscripts and Archives has an oral interview conducted by Gould F. Colman on December 19, 1963, at Waterloo.

Gray Silver left no papers concerning his Farm Bureau career. Nor are there any Silver papers in the AFBF's Washington office. His most informative biographer is his granddaughter, Mary Anne S. Young, whose unpublished "Gray Silver, Washington Representative of the American Farm Bureau Federation, 1920–1924" (27 pages, notes, and bibliography) is in the University of Virginia Library. It was written in 1979 for a legal history seminar. The Silver papers in the University of West Virginia Library deal only with his farming operations. The Howard papers contain considerable miscellaneous information about Silver.

As for the founding years, the archives of the American Farm Bureau Federation at the Park Ridge, Illinois, general office are limited to transcripts of conventions and meetings of the executive committee, the official True-Howard agreement, and the AFBF newsletters.

Orville M. Kile, who was Silver's original assistant in Washington, wrote the two definitive early histories—*The Farm Bureau Movement* with Introduction by James Raley Howard (New York: Macmillan Co., 1921) and the work already cited, *The Farm Bureau through Three Decades.*

The most thorough state Farm Bureau history is John J. Lacey's *Farm Bureau in Illinois: History of Illinois Farm Bureau* (Bloomington: Illinois Agricultural Association, 1961). The Ohio Farm Bureau Federation has an excellent unpublished history by Perry L. Green, former president. Important sources on which the various chapters of this book have been based are as follows:

In Chapter 1, the hotel room scene in which Coverdale notified Howard of his election is taken from Howard's miscellaneous papers.

For much of the information in Chapter 2, and in following chapters, the author is indebted to his siblings and cousins. Lenora Howard Moninger's recollections of Jennie Howard and of her father and uncles were contributed by her daughter, Mary Louise Mitchell.

Most of Chapter 3 comes from "Making an Iowa Farmer." The description of the shanty in which Howard was born was part of three pages of recollections written on January 30, 1947, when Howard's thoughts turned backward on a stormy night. The account of the death of Mamie was written as a separate essay.

The account in Chapter 4 of Howard's country school and academy career is taken from "Making an Iowa Farmer." The academy report cards are among his papers. He wrote three nonconflicting accounts and talked frequently about his New York trip and the red bananas adventure. He mentioned a little about Penn College but virtually nothing about Grinnell College, Guilford College, and the University of Chicago. Officials of those institutions contributed information from their archives; John D. Wagoner of William Penn College was particularly helpful. At no place does Howard reveal whether as a bridegroom he aspired to a doctoral degree from the University of Chicago. The text of the 1900 speech at the Eldora teachers' meeting suggests that he was teaching in the New Providence town school at the time.

Chapter 5 is largely a montage of Howard's writings. Much of the information, including the account of his father's economic beliefs and his own early investments, is from "Making an Iowa Farmer." In various documents he gave details of his banking career and his sudden decision to buy a farm. The most revealing information on that point is contained in his January 30, 1947, confession that it was a blunder to leave tenant farming to become a banker. He hoped that document, three single-spaced pages, might "prove of sentimental or historical value to younger and perhaps unborn generations."

To a large extent Chapter 6 is based on family recollections, especially those of Henry Howard. On several occasions Jim Howard wrote without continuity about his early farming career. For several years around 1940 he contributed annual year-end essays to the *Annalist*. Although he discussed trends throughout the Corn Belt and plains states, to a large extent he focused on his own farm. These articles are informative, perceptive, and pleasant reading. The text of the White Sulphur Springs speech referring to the electric light plant is one of many in the Howard papers.

At various times, in "Making an Iowa Farmer" and elsewhere, Howard wrote about the need for school consolidation described in Chapter 7, but he modestly said little about his own part in establishing Liberty Consolidated School. Although the author of this book attended the school for six years he has depended primarily on the memories of others for the material in this chapter. For background, see M. L. Cushman, "Schools for the Farm Boy and Farm Girl," in *A Century of Farming in Iowa, 1846-1946* (Ames, Iowa: Iowa State College Press, 1945). The brief record of *Ingold Unit System* v. *Independent Consolidated School District* can be found in Equity Docket 11298 of Marshall County District Court. Howard spoke on November 3, 1921, before the Wisconsin Teachers Association in Market Hall, Milwaukee. In the Langer interview, Howard told of his stage fright at Iowa State College but gave no details of other speeches. School board secretaries, like the early Farm Bureau officials, had neither the training nor the facilities for preserving their records.

Chapter 8 is based on Howard's papers. He wrote at length about the Bevins Grove picnic but recorded less about the New Providence short course and Perry G. Holden. Other details are found in his extensive writings about the predecessors of the Farm Bureau movement.

Some details of Chapter 9 are from Howard's memoirs, which tell about the Thanksgiving barbecue but do not name the signers of the membership pledge. Although the memoirs contain little information about Howard's two years as county Farm Bureau president, they do tell of the emphasis on improved livestock. The county Farm Bureau has brief minutes of board meetings and some other early meetings, but nothing about the organization meeting. See *Fiftieth Anniversary, Marshall County Farm Bureau* (Marshalltown, Iowa: 1968), and Gerhard Schultz, *History of Marshall County, Iowa* (Marshalltown, Iowa: Marshalltown Printing Co., 1955).

Chapter 10 relies heavily on Coverdale's recollections in "Early Days," his oral interview, and biography. For the genesis and growth of the Farm Bureau movement nationally, see: Orville M. Kile, *The Farm Bureau Movement* and *The Farm Bureau through Three Decades;* Alfred C. True, *A History of Agricultural Education in the United States, 1785-1925* (Washington, D.C.: 1929); Gladys Baker, *The County Agent* (Chicago: University of Chicago Press, 1939); M. C. Burritt, *The County Agent and the Farm Bureau* (New York: Harcourt, Brace & Co., 1922); Roy V. Scott, *The Reluctant Farmer: The Rise of Agricultural Extension to 1914* (Urbana: University of Illinois Press, 1970); and George A. Works and Barton Morgan, *The Land-Grant Colleges,* vol. 10 (Washington, D.C.: Advisory Commission on Education, 1939).

Iowa sources include: D. B. Groves and Kenneth Thatcher, *The First Fifty; History of the Farm Bureau in Iowa* (Lake Mills, Iowa: Iowa Farm Bureau Federation, 1968); Ralph K. Bliss, *A History of Cooperative Agriculture and Home Economics Extension in Iowa* (Ames, Iowa: Iowa State College Press, 1960); Barton Morgan, "Movements Leading to the Establishment of the Extension Service in Iowa," in *The Extension Service in Agriculture and Home Economics in Iowa* (Ames, Iowa: Collegiate Press, Inc., 1934); Earle D. Ross, *A History of Iowa State College of Agriculture and Mechanic Arts* (Ames, Iowa: Iowa State College Press, 1942).

Chapter 11 is based on a two-page, single-spaced, typewritten "Report of Transactions by Iowa Federation of Farm Bureaus since Organization December 27, 1918," with the constitution attached, which was issued after the Marshalltown convention. Other details were taken from various 1918, 1919, and 1920 issues of the *Marshalltown Times-Republican, Wallaces' Farmer,* and *Iowa Homestead.* Also see "Early Days," and the Coverdale and Howard oral interviews. Howard wrote an account of his troubles with the *Homestead.*

The biography of Coverdale in Chapter 12 was taken largely from the "History of John Walter Coverdale." The Iowa Farm Bureau Federation has abbreviated minutes of committee meetings. As well, Howard wrote about the Non-Partisan League. See also "Early Days."

Many details in Chapter 13 can be found in the Howard memoirs, particularly accounts of the audience with President Wilson on the cost-of-living issue and of his lobbying against Daylight Savings Time. His account of Wilson's summons to Howard and Silver on the League of Nations issue was printed in the *Des Moines Register,* March 17, 1938. In this and some other cases, Howard omitted time references. No record of the League of Nations meeting is found in the Woodrow Wilson Papers in the Library of Congress.

The minutes of the Ithaca conference referred to in Chapter 14 are in the Olin Library, Cornell University. Howard wrote at length about the meeting and about his discussions with Henry C. Wallace concerning the future of the Farm Bureau movement.

Information on the Chicago convention discussed in Chapter 16 is largely from the American Farm Bureau Federation, which has transcripts of all conventions, beginning with the founding convention, and executive committee meetings. At various times Howard wrote about the 1919 convention, but in this case and some others he said little about his own activities. A large share of incidental information comes from *Prairie Farmer* 1920 issues of January 24, February 14, and February 28.

Both Howard and Coverdale wrote at length about the launching of the AFBF discussed in Chapter 16. See also Kile's *Farm Bureau Movement,* and Murray R. Benedict, *Farm Policies of the United States, 1790–1950, A Study of Their Origins and Development* (New York: Twentieth Century Fund, 1953). Coverdale's oral interview told of H. C. Wallace's premature appearance before the Republican platform committee with the Farm Bureau planks.

Parts of Chapter 17 on Gray Silver are from Howard's papers. He wrote extensively about his experiences in Washington and included details about Gaston Means, the two persistent women, and the tapped telephone. Kile's *Farm Bureau through Three Decades* tells about the Muscle Shoals appropriation and the Howard letter to congressmen. Howard wrote a full account of the committee hearing that followed. He frequently talked about the hearing but by 1927 he had forgotten the name and corporate affiliation of the lobbyist. *Prairie Farmer,* January 15, 1921, reported the cross-examination without mention of the lobbyist.

Detailed information about the Committee of Seventeen and the U.S. Grain Growers mentioned in Chapter 18 is found in Howard's speeches, Coverdale's reports as executive secretary, and Kile's books. Although C. V. Gregory strongly supported Sapiro, the columns of *Prairie Farmer* in the years 1920, 1921, and 1922 give valuable insight into Farm Bureau activities, which it covered more fully than other publications. The definitive work on Sapiro is Grace H. Larsen and Henry E. Erdman,

"Aaron Sapiro: Genius of Farm Cooperative Promotion," *Mississippi Valley Historical Review* 49(September 1962):242–68. See also Coverdale and Howard oral histories.

Howard's writings are the major source of details in Chapter 19, concerning the impact of the rural depression, the farmers' donation of surplus corn, Howard's first meetings with Herbert Hoover, and the Brauer episode. See also Coverdale's annual reports.

The account in Chapter 20 of the Howard-Silver confrontation with President Harding is in the Howard papers. His evaluation of farm success while the U.S. Grain Growers floundered is in the Langer interview. For farm bloc achievements, see Arthur Capper, *The Agricultural Bloc* (New York: Harcourt, Brace & Co., 1922); Murray R. Benedict, *Farm Policies;* AFBF weekly newsletters of 1921 (March 15, August 15, October 20, 27, and December 8, 15) and 1922 (April 7, May 25, August 7); Coverdale's second and third annual reports; and Howard's Minnesota Farm Bureau speech. The *New York Times Index* was invaluable in tracing the reaction to the bloc and the sequence of other events. Howard wrote a full account, with confirmation by Wilson, of the Wilson-Armour conference that made possible the Packer and Stockyards Act. His papers do not mention suggestions that he be appointed senator to replace Kenyon. See the *Des Moines Register* and the *New York Times* for February 1, 2, 3, 17, 18 (1922) and 17, 18 (1923).

Howard's own account of the freight rate reductions discussed in Chapter 21 is found in "Early Days" and in his January 10, 1922, speech before the Iowa Farm Bureau convention. See also AFBF newsletters and Coverdale reports. See letters to Howard from S. J. Lowell, 12-5-27; N. W. Willard (Santa Fe) 12-14-27; and F. R. Todd, 12-20-27. Accounts of the Cadence of the Corn speech and the "rabbit sausage" rejoinder are also in the Howard papers.

Information for Chapter 22 on Howard's retirement comes from the Des Moines speech, in which he defended his railroad policies and stated his determination to retire. The Esch-Cummins and merchant marine issues were discussed in full in an undated and possibly unmailed letter to Andrew Stevenson in 1923 or 1924. For the 1922 AFBF convention, see the official transcript and the 1922 *Prairie Farmer* issues of December 9, 16, and 23.

The most extensive information about Sapiro's farewell described in Chapter 23 can be found in Coverdale's papers, including "Early Days." Coverdale discussed the matter at length in his oral history. His papers also contain details of press coverage of the 1923 convention, and of Lowden's involvement. Coverdale also told of his brief involvement with the Grain Marketing Company. Senator Styles Bridges several times told Roger Fleming of his disappointment in not becoming AFBF secretary. The Howard papers contain full details of the Saskatchewan encounter with Sapiro. For Howard's final judgment of Sapiro, see letters to C. H. Gustafson, February 17, 1945, and to M. R. Myers, August 15, 1933. Except for the speech before the 1923 AFBF convention, information about the National Transportation Institute mentioned in Chapter 24 is limited to some promotional material and texts of speeches in the Howard papers. Details about his poor health and recuperation are in private letters. Wheeler McMillen is the authority for the anecdote about Howard's delivery of Hoover's unidentified material objecting to McNary-Haugenism. The Herbert Hoover Presidential Library has considerable Howard material, including the listing of his name as a possibility for secretary of agriculture. Other information in this chapter, including his prolonged efforts to become a recognized writer, are from his private papers or family recollections.

FURTHER REFERENCES

Agricultural Depressions, 1785–1920, A Preliminary Summary of a Report by Agricultural Service. Washington, D.C.: U.S. Chamber of Commerce, 1925.

Battin, William, and Moscrip, F. A. *Past and Present of Marshall County Iowa.* Indianapolis: B. F. Bowen & Co., 1912.

Block, William J. *The Separation of the Farm Bureau and the Extension Service.* Illinois Studies in Social Services, no. 47. Urbana: University of Illinois, 1960.

Campbell, Christiana McFadyen. *The Farm Bureau and the New Deal: A Study of the Making of National Farm Policy, 1933–40.* Urbana: University of Illinois Press, 1962.

Evans, James F. *Prairie Farmer and WLS: The Burridge D. Butler Years.* Urbana: University of Illinois Press, 1969.

The Farm Bureau Carries On: The Growth of an Idea. Ithaca: New York State Farm Bureau, n.d.

History of Marshall County, Iowa. Chicago: Western Historical Co., 1878.

Lacey, Mary G. *Food Control during 46 Centuries: A Contribution to the History of Price Fixing.* Typescript of March 16, 1922, address before Agricultural History Association, Washington. Reprinted by Swift & Co.

McConnell, Grant. *The Decline of Agrarian Democracy.* Berkeley: University of California Press, 1953.

Peek, George N., and Johnson, Hugh S. *Equality for Agriculture.* H. E. Harrington, 1922.

Reck, Franklin M. *The 4-H Story: A History of 4-H Club Work.* Ames: Iowa State College Press, 1954.

Robotka, Frank, and Bentley, R. C. *Cooperation in Grain Marketing in Iowa.* Agricultural Experiment Station Research Bulletin 276. Ames: Iowa State College, September 1940.

Sage, Leland L. *A History of Iowa.* Ames: Iowa State University Press, 1974.

Schapsmeier, Edward L., and Schapsmeier, Frederick H. *Henry A. Wallace of*

Iowa: The Agrarian Years, 1910-1940. Ames: Iowa State University Press, 1968.

Schlebecker, John T. *Whereby We Thrive: A History of American Farming.* Ames: Iowa State University Press, 1975.

Schuttler, Vera Busiek. *A History of the Missouri Farm Bureau Federation.* Jefferson City: Missouri Farm Bureau Federation, 1948.

Winters, Donald L. *Henry Cantwell Wallace as Secretary of Agriculture, 1921-24.* Urbana: University of Illinois Press, 1970.

INDEX